Praise for *Undocumented*

Undocumented gives a voice to people who have been forced to flee their own homelands to come to America in search of a better life. This is a story of bravery, resilience, and courage.

—**Katye Anna**,
Author, *Conscious Construction of the Soul*

Veronica Lynch has broken through the walls of fear and trepidation to write a story of undocumented Black immigrant lives rarely shared before. It is a courageous telling of one woman's harrowing journey to succeed at all costs and conquer the countless obstacles tossed into her path as she reaches for the dream of U.S. citizenship. Ms. Lynch dares to relive the perilous struggles, the tears and the terror, the longing for safety, and a place of belonging. *Undocumented* is written with unvarnished truth, undaunted determination, and exemplary storytelling. It is a shining example of the triumph of will, a book that needs to be in the hands of all who call themselves American citizens and those who still strive to be.

—**Dorothy Randall Gray, MSC**,
Author, *Soul Between the Lines*

The undocumented immigrant spends days in constant fear, pain, and in alone spaces while navigating another culture, language, and another way of being in the world. Dr. Veronica Lynch walks us through the physical and emotional frailty and instability facing the undocumented while sharing, along the way, how she persevered and grew herself forward. This is the story of the undocumented immigrant and a handbook for the undocumented as well as for all who strive to move life forward, to learn, to grow, and to live their best life.

—Marilyn Mackel,
Attorney, Law School Professor,
and Juvenile Court Commissioner (ret.)

Undocumented puts to paper the main ingredients for achieving success: a pound of perseverance, some resilience and hope, and a large portion of "knowing what you want" served on a platter with a Caribbean flavor. After reading just a few chapters, I could appreciate how this story could represent everyone's story: the struggles of an immigrant woman against all odds in a cultural quagmire who overcomes and achieves her dreams. But especially for an immigrant, to recognize oneself within the pages of this story and identify with it allows you to believe and hope and anticipate.

—Angela D. Kerr, MD,
Fellow of the American College of
Obstetricians and Gynecologists

I love its readability and its mind-bending opening in which we are given a step-by-step account of what happens to a young teenage girl as her life stands still for the moment. Her fears of isolation develop a tenacious spirit within her that creates her set of values that will motivate her to pursue her life's journey. We learn about culture transitions wherein the premise is not just to improve one's circumstances but to improve oneself. *Undocumented* is a must read for anyone who wants strength for the journey of life.

—**Ida White, MAEd**,
Author, *You Can Be Anything You Want to Be*,
Educator, Mentor, and Speaker

Captivating! The immigrant experience. While not all immigrants to this country have followed the exact same path, their experiences are similar. Dr. Lynch's description has put them into words. The book is so well written that you will not be able to put it down.

—**Frantz Backer, DDS**

Undocumented pulled me in from the very first sentence! Even though some of Veronica's experiences were foreign to me, I felt I was reliving everything with her. Definitely a great read!

—**Michelle Currie, MEd**,
Intuition Mentor

Join Veronica as she shares with us her courageous journey to U.S. citizenship. This is a wonderful and fascinating story to help us gain a deeper understanding of the many trials and risks our immigrant brothers and sisters take for a better life of opportunity.

—**Jane Caffrey**,
Yoga Instructor, Community Volunteer

Undocumented will make you laugh, cry, and experience many moments of empathy and sympathy as you travel along this journey with the author as she comes of age in a new culture that she found not so welcoming to her.

—**Joyce O. Chavers**, MA, RMT,
Co-author of *How Big Can You Dream?*

Undocumented offers us a very intimate lens into a very emotional story of a woman whose desire for freedom leads to an awareness of imprisonment. Her inner strength leads us to know the human spirit is resilient when the soul knows love. Great read.

—**Rebbe TZiPi Radonsky**, PhD,
Author, *The Spiritual Pilgrim Discovers Home*

With the current laser focus on immigration worldwide, *Undocumented: One Woman's Traumas and Triumphs in Becoming a U.S. Citizen* shares a timely insider's journey in this deeply inspiring memoir of a teenaged immigrant's experience through her own eyes. Lynch relates her tale in narrative so strong, clear, and believable that a lovely, lilting, Caribbean singsong sometimes seems to emerge amid brought-to-life 1970s Brooklyn. The author's language reveals complex emotions in dead-on descriptions of a pit-of-the-stomach terror so real, she takes readers with her into the depths of unrelenting fear. Only this determined young woman's courage and soul-deep trust—strengthening her *faith muscle* and creating her own *palette in life*—can lift her back up to the joy of embracing the daylight in her heart. *Undocumented* is a moving story of the power of faith against the odds.

—**Katherine Tandy Brown**,
Freelance Writer

Read it twice! Veronica Lynch has composed a compelling life drama! I highly recommend this treatise.

—**Samuel J. Scott Sr.**,
NASA Aerospace Research Engineer
(ret.), Author, *Obama: Out of Genesis*

Veronica Lynch's writings are bold and compassionate and politically astute. In our current age of divide, this book will bring readers of all backgrounds and experiences together as the author brings the struggle of children and families to bear and allows us to delight in their fortitude and kindness. This is an important and precious book! Timely, soulful, and hopeful. Full of twists and turns, keeps you on your toes! Her words will enrich your life.

—**Catherine Paykin**, **MSSW**,
Author and Playwright

Out of the deep, dark shadows of pain, anguish, and shame, she had to endure, Veronica Lynch has triumphantly emerged, has found her voice, and can now unequivocally be unafraid to tell her story in her own words of the despair, rejection, and sadness she endured of being an undocumented person/woman in the United States of America.

—**Annetta/Adaebola**,
Artist and Fashion Designer

Undocumented is the story of a lifetime—of a life of a brilliant, gifted Caribbean woman of great courage, determination, faith! Veronica Lynch's book lays out for us her personal journey from a child losing her mother at ten years old to a high school student needing to leave her temporary home on St. Thomas upon graduation, to being a traumatized *Undocumented* citizen of NYC, to becoming a gifted and compassionate healer. This is a powerful story of healing, of overcoming, of actualizing, of ascending.

—**Ifetayo White**,
Usui Shinpiden Reiki Master

An important and necessary book. It brings solace and liberation and will strengthen all immigrants in this country today. This book is filled with resources that can be kept on your library shelf as a point of reference or a required reading in schools or social meetings. I highly recommend *Undocumented* as a must read.

—**Pamela A. Young**,
Minister, United Pentecostal
Churches of Christ

UNDOCUMENTED

One Woman's Traumas and
Triumphs in Becoming a
Documented United States Citizen

VERONICA R. LYNCH, PhD

UNDOCUMENTED

One Woman's Traumas and
Triumphs in Becoming a
Documented United States Citizen

For J. Olinda

UNDOCUMENTED
One Woman's Traumas and Triumphs in Becoming a Documented United States Citizen

Copyright © 2020 Veronica R. Lynch, PhD

The views expressed by the author in reference to specific people in this book represent entirely their own individual opinions and are not in any way reflective of the views of Capucia, LLC. We assume no responsibility for errors, omissions, or contradictory interpretations of the subject matter herein.

Capucia, LLC does not warrant the performance, effectiveness, or applicability of any websites listed in or linked to this publication. The purchaser or reader of this publication assumes responsibility for the use of these materials and information. Capucia, LLC shall in no event be held liable to any party for any direct, indirect, punitive, special, incidental, or any other consequential damages arising directly or indirectly from any use of this material. Techniques and processes given in this book are not to be used in place of medical or other professional advice.

No part of this book may be reproduced or transmitted in any form, or by any means, electronic or mechanical, including photography, recording, or in any information storage or retrieval system, without written permission from the author or publisher, except in the case of brief quotations embodied in articles and reviews.

The material in this book is provided for informational purposes only. It should not be used as a substitute for professional medical advice, diagnosis or treatment. It is your responsibility to research the completeness and usefulness of opinions, services and other information found in this book. The reader is responsible for their own actions. Some names have been changed to protect the privacy of some individuals.

Published by:
Capucia, LLC
211 Pauline Drive #513
York, PA 17402
www.capuciapublishing.com

ISBN: 978-1-945252-79-2
Library of Congress Control Number: 2020910868

Cover Design: Ranilo Cabo
Front Cover Photo: Joyce O. Chavers
Layout: Reggy delos Santos
Book Midwife: Carrie Jareed

Printed in the United States of America

CONTENTS

Preface	1
Part I – Coming to America	3
Chapter 1: Hopeful Entry	5
Chapter 2: Adjusting and Assimilating Into the American Culture	17
Part II – Life Before America	37
Chapter 3: Tropical Lifestyle	39
Chapter 4: My Childhood Dream of Going to America	63
Chapter 5: Mourning	87
Part III – My Personal Odyssey in America	105
Chapter 6: A Cultural Melting Pot	107
Chapter 7: What I Did to Accomplish My Dream	129
Chapter 8: Ditching the Confines of Fear and Grief	163

Part IV – Breakthroughs in America 213
Chapter 9:   Turning Point 215
Chapter 10: Soul Stuff—A Recounting of
             What I've Learned 257

Acknowledgments 321
Bibliography 323
About the Author 331
Contact Author 332
Free Resources 333

PREFACE

Prior to coming to America, I was constantly worried about what would happen in my life. The day my school bond expired—the legal documentation that allowed me to stay in St. Thomas until I graduated from high school—the immigration authorities would be waiting to deport me back to my native island. That fear almost crippled my human self, but something deep inside kept me going: I had knowledge of a power that was greater than the immigration authorities. Because of my trust in the power of God, I believed a way was being made for me to get to America, to find what I thought would be freedom.

But the thought of coming to America and being allowed into the country—or not—by the immigration authority figures created within me untold paranoia, fear, distrust, and physical shaking. Thinking about it made me want to hide in a closet and curl up into a fetal position until I thought it was safe to come out. I was lost in this tunnel of fear. I knew the immigration authorities could determine the outcome of the rest of my life.

Anyone who wore a uniform with shiny buttons would send me into a tailspin. To me they represented the *Man*, and that meant they had power over me. Still, I persevered.

UNDOCUMENTED

That was over thirty years ago, and even as I write these words today, I experience trembling in my body. Now, thirty years later, I have legal citizenship, one doctorate, several master's degrees, and years of experience as a psychotherapist helping others to heal their traumas. Yet, that same fear I felt that night when the local immigration officers pounded on my door in the middle of the night still lives in my bones. It was the fear of being discovered and deported, fear about being an undocumented immigrant. Fears that I, and millions of other immigrants, have experienced.

PART I

COMING TO AMERICA

My Beginning Journey of Faith, Love, Hope, and Determination

CHAPTER 1

Hopeful Entry

Have you ever been so determined to create your own life's journey from surviving to thriving that you would choose to rely on faith and watch things work for your greater good? Well, I did. I was so tired of wearing a face of anger, shame, disappointment, and abandonment after the loss of my mom and my homeland that I knew I needed to create more peace and joy in my life.

My biggest goal at that time was to get a college education that would prepare me to help myself and others. I desperately wanted to minimize the sadness and loneliness that can accompany fear, grief, and abandonment for many people and help them learn how to better cope with life.

When I was eight years old, my mother migrated from our native island of Antigua to St. Thomas in search of a better life. When I was ten years old, she sent for me and my younger brother, and we were able to get on her work bond in order to attend school in St. Thomas.

Two years later, due to Mom's illness, she, my brother, and I had to return to Antigua. After only two months there, my mother died. After her death, I returned to St. Thomas to live with my sister and her family. At that time, I was granted a school bond that would expire upon my high school graduation.

After graduation, I was hoping to go to the States to be with two older sisters who already lived there. I desired to meet other distant family members. Now that I had reached the age of seventeen, it would soon be time for me to make my way in creating my own fulfilling lifestyle. I would have to leave St. Thomas and the guardianship of my sister and her family because the law only allowed students to stay there on a school bond until their high school graduation, and mine was quickly approaching. I had prepared myself to go out into the world by obtaining excellent clerical skills to fall back on if I couldn't create something else to sustain me along my life's journey.

Each day of the last two weeks of high school was a day of excitement and a sense of completion for my graduating classmates, while my excitement was shrouded by nerve-wracking anticipation and fear rapidly encroaching upon my psyche. The immigration authorities would be coming to deport me to my home island where there was no one there to receive me. I needed to believe God would be there to provide for my needs while I pursued my heart's desire. I had to totally trust in this belief. I believed that my trust in a Higher Power had already begun supporting me as my friends and family procured a safe place for me to stay to avoid deportation while arrangements were being made for my departure to America.

HOPEFUL ENTRY

My escape route began on St. Thomas, U.S. Virgin Islands, the third day after my high school graduation. My teenaged heart filled with fear when someone pounded on the door of our island home at two o'clock in the morning.

"Immigration!" shouted a voice from outside the door. The immigration authorities made a habit of showing up at people's homes unannounced after their bond or legal documents expired. Those who didn't have legal status were constantly in fear and were harassed. It was common to hear the loud banging of the officers pounding on doors and people running, trying to get away from the authorities for fear that they would be immediately deported or sent to jail.

In her Caribbean dialect, my sister yelled, "Hol' on, hol' on," as she hurriedly threw her tattered bathrobe over her nightclothes and headed for the door.

I heard the ruckus but was paralyzed with fear when my uncle ran into my room and pulled me out of bed while barely audibly whispering, "Quick, girl, put on your clothes and jump out the window. Immigration is at the door! You must run to Miss Ella's house. She will know what to do."

I was scurrying about in the dark to find and put on the clothes I had on the day before, when my uncle handed me a suitcase that had already been packed in preparation of the authorities' arrival. In my haste, I forgot to put on my shoes, but I continued to jump out the window into the night and raced down Mango Road, leaving loud voices of anger and authority behind me.

There were no streetlights to guide me through the darkness, but I ran as fast as I could through the alleyways and high bushes. My bare feet began to ache from the sharp rocks I encountered as I ran for my freedom. Tears streaming down my face, I finally arrived at Miss Ella's door, praying that she would receive me at that time of the night. As soon as she opened the door, I fell into her arms and continued to weep from fear.

Miss Ella, a native of St. Thomas, had not only bonded my mother and sister as housekeepers for her and her family, but she had always been a supportive friend to my mother.

"Lord, chil', you made it," Miss Ella cried in her Caribbean dialect, holding me firmly in her arms. In a calm, welcoming voice she whispered, "You're safe now."

She grabbed my suitcase and helped me into her house. Though her pleasant face showed signs of relief, she looked tired and sleepy. I felt guilty for arriving at her home in the middle of the night in my sweaty, ripped dress—guilty that I was disturbing and burdening her.

She fixed me a cup of peppermint bush tea, but fear was shaking my body so much I couldn't hold the cup steady. "You must keep up your strength," she said, pulling up a chair to sit closer to me. "Drink, chil'," she insisted, putting the china teacup to my mouth. "It will make you feel better."

Miss Ella didn't seem too surprised at my showing up on her doorstep, and from the tone of her voice and actions, she had been expecting it to happen—it was just a matter of when. "You're a strong girl," she said.

HOPEFUL ENTRY

I didn't feel strong. I felt afraid, dependent on others, and still unsure of my future.

"Don't worry, baby. Everything is going to be alright," she said, as she put her arm around me and gave me one of her nightgowns to put on. Just then she noticed my swollen, bloody feet. She quickly brought in a basin filled with warm water, poured the antiseptic Dettol in it, and began washing my feet. After drying them and applying aloe vera gel, she said, "This will help with the healing."

I trusted Miss Ella and she trusted me. When I was fourteen years old, Miss Ella had allowed me to work in her mother's home and in her apothecary after school. I would often sit and read the philosophical books in her library, which fed my quest for learning. She always encouraged me to pursue an education.

After drinking the tea, I felt a little calmer, yet very tired. I looked at the clock. By now it was about 5:00 a.m., so I decided to close my eyes for a second. I must have fallen asleep because when I woke up it was dark again. I felt disoriented and didn't know where I was. Looking about the room, I saw books in a tall bookcase and pictures of Miss Ella's son and her husband. Her husband was a military man and stationed in the United States. Seeing these things helped me to recognize where I was, and I felt safer and grounded.

A clock showed me it was now 5:00 p.m.—I had slept for twelve hours! I started to get up and look for my clothes and realized that there was still a dull ache in both my feet, although the swelling had gone down. I managed to make it across the room and opened my suitcase to see if my graduation pictures were there, but they weren't. I remembered how proud I had felt walking down the aisle at Charlotte Amalie High School just a few days before to receive my high school diploma.

"I'm glad you're awake," Miss Ella said, entering the room with my clothes. She'd washed and sewn up my dress. "You're a brave girl. Your life is about to be transformed."

Again, I did not feel brave. It was the summer of 1977 and graduation had come and gone. My school bond had expired at midnight on graduation day, and I had no definitive plans for what was next in my life.

"I know you're hungry by now," Miss Ella smiled.

"Yes," I whispered and tried to return her smile.

"Me soon come back," she said in her native dialect as she briskly left the room.

"Okay," I replied, smelling my freshly cleaned clothes as I began to put them on.

Miss Ella returned shortly with a tray of food and stood in the doorway. With a smile she said, "You're not going to need clothes right now. It's almost time to go back to bed."

So, I took off my clothes and replaced them with Miss Ella's nightgown once more. I quickly ate the stewed fish with peas and rice she had prepared and brought to me. I learned from Miss Ella that my sister had left a message earlier and would be visiting me the next day.

"How are your feet doing?" she inquired. "Let me see them." She noticed that the swelling had receded, so she massaged my feet with cocoa butter, which helped to soothe the dull pain.

The next day I eagerly awoke, anticipating seeing my sister. She came during her lunch hour and brought a package for me. Among the things my sister brought to me were my shoes, my high school diploma, a notebook, and my unframed graduation pictures. In the package was a separate manila envelope in which was an airline ticket to Puerto Rico, en route to New York City. She informed me that I would not be returning to my home in St. Thomas but would be leaving for the U.S. that night. She then pressed $200 into my hands, more money than I had ever seen at once. She was not able to stay long because she had just started a new job at the local bank and did not want to return late. We said our goodbyes quickly as we hugged and cried.

For the next few hours, Miss Ella and I talked about my goals and dreams as I prepared for the trip. Before I knew it, I was in Miss Ella's car, speeding to the airport. My heart was beating so hard it felt as if it would burst through my chest at any minute. I felt torn because I would be leaving my home, yet I realized it was time for my escape. I had little time to say goodbye to Miss Ella, who hurriedly checked me in at the gate where I presented my birth certificate to the attendant and was given my airline ticket and boarding pass to Puerto Rico en route to JFK in New York City.

Shortly thereafter, I boarded a six-seater plane for the short flight to Puerto Rico. Upon arrival in Puerto Rico, the airline attendant announced there would be a delay on my flight to JFK.

The anticipation of sitting in the airport while waiting to board the flight was not exactly fun-filled for me. I was too afraid my secret of escaping would be discovered.

I had no way of letting my family in the States know of the delay, so I began to worry, not realizing that my family would call first to check on the arrival time of the incoming flights from Puerto Rico.

I sat quietly for about two hours until they announced that the next 747 jumbo jet heading for JFK airport in New York City would be boarding shortly. Miss Ella had already told me that *red-eye* flights were the best time to travel because travelers were less conspicuous. My instructions were to board the jumbo jet heading for the States to begin my new life.

Finally, an announcement was made that we were beginning to board the plane for JFK.

Once on the plane, when the flight attendant announced over the loudspeaker that we would be taking off shortly and to fasten our seatbelts, multiple emotions enveloped me. I felt sad, alone, and displaced because I was leaving behind my sister and St. Thomas, the place that had become my home since my mother's death. Yet at the same time, I felt excitement because I was going to the States to meet my two older sisters, who had immigrated there five years prior. I felt fear because I was going to a place I had never been before, and I didn't know what to expect or even if I would like it. I also felt concern about my legal status. In addition, I was not sure which of my sisters I'd be staying with when I arrived in New York.

When the jet started moving and lifted off the runway, I looked out my window and could see the lights of Puerto Rico getting smaller in the distance. I started praying and thanking God. This was the point of no return.

My feet were beginning to burn, so I removed my shoes. I must have fallen asleep because the next thing I knew they were announcing we would be landing soon. My anxiety immediately increased, and my hands began to sweat when a man in an official-looking uniform walked down the aisle. I held my breath and felt relief after he passed my seat.

I looked out the window, hoping that no one would discover me, and saw the vastness of the bright, colorful lights like a never-ending quilt below me. I took time to reflect on the words of Miss Ella and my sister. They both believed in me and encouraged me to believe in myself and to stay focused and dedicated to my goals and aspirations. They knew I had the potential to create a life of empowerment and reminded me that prayer changes things. I had to rely on the God Source with which I was familiar from the foundation my mom laid for me as a child. Again, having strong faith and belief in a Higher Power would be my source of survival. The land of *milk and honey* was finally in my view.

It was about two o'clock in the morning when we landed at JFK. I calmed myself by checking to make sure I had all my documents in the manila envelope as we prepared to deplane. I grabbed my suitcase and my purse and followed the few passengers to the United States customs. Afraid, alone, and very nervous, I began practicing my spiel quietly, "I am Sarah Whitehead, African-American from Brooklyn, New York." Saying these words, I felt as phony as the piece of paper that the name *Sarah Whitehead* was written on.

There were only two customs officers working that night. I stood in line briefly. When it was my turn, I walked up to the counter and handed my birth certificate to the customs officer, who looked at it briefly, stared into my eyes, then motioned for me to go through.

"Thank you, God," I quietly whispered to myself and continued to follow the signs to retrieve my luggage.

I was finally realizing my dream of coming to America.

On route to claiming my luggage, I recall the joy I felt when I saw my sister, who was standing at the bottom of some moving stairs—my first introduction to the escalator. She and her boyfriend beckoned for me to come down the escalator. Even though I was thrilled and excited to see my sister, I still had trepidations about my well-being. We went to retrieve my luggage and then called our third sister to let her know we had united safely. She gave a big sigh of relief too.

I looked forward to spending time with the two of my three sisters whom I hadn't seen since our mother's funeral, six years prior. They were the first to immigrate to America. I remember the first time they returned home to Antigua from New York. They were dressed like Caribbean queens in their maxi dresses, platform heels, and afros. I dreamt of being just like them in America. Everybody I knew in the West Indies who went to America came back wearing nice clothes and shoes.

They said that in America things were plentiful and abundant.

What I Expected to Find in America

They said in America the streets were paved with gold, you could find money on the streets, and the place is so clean you could eat off the ground. But when I got to America, it was different. There were homeless people and rubbish on the streets.

They said that in America, children wear shoes and socks. When I heard this, I was glad because on the island children hardly wore shoes, much less socks. Where I come from is so small you can walk everywhere you go, ride your horse or donkey, or you can ride in a rugged old bus.

It was said that when you walked on the roads in America, if you were lucky, you'd often find furniture, equipment, and even money that had been thrown away by rich people. In America, children are driven to school and eat their lunch there. The roads are paved with tar, and there are different kinds of motor cars.

They also said that anyone could make it in America, but they had to work hard. I was determined to work hard, go to school, and make something of my life.

I expected my family to be more receptive of my coming to the States to get an education. I expected more congenial interactions with my family and was surprised to experience discord, especially with my sisters. I expected the culture and values from home to have remained in place. Because of our early loss and not continuing to grow together, it was like meeting new people.

Finally, I expected people to be nice and kind, but my impressions were disappointing.

We took a yellow taxicab, and my sister and I sat in the back, chatting and laughing with excitement. The roads in the city were wide and long, and the buildings seemed large, like giants standing at attention. She pointed out the Conduit and Belt Parkways as we drove down Atlantic Avenue through the twists and turns from Queens to Brooklyn. Amazed and befuddled, I couldn't understand how the earth beneath these tall buildings could withstand the weight.

I took in as much of the sites as I could and was glad when we arrived at the building where I would be staying with my sister. Because she only had one bedroom, I would have to sleep on the sofa. I was very grateful and knew I would soon need to move on. I was afraid of everything, being new and knowing I must ultimately fend for myself. However, I was ready to grow up and have wonderful coming-of-age experiences, except for one major fear: my immigration status. I knew I was undocumented.

They said that life in America was sweet and bountiful. They said that in America you could obtain your dreams and be free. So, I came looking for these things in America. I wanted liberation, not deportation.

Having strong faith and belief in God would be my source of survival. I was determined to ditch the confines of fear and grief. However, it would take another thirty plus years before I finally shed my fear of deportation. Ditching the confines of fear and grief has truly been a work in progress.

CHAPTER 2

Adjusting and Assimilating Into the American Culture

I came to America to pursue a better life. I came to pursue an education and reconnect with family.

My sister was happy, I believed, to have me in her neat, fancy apartment and gave me my own set of keys to go and come whenever I wanted. The following day, my oldest sister and my younger brother came over, and we reminisced about life back home on the island. We cooked and ate West Indian food, like calaloo, fungie, peas and rice, and curried goat. We also played and danced to calypso and reggae music. I was so glad to see my family had held on to some of our culture. I realized my sisters and my brother didn't speak with a heavy Caribbean accent anymore; they had begun to *yank*. I felt very self-conscious about still speaking that way.

From time to time, my siblings and I would gather and laugh or cry about childhood experiences. One evening, my oldest sister reminisced about the Weston's Dance School. She played the song, "Pata Pata" by Miriam Makeba, and we all joined in as my sister demonstrated the African dance moves.

I loved telling the story of finding and hiding money that fell through the floorboards of our house and using it to buy sweeties to share with cousin Lenore at school. However, the big landfall was the time Lenore found a $20 bill. She came by my house and showed me a crisp $20 bill that she had found. We were so excited, and I volunteered to keep it safe under my house. I put a big rock over the $20 bill to keep it hidden.

I couldn't wait to get home from school the next day to make sure it was still there, and it was. After hiding the money for a couple of days, Lenore suggested we cut school and walk into town to buy foods. We walked around all day until it was time to come home from school. Whatever change was left from the twenty-dollar bill after the day's adventures, we would hide under the house again. Within the next couple of days, Lenore and I decided to take the remainder of the $20 from under the house and have one more eating spree in town.

We met early that morning, cut school, and went to town to eat and walk around all day again. We wanted to eat all of our favorite foods. We first bought fresh popcorn, wrapped in small brown paper bags and drenched in the grease from the lard used for popping, then snow cones from Mr. Flako. We squealed with excitement as he shaved flakes from a large block of ice, forming balls of snow to make the cones that were then saturated with our favorite tropical flavorings, like coconut, banana, or guava.

The next stop was the beach, where we played and relaxed until lunch time when we returned to town to continue eating with the rest of the money. This time we ate more of our indigenous dishes, like ducana cooked in grape leaves and served with codfish mixed with onions, tomatoes, and peppers. For dessert, we bought ice cream. By then, we didn't care that our school uniforms were soiled with foods from our excursions.

After a full day of fun, we returned home as school was being dismissed. In our naïveté, we didn't expect anyone to tell our parents or guardians we had cut school, though we both were dressed in our school uniforms.

When Mom got home from the baker shop, she asked me about cutting school and hanging out with Lenore all day. I was verbally reprimanded, and I promised not to do that again. Unlike my Mom's response, Lenore's grandmother contacted Lenore's mother in England and told her that she was going to send Lenore to England to live with her because of her disobedience. I felt so sad. I missed my cousin who had taught me many things, including how to ride a bike. I never wrote to her or spoke to her again. Thus began my second loss after having lost our dog, Tarzan, earlier on. I never thought of asking for Cousin Lenore's address, though I missed her terribly.

After being in America for a few days, I started venturing out on my own. I began to explore the surrounding neighborhoods. There was a hospital, a funeral home, a high school, and a subway station, all within walking distance. On every corner, there was a shop selling either food or clothes. Walking from one corner to the next was called a block, and there were streetlights on every corner.

To become acquainted with the public transportation in New York City, my sister showed me how to navigate the subway and bus systems. When you entered the subway station, you had to buy a token for twenty-five cents to pass through a turnstile in order to get on the train.

The first time I got on the train I was frightened because the train went underground, and I didn't know where I would end up. Yet, I was excited about the experience of riding the train. I also didn't realize the train could not only run underground, but also above ground, through tunnels, and over bridges.

Riding the train underground made me feel closed in and stifled like being in a cave or a dungeon. "How funny," I chuckled. I laughed to myself, knowing that bikes, cars, trucks, busses, and people were walking and driving over my head on the streets, as I observed when the train ascended from beneath the ground.

The entire city transportation system seemed like a rat race to me—this car, that bus, that train, even lots of planes overhead. Inside the subway station was like a different world. Vendors set up stands for magazines, newspapers, and sweets. Old A trains heading to Brooklyn made loud rusty noises, and C trains heading to Queens collided with the muffled sounds of the wind as the train ascended from underground. The screeching of train wheels on those rusty tracks was so loud it felt like my eardrums would burst. I had a ringing in my ears for a very long time.

Riding the crowded train was a sight to see. People huddled together, always seeming to be in a hurry. "What confusion," I thought. You'd think they had all gone mad—rushing, fussing, getting stuck in closing subway doors, and pushing, like they were running out of time. Some people had to stand up all the way until they got to where they were going. Some people looked tense, frustrated, depressed, and sad. Their faces looked stiff and stoic. If they dared to smile, their faces looked like they would crack. I saw people reading books, newspapers, magazines, and listening to their Walkman devices.

I was told not to make eye contact with people while on the train or on the streets because I might get cursed off, or look too excited, like a tourist, because people could see me as a target to approach. I was also told to put my pocketbook strap around my neck, stay off the trains late at night, and always stand in a well-lighted area.

I was shocked to see a policewoman carrying a gun. This was all so different from the island home I had left behind. There were no policewomen, and policemen did not carry guns. They carried clubs.

As I continued to check out the neighborhoods in Brooklyn where I lived, I was surprised to see bars on the doors and windows of people's homes.

Groups of men were hanging idle on stoops and street corners. I wondered if they had to go to work, because my dad was always at work performing one of his many jobs.

I had not seen many drunken, homeless people on the streets, but as I strolled down 42nd Street in Times Square on a warm summer night, I saw a man nodding and bowing down low to the ground. I thought he was sick, maybe fainting or something. I walked over and asked him if he was all right, and all of a sudden, he lifted up his head, straightened himself up quickly, and walked away as if nothing happened. A woman on the other corner did the same ritual. It was amazing to see. I didn't know if they were high off some kind of substance. I continued to see that to make it in America you'd have to be tough, brave, and patient.

Barely out of high school and transplanted to a new culture, I felt like a fish out of water. I was not sure if I was prepared to handle all my new life would entail. I had very mixed emotions because I had left my sister and her family, who had taken care of me and given me a home in a familiar culture. However, I had already reached my point of no return when I achieved my dream of coming to the United States. I had to choose to adjust to my new environment, find ways to survive, be strong, brave, courageous, feel good about myself, and stay inspired. More than ever, I had to work hard to achieve my goal of going to college. I was now in the position to take on the challenge of creating the peaceful, blissful life I wanted.

After my mother died, I felt alone, abandoned, and less than my peers, with an emptiness that lasted for years. Because of the emptiness that left me feeling broken, disconnected, afraid, and hopeless, I knew I would have to embark upon a journey of healing to feel whole again. I needed to find a spiritual connection; a source greater than myself for support. My knowledge and belief in a higher power led me to know that I was not alone in this process and could come out unscathed.

I set out about strengthening my faith muscle, which resulted in living in a state of expectancy and creating my own palette in life. I had to find a way to remember that all was not lost and there was a light at the end of the tunnel.

The death of the matriarch affects the entire family. As a result, my relationship with my siblings was greatly impacted. We did not discuss our feelings about Mom's death or what it meant to us, personally or collectively. Consequently, I did not know I had a choice in how to deal with grief and never considered that what I thought or felt mattered since I came from a family where children were seen and not heard.

As a family, we did not know how to cope with the myriad of emotions that accompanied such a loss, and there were no instructions on how to cope with bereavement.

Sadness and Loss

Though I was happy to reconnect with my sisters and brother in America, I felt displaced, alone, and sad. My sadness and a profound sense of loss were still an albatross around my neck. I felt we were all deeply impacted by the death of Mom, but still no one talked about it whenever we all got together. Maybe my younger brother and I were impacted the most because we were the two youngest of twelve children. I still desired to talk about it and to bring some closure after those many years.

I didn't feel we ever expressed our feelings to each other to provide comfort and support during that time of loss.

My Emotional Reaction to Losses

Losing my mom was a traumatizing, emotionally impactful experience. Among my emotions were fear, abandonment, anger, distrust, insecurity, rage, blame, doubt, guilt, shame, and resentment, in addition to a deep sense of inadequacy, loss, embarrassment, and unworthiness.

Though I still felt a lack of family support or discussion about our major loss, I had to *woman up* to cope with the persistent sadness and move on with my life.

The death of Mom impacted all of us. We did not handle her death well, and though we swept our feelings under the rug, I still felt a sense of profound loss and sadness.

Immigrant Fears

Because of the way I entered the States, I lived in constant fear of being discovered and deported. I even had dreams about being stopped by the authorities and unable to speak.

Inside, I was anxious and feared that I would be found out, be seen as a fraud, be placed in jail by the *Man* because I was not an American, and eventually be deported back to Antigua. Deportation was at stake for me. I had no mother, parents, nor home to return to. My struggle for survival and even the fear of my own death was also in play.

When my sister had to work late one night, I decided to make dinner for her. I decided to go to the corner store to buy groceries. The store was closed, so I had to walk an additional block further to the supermarket. I bought red herring, ripe plantains, and a red cabbage. When I was on my way back home, I noticed someone walking swiftly behind me. I clutched the brown paper bag in my arms and began to run. I noticed the man started running behind me so I dropped the bag of groceries and ran down the back alley and didn't stop running until I got home. When I entered the apartment, I was out of breath and so afraid that I ran to the bathroom and vomited.

Later when I explained to my sister what had happened, she said I did the right thing to run home. She explained she was familiar with this experience because a similar situation happened to her. "It's a feeling that you don't easily get over," she explained. "It's not safe for a young girl to be outside at night."

This experience made me so afraid that I dreaded leaving the apartment and only wanted to stay inside and hide. All these unsettling events made it difficult for me to adjust and assimilate in the new culture.

After being here and living with my sister for a few weeks, I wasn't comfortable not contributing financially to the household. I knew I needed to find work. I learned my work ethic from my parents and knew I could make my own way. Though I encountered that horrible, frightening experience coming from the grocery store, I couldn't allow anything to stop me from moving on with my life and becoming acculturated into my new environment, so I ventured out again to discover my new neighborhood.

One day while walking in the neighborhood, I came upon a little storefront church where I heard gospel music being played on a piano. Curious about the church name, I read it aloud, "Bright Light COGIC."

I did not know what those letters meant. I couldn't resist going inside to listen. From the pew on which I sat, I looked up at the pulpit and saw a pleasant looking woman reading the Bible. As the pianist continued to practice, the woman walked over and welcomed me to the church.

Another day, I couldn't resist returning and entering the little church I'd wandered upon when I met Mrs. Winters.

"Hello young lady, I am Mary Winters, one of the missionaries in the church," she said with a welcoming smile.

"Nice to meet you," I smiled back.

Mrs. Winters talked to me about the history of her church. Bright Light Church of God in Christ, a Pentecostal church, took a fundamentalist approach to understanding life and meaning. I was familiar with going to church, but this church was different in that they believed in *getting saved* and living your whole life in service to God. I was impressed by the way she spoke about the power of God, and she invited me to give my life to Christ. She told me that God loved me and wanted me to commit my life to Him.

She asked me questions about who I was and if I were new to the neighborhood. "Are you looking for a church home?"

I immediately replied, "Yes." Somehow, I felt safe enough with her to divulge information about myself.

She seemed delighted to know she may have recruited a new church member. She explained the schedule of church services and invited me to attend. I said I would attend one Sunday at a later date. After talking and sharing for a while with Mrs. Winters, she asked if I'd found a job yet.

I replied, "No, but I need one." I told her I was proficient in clerical skills—shorthand, typing, etc.

She dug into her bag and gave me a card with the address of an employment agency and the name of a contact person at the agency.

A few days later, I contacted the agency about a job placement interview. I felt hopeful I could be placed as a secretary or a stenographer.

After contacting the job placement agency, I was told to come in the following day for a job placement interview in Brooklyn, which required me to have my first bus ride experience. On the day of my appointment, I got on the B44 bus and gave myself plenty of time in case I got lost. I was proud to venture out and get my footing. I was wearing a nice dress with a half-slip under it and my lavender spring coat that my sister gave me.

After completing the placement application, taking and passing the typing and shorthand tests, the interviewer saw that I was very skilled. I typed 90 words a minute and wrote shorthand at 120 words a minute. I was accepted into the clerical work pool on the spot. I was also given a referral for a job interview the next day in Manhattan.

On the day of my first job interview, I was confident I would get the job. I had been on the train alone only a few times before and felt nervous about going to Manhattan by myself. When I arrived at the interview, to my disappointment, I was informed that the job had been taken, so I began making my way back to Brooklyn by train.

Because I still had a tremendous fear about the immigration authorities, I was always on the lookout. As I left the office building and stepped off the elevator, I saw two husky, approximately six-foot white men who reminded me of the immigration authorities. I just knew they were looking for me, so when they began to walk in my direction, my heart began to palpitate, my knees wobbled, and bullets of sweat ran down my face. I knew this feeling all too well. Once again, I held my breath until they walked past me. I panicked and hurried to get to the A train that would take me home.

As soon as I got into my sister's apartment, I locked the door and went to sleep on the couch. Though I was petrified from the day's experience, I knew I had to get up, shake it off, and persevere.

Soon after, the placement agency referred me to be interviewed for another clerical position in Manhattan. On my way to my second job interview I sat beside this kind-looking gentleman on the train reading the Daily News. I just glanced over at the newspaper, and, Lord, have mercy, the man started cursing me off.

He looked like he was ready to fight and told me to "buy my own damn newspaper." His eyes grew big and wide, as if they were going to pop out of his head. The man stopped reading the paper, put it in a plastic bag, and sat on it. I was so afraid, I just stared straight ahead. I tried as much as I could in every way to avoid his attention. When my stop came up, I hurriedly got off the train. Climbing the stairs, I came up out of the subway and walked a block to my job interview.

After completing a typing test, I was told that they were still interviewing applicants and would contact me within a few days.

Returning home on the train that day, the only seat available was next to a man dressed in a dirty white tee-shirt and washed-out dungarees. The man was bent over the whole time, scratching off a quick pick lotto ticket with a penny. The man just kept bending over, going down as if he were going to fall. He seemed to have fallen asleep. The penny fell to the floor and rolled under the foot of a heavy-set white man dressed in black pants, black shirt, and big, brown boots. A few seconds went by when, all of a sudden, the man woke up, reached over, and picked up his penny. I just sat right there pretending not to notice, but I saw everything. I was careful not let him see me looking directly at him.

The following day, I was contacted by the job placement office regarding another job offer as a receptionist or secretary in Brooklyn. They were looking for a receptionist who would be paid $300 every two weeks. I contacted the agency and an appointment was set for a week later. The interview was held in Brooklyn, which meant I had to take the bus.

Somehow, I developed enough courage to get on the bus and arrived on time. Riding the bus was a more pleasant experience this time. It was difficult to find the exact address.

I was grateful that I was at least ten minutes early and had time to walk an extra block to the place where the interview was being held.

When I arrived at the interview, I was ecstatic to see that the interviewer was Mary Winters, the lady from the church who initially referred me to the employment agency. In my mind, I surmised that since she knew I was looking for work, she had called the agency and requested me.

She interviewed me, gave me a short typing test, and hired me the same day as the receptionist in the real estate management office where she worked. My salary would be $300 every two weeks, plus health insurance. I was overjoyed to report to work at nine o'clock the following Monday morning. I was happy because I could now contribute to the household as well as save money to get my own apartment. I felt very proud of myself.

The following Monday morning I felt happy to report to work at ten o'clock. Mrs. Winters had not yet arrived, so I waited in an empty room. My responsibilities as a receptionist entailed answering the telephone, greeting callers, and taking messages. It also consisted of recording admissions to the apartment complex, keeping a tally of filled and open apartments, translating shorthand dictations, and reporting directly to Mrs. Winters.

During lunch, Mrs. Winters shared that she had three young sons and was the church secretary. Born in Mississippi, she and her three sons moved to Brooklyn in the early 60s in search of a better life after losing her husband in the U.S. Military.

She met the pastor and his wife and supported them in starting a church in the community. After accepting Jesus Christ into her heart, she was *saved*. She often talked about God's love. She said that God loved me. He had a call on my life and wanted to save my Soul. I thought that because God wanted to save my Soul, I must have done something wrong. I knew there was something else that needed to be done with and for the Soul. Though I did not know what it was, I was curious to find out.

When I received my first paycheck of $250 after taxes from the real estate management office, I was very happy. I took out $50 to prepare a parcel to send back home to my sister in St. Thomas, which I did religiously each pay period because that's what I thought I was supposed to do. People would come to America, get a job, and contribute to help their family back home. I wanted to contribute to my sister and her family because she took me in after my mother died when I had no place else to go.

I contributed $75 each pay period for room and board at my third sister's. I opened a savings account in which I deposited $50 each pay period, tithed $25 each pay period to the church, though it was a struggle, and survived off $50 every two weeks for transportation, food, and pocket change. Over time my income increased, and I deposited more money into my savings account because I was on a mission to procure my own apartment.

With all the preparations I received in how to navigate in my new environment, I was still robbed. I was coming home from work one afternoon, walking through the neighborhood park when I encountered a man who said he was from Africa visiting his relatives here in New York and needed to call them. He asked if I could give him some money to make a phone call to his relatives. I only had a $20 bill, and I wanted to help him because I could identify with feeling displaced in a new country.

I trusted what he said. He gave me a package to hold to assure me that he would come back with my change after he made his phone call. I held the package and waited for a couple of hours for him to return. Needless to say, he didn't return for his package, which was filled with newspaper, nor to bring back my change. In my naiveté, I finally realized I had been robbed. I felt violated, abused, exploited, depressed, embarrassed, and angry.

Was this the kind of adjustment I'd have to make to survive in this new culture? My trust in people was rapidly waning. Of course, I was afraid to go to the police station to report the incident for fear of being deported. Not being able to go to the police for help confirmed that I was still unvoiced and had to remain marginalized. My dream of coming to America had been slightly dashed, but I had to persevere to make it in America until I could fix my immigration status.

After working at the rental company for a few weeks, Mrs. Winters invited me again to come to her church, and I agreed to attend the following Sunday. It was a beautiful, bright Sunday when I first attended church. I was introduced to the whole church. Mrs. Winters, who was not just the church

ADJUSTING AND ASSIMILATING INTO THE AMERICAN CULTURE

secretary, but also a missionary, sat one chair below the pulpit where the pastor and deacon sat. On the next row down were church ushers on both sides. She sat with a big welcoming grin on her face.

I enjoyed the service and the message, "It's Time," delivered by the pastor's wife. It was a small church and the choir consisted of all ages. Someone played the piano and a boy played the drums. It was very exciting for me to see.

I was curious about the demonstration of some of the members who became very excited and emotional; that was called *getting happy*. During that time, a member might get carried away with the music and begin to express emotion through dancing, jumping, screaming, or falling and rolling on the floor. The church mothers would then surround the member and stand ready to support or wrap them with a sheet or blanket until they came back to composure.

I also enjoyed the non-Caribbean lunch which consisted of potato salad, string beans, and fried chicken.

After my first visit to Bright Light, I started to spend time with Mrs. Winters at the church where we often talked about God's love and salvation, and why it was important to study the Bible.

Bright Light Church consisted mostly of family members who comprised the congregation.

Needless to say, I joined that church. I began to spend most of my after-work time in church where there was peace and harmony. I attended Tuesday and Thursday night services and Sunday services throughout the day from 9 a.m. to 9 p.m.

I felt blessed to have found a church home to reinforce the teachings of my upbringing. I drew close to Mrs. Winters, who eventually adopted me as her goddaughter. I felt like I had a mom again. I felt she was the angel whom God had sent to protect and take care of me at that point in my life.

During Bible classes, Mrs. Winters taught that in order to be saved, you only needed to ask God to forgive you for your sins, accept Jesus into your heart, and receive Him as your Lord and Savior. Belief in God would be the Source of my strength and power to manifest my needs. I would develop my faith muscle through believing in the Supreme Being and reading His word, the Bible.

After attending church for a short while, I began to feel a stirring in my heart to dedicate my life to serving God. I accepted God in my heart one sunny Saturday morning in the 70s and began developing a personal relationship with the divine Source.

I started spending more time in church after work, studying the Bible, singing in the choir, and preparing my youth ministry mission. This helped to improve my confidence, but I was still guarded and didn't trust divulging any information about myself for fear of it being used against me. I marginalized myself by only spending time with people inside the church environment. I continued to be reclusive.

Assimilation into the American culture proved to be more difficult than I anticipated, but I knew I had to stay in an environment like church to keep me motivated. By spending so much of my free time in church, my extended family was developed. I knew it was essential I find a support system where I could feel safe, secure, and more accepted in this new culture. Because I believed God had a service for me to perform, I became obsessed with studying the Bible, seeking answers to questions about my life's purpose, and developing my spiritual practice of praying for the next few years.

I had problems socializing and making friends, so apart from my conversations with Mrs. Winters, I did not interact nor socialize with the youth in the church and stayed mostly to myself to protect my secret.

I experienced Americans as inquisitive, probing, and asking too many questions: *Where are you from? How long have you been here?* and *Where did you go to school?*

Those kinds of personal questions made me more introverted. Consequently, I avoided intimacy with others, and thus, my challenge with trust continued. I imprisoned myself. Except for the need to go out for the bare necessities, I never went outside and was always looking over my shoulder when I did. I didn't want to have to report to or be accountable to anyone, have anyone knowing my every move, or getting too close. Not allowing myself to make friends made me feel ostracized and guarded. This impacted my ability to communicate my feelings in social situations, which affected my ability to make friends and form trusting, healthy, authentic relationships.

After arriving home from work one day, I took a quick nap before going to church. In my dream, I was coming down the hallway at work when I saw a group of people walking and coming my way. I felt so scared my knees were weak. I started to shake, my heart began to palpitate, my palms became clammy, and my innards began to quiver nervously. I knew I was busted. I broke out in a cold sweat. As they passed me by, my eyes welled up with tears.

Awakened by a light touch of my sister's hand on my shoulder, I realized it was one of my many frightful, recurring dreams of hiding. I lived a hermetic existence going only to church and work. However, I knew I could not hide myself away from the world forever.

PART II

LIFE BEFORE AMERICA

CHAPTER 3

Tropical Lifestyle

There were times I'd sit and think about where I had come from. I'd start with my journey from childhood, which was filled with sadness and loss, to having arrived in the States and embarking upon my new life in a new culture. Though I had no desire to return to Antigua, I enjoyed reminiscing about my beautiful home island.

There was a certain freedom of expression that occurred on my island, especially uptown when the country folk came to shop for their weekly goods. Yearning for my island became a daily occurrence, which gave me the opportunity to express my love for it in this poem.

My Beautiful Island

I love the freedom of my tropical lifestyle—
In the islands, between the Atlantic Ocean and
    Caribbean Sea,
The pure large sun shines, seemingly

Burning hotter than anywhere;
Antigua, being not too far from the equator,
Feels like winter is absent there.

I love the freedom of my tropical lifestyle—
In the islands, crisp, fresh air softly tingles
Fragrant flowers, sweet-scented perfumes of
Daffodils, hibiscuses, and morning glories,
African violets, lilies, and poppies,
Paradise birds flying, bees humming,
Butterflies flitting, stopping occasionally
Communing with trees, swaying and
Bowing in grand flamboyancy.

I love the freedom of my tropical lifestyle—
In my beautiful island, grass looks greener
Like plush velvet and silk-jade, blanketing
Potent mother earth who stands poised, ready
Waiting to welcome the arrival of
Nourishment from liquid rain.

I love the freedom of my tropical lifestyle—
When lightning is striking, thunder is
Rumbling, and rain is beating on cocoa earth
While diverted spouts yield fresh rainwater
into cisterns, wells and drums,
Creating sounds of African rhythmic patterns.

TROPICAL LIFESTYLE

I love the freedom of my tropical lifestyle—
Looking over the horizon, sunset explodes
Rainbows unfold, in kaleidoscopic hues
Shades of reds, greens, yellows, and blues
As white cottony clouds create mysterious
Shapes and symbols like angels and dragons
Wafting gently across the sky.

In the freedom of my beautiful island
The fierce glistening seawater bubbles,
Waves dancing, curling, rolling, tumbling
Whoosh, whoosh, splish-splashing.

Sauntering across the ocean shore
Sinking my feet in blazing hot sand
Waves perform their tireless task of
Pulling and pushing, tugging and rolling
Crashing powerfully against my bare feet,
With toes I brace myself
Sinking my feet into cool wetness.

Above me, seagulls are squawking
Seaweeds wrapping around my feet
Lukewarm sensations from the water
Tickling my excitement as I smell the
Bouquet of the ocean breeze.

UNDOCUMENTED

On my beautiful Caribbean island
Motorboats dock at Fisherman's Wharf
Where tourists and natives come to shop
The stalls are crammed with multitude of
Fishes for sale: "Fresh fish, w'at you want?
Ol' wife, Queen Mullet, Doctor, Flounder,
Octopus, Conch or Lobster Tail—
Two shillings a pound."
"Get your fish, w'at you want? No better price
To be found, it's the cheapest price in town."

In the freedom of my unspoiled, exotic island
Cotta-headed women wear seersucker dresses
With pregnant hips sashaying, sauntering,
Moving gingerly in marketplaces
Bearing trays of produce and fruits: Dasheen,
Cassavas, guavas, papaya and ground nuts
Mixed with aromas from local eateries and
baker shops.

Bouncing with rhythm in hips and smiling faces
Spoke with bold voices, "Get your breadfruit,
Eddoes and yams, tomatoes, green figs, buns,
Bread pudding and macas; one shilling a pound."

In the freedom of my beautiful island
Daring voices void of fear or worry

Exude great joy in orating, playing baseball
Water sports, cricket, golfing, or Warri.

I love the energy in my beautiful island—
Natives in colorful attire are swinging and singing
Moving to lively sounds of Calypso rhythms
Steel drum pans musicians playing
Winding and grinding, twirling and dancing,
Saluting each other with plenty pride and dignity.

Antigua, one of the Leeward Islands and a former British colony of the Lesser Antilles, is a small island, though one of the largest islands in the West Indies. It rests on the north side of the equator with a tropical climate and little change in seasonal temperatures.

Antigua gained its independence from Britain in 1981. Today, Antigua is developed and prosperous, due to tourism, offshore banking, internet gambling, and educational services. However, sugarcane and tourism are the main industries. Tourists come from overseas to enjoy the beautiful beaches with the crystal-clear waters, soft sand, and warm tropical breezes passing through the lively trees.

There was freedom and beauty in my tropical lifestyle, for its relaxing quietness was always vibrantly exotic. After reading the rich history of my island, I began to understand there were so many that came before me who inhabited and developed my island paradise.

The whole of Antigua is divided into parishes or villages; St. Johns, Bolans, Sweets, Old Road, Grays Farm, and Jennings are just a few. My parents were ambitious and creative and settled in the parish of Grays Farm to rear their children and raise pigs and chickens. This parish was once considered a poor, rural, Creole-speaking community, small enough that everyone knew their neighbor and gossiped and talked about each other.

Most people in our community lived in small, cramped homes, topped with flat roofs built with wood, very rarely cement.

Though we were not wealthy, our house was one of the better houses in the village. I spent many days sweeping the front yard with the bramble bush broom from the shack tree to make sure the curb appeal was neat and clean. First, I began by sprinkling water in the dirt on the ground to keep the dust down, especially if it were windy, then I used the fullest bramble from the shack tree to briskly sweep the yard until it was clean. Then I would pick up and sweep up twigs and brambles that had fallen from the tamarind tree to be added to the coals in the coal pot to build the fire for cooking. We owned and lived in a white-painted, one-bedroom house with a gallery in the front of the house facing Parliament Street in Grays Farm.

Except for the big beige and white house on the corner in front of the lamp post, which belonged to the strange woman from America, our house stood out from all the others on Parliament Street. Where we lived was prime property and having a house with a gallery was a status symbol. Most families sat on their gallery in the evenings after chores were done. The gallery was where most of the gossiping took place as folk gathered to talk about what was going on in the neighborhood. It was easy to hear their voices from under our house or behind the fence.

Our gallery was in the front of our house, and we had a crawl space about two feet high under the house. My delight was crawling under my house, scraping and searching while looking for money, combs, hair pins or afro pics—anything flat that fell between the cracks and crevices of the floorboards. I was always excited whenever I found money under the house to buy sweet treats, like ginger beer, ice cream, Fanta soda, or scorched coconut sugar cakes in the hard coconut shell.

I remember the day I discovered an old, round rusted coin, which had been maltreated by time and buried under our house. It was a joyful day. While washing away the dirt in soapy, sudsy water, rugged edges slid and slipped into my palms as a ten-cent coin with the image of a white lady wearing a crown with a smooth silver background appeared before my eyes.

Mom said she was our queen, a very important person because her face was on money, clothes, food, everything. She ran our island from where she lived in England. I had never seen a white queen before. Mom said the queen seldom visited, so whenever she came to town, it was a royal holiday.

Seeing her majesty was a big affair, a celebration. We celebrated her like it was carnival. School was dismissed, businesses shut their doors, and parades and motorcades mingled with shouts and laughter of children bouncing on their fathers' shoulders. We lined narrow ditched roads with jovial faces jumping, pushing, and shoving to catch a glimpse of her majesty as people raved over her beauty. We waived a British flag in her honor, singing and chanting the lyrics of "God Save the Queen."

Though my island was beautiful and serene, the energy in my neighborhood was not always peaceful and full of love. Right outside our kitchen window, between the stone heap and the galvanized fence, Violet lived in the small wooden house. Anyone could tell when her boyfriend, Victor, came to visit because he always got upset and instigated fights with her in the house. He lived elsewhere and often bragged about his need for *rudeness*. When he wanted it, the whole neighborhood knew because she would deny his advances and he would run her out of the house when he was not able to attack her inside the house. Yet, no one said a word.

Victor, they said, was a functional drunk. He worked as a grave digger and used to be a deacon at Green Bay Church, but every Friday night after six o'clock we could expect to hear them arguing and fighting. They said that Victor drank rum like fish drink water. They said he used to be very active in the church, but when he started drinking, he stopped going. One afternoon my friend Lillian and I were playing hopscotch in my front yard, when all of a sudden, we heard the shouting, screaming commotion.

"You're a crazy drunk," Violet shouted, running out of her house.

"Me go kill you, nasty woman," he screamed, running behind her with a cricket bat.

"Me no want you," Violet shouted as she ran to our yard for shelter.

This was a regular occurrence, and again, no one bothered to say anything about it.

"Me no want you," Violet would retort time and again as she would escape his chase and run back into her little house.

Victor was very persistent and would pound on the door for her to let him in. I always felt embarrassed when a crowd of people in the neighborhood stood by to enjoy the spectacle instead of trying to support the safety of the woman. No one seemed to want to get involved in domestic squabbles.

Not only were there a few dysfunctional families creating unrest in the neighborhood, there were many superstitions about the indigenous folk—people believed they could hex you or send you to an insane asylum. This kept people afraid and non-trusting of people's ulterior motives. If you didn't assimilate and socialize with other neighbors, you could be targeted to receive ill wishes from those who may have envied or begrudged you, or from people who felt you acted like you thought you were better than they. It was a fearful experience for me.

We were a large close-knit family who were supportive of each other and did many things together. Some people thought we were proud, haughty, and judgmental, and not very welcoming to the ways of the islanders.

Mom tried to insulate her children from those who might be able to lead them astray from our strict rules and boundaries, our moral values and aspirations of achieving a better education, and the wholesome lifestyle our parents had imparted to us. Because my Mom didn't spend time with the people who spent time on their galleries gossiping about others, they lashed out at us. As a result, bullying began. We suffered physical and verbal attacks from people who thought we thought we were better than them.

In the evenings, people would sit on their galleries and share gossip about everyone in the village. As a child, I would hide and listen to the gossip and realize that my Mom didn't spend time gossiping and contributing to the negative energy of the gallery-sitting people. My mother was very concerned about how the influences of our environment would impact her children's experiences. She had strict rules, which kept her children away from other kids who didn't have boundaries or guidelines.

As a result, the bullying continued. Rocks were thrown at our house to break the glass in our front door and windows. Garbage and human feces were thrown in our yard. We noticed that our half-acre lot grew narrower over time, as our galvanized fencing slowly moved to gradually take inches of land from our property to add to the adjacent property.

These behaviors unnerved me. I couldn't figure out why they didn't like us or mistreated us so. My mom was soft-spoken and didn't speak up and I, a child, was afraid to speak out against the injustices. I couldn't understand why my parents didn't follow up with the complaints about the injustices of stealing our property or mistreatments against our family. Thus was the early beginning of my becoming unvoiced out of fear, distrust of people, and retribution. I became more and more introverted. I became fearful of the people who bullied us.

This experience impacted my confidence and my feeling *less* than others. I felt ostracized and afraid of what people could do to me. I wanted them to stop the mistreatment.

As fearful and as disillusioned as I was about people's motives and actions, I was still inspired by the few upwardly mobile people who thought differently from the small-town mentality of some of the islanders. I remember Mom wanting a more sophisticated environment for her children. My parents tried to give us good values.

Our yard was fenced in on both sides as well as the back. Both front and back yards were unpaved, clear of shrubs and grass, making it easier for our large family to play and socialize together. However, it was customary to see the neighboring children playing hopscotch, jacks, or marbles in the street.

I was a quiet child and didn't have many friends. I didn't mind because I liked being alone to play with my baby dolls in my dollhouse, creating my own games and playing with my cousin, Lenore, with whom I felt safe. Lenore lived with her grandmother who wasn't as strict as my parents. She was a freer spirit. I admired my cousin Lenore because I saw her as brave and adventurous. She wasn't afraid to take chances and be a little disobedient.

Sometimes on Saturday mornings, she would come to my house and help me deliver the wash that my mom had done for the people in the neighboring villages, and sometimes we walked about the island. We would then return home and enjoy my favorite thing, which was to watch and help Mom as she parched peanuts for sale. She bought ten-pound bags of peanuts in the shell and roasted them on the coal pot. I can remember the days when my sisters shelled them. Mom made the peanuts into candy with coconut, sugar, and spices. Occasionally I would run back and forth from our house to Salmon Shoppe to buy sweet oil and yellow-salt butter, which Mom used to make the candy. If they didn't have what we needed, I would walk up the hill to Mr. Coalbin, a short, stout burly man who could often be found outside his congested shop, where our family maintained a weekly running tab. Among the items we bought from Mr. Coalbin were brown sugar, white flour, cornmeal, charcoals, and coconut for baking.

Sometimes Lenore would even come home with me from school for lunch and help me pick up the dry lodging on which my family slept the night before from the stone heap before it would rain again, since it often rained intermittently during the day and would rewet the lodging.

We had many modes of transportation on the island, including buses, donkeys, and horses. Fortunately, everything in the neighborhood was accessible by foot, so if it didn't rain enough to fill the drums that collected the water, the children had to walk for miles to the public pipe and bring home buckets of water for cooking and drinking. We also had to use the community shower across the street from our house, which always seemed to have clean running water.

My family was a typical island family with traditional African values. My parents were both hardworking, creative, resourceful, and self-sufficient. What I remember most about my parents was their entrepreneurial spirit and work ethic. Dad was a fisherman, farmer, and father; he tended his own farmland and sugar cane fields and livestock with the help of his donkey, Jim. Mom was a baker, housewife, and mother, who desperately desired to have a large, fully-equipped kitchen. I learned the value of hard work, ambition, and a good work ethic from my parents. They believed in working hard and contributing to the community.

Mom was a typical poor, working-class woman who took pride in fulfilling her domestic duties at home for her family. Mom was also on the Women's Fellowship Board and Armor Bearers' group at church. On special occasions, Mom was contracted to provide her baked goods to the church for sale.

As early as five o'clock every morning after Big Church's bell rang, she began her ritual of gathering up her risen kneaded dough to take to Mrs. Brown's Baker Shop to bake for the day. By three o'clock in the afternoon, she would hurry to go uptown, carrying a tray of her wares on top of a cotta on her head. A cotta is a wound piece of fabric forming a crown to help balance and cushion the weight of the tray.

Head carrying was common on the island as women, children, and some men carried buckets of water from the community pipes. Women also carried baskets and bundles of folded clothes on their heads from doing and delivering laundry to their employers. Some women showed how dexterous they could be by balancing their tray so well they did not use their hands. It was always an exciting experience to go uptown and see business owners selling goodies: ice cream, popcorn, blood pudding, and soda pops. I felt proud to see my mom selling her cakes, buns, and tarts among them.

When Mom came home about nine o'clock at night, she would begin her other rituals. These duties included washing clothes by hand or on a wash board, cleaning the house, and cooking on the coal pot in the yard under the tamarind tree, after having spent a ten-to-twelve-hour workday at Mrs. Brown's Baker Shop.

Our coal pot was the heat source we used to cook our meals. A coal pot is made of clay and holds the hot coals for cooking. The coal pot has an opening in the bottom to catch and release the ashes.

From the early age of six years old, I learned how to cook from my mom. I watched her long, bony fingers that looked like mine knead bread at night and set it to rise by morning in preparation for the shaping of the loaves of bread, buns, and tarts she would sell in the afternoon at the market in town. Often, while Mom was still at the baker shop, she would send one of my older sisters ahead of her to town with a tray of her wares to catch the morning crowd.

I also had the opportunity sometimes to watch Mom with her favorite red-plaid headband around her head, covering her shoulder-length, braided hair to help control the perspiration running into her eyes. She wiped away the moon-lit, glistening sweat off her dark, worn face with the back of her hand as she finished her chores for the night.

In the morning, she would give us the biggest smile with her brown dancing eyes, her white porcelain teeth, and her deep dimpled cheeks before leaving the house to work in the baker shop all day.

Dad was a tall, strong, proud, stately-looking, medium brown-skinned man who was a talented fisherman. He had no formal education but lots of natural talent. He taught himself to make fish pots and mend fish nets while standing outside in the front yard so everyone could see how inventive, innovative, and creative he was. This enabled him to feed his family from the sea. As previously stated, Dad tended his own farmland, sugar cane fields, and livestock with the help of his donkey, Jim.

Some of my happiest moments with Mom included singing hymns from her red song book and cooking macaroni and cheese. Some of my happiest moments with my dad included watching him make fish pots and visiting him at the fish market.

Though I would rarely see Mom until late at night, I always felt comforted by her soft-spoken and caring words. It encouraged me to live up to her expectations. As a child, I hardly spent time with my parents because they worked all the time, so my older siblings had to be around to supervise my younger brother and me.

Though my parents weren't around much during the day, they were strict disciplinarians and we obeyed their rulings.

Whenever Dad thought I had disobeyed an order and deserved punishment, he'd always have trouble catching me to spank me because I was a fast runner.

On my small island, it was our culture to eat in harmony with nature. We didn't have big supermarkets with imported foods. We grew our own provisions, which were free of pesticides and deadly chemicals. We ate organically. We grew primarily whole-root vegetables like: cassava, sweet potatoes, eddoes, yams, and carrots. Other vegetables were tomatoes, corn, okra, eggplant, cucumbers, cabbage, and lettuce.

Sometimes on my way home from school, I would stop by Mrs. Walter's house to pick spinach, which grew wildly over her fence. We also picked wild-grown cassi (nopales cactus). Our fruit trees included: banana, plantain, sugar apple, dumps (jujube fruit), guava, soursop, breadfruit, and avocado. I enjoyed gathering the fruits from climbing coconut, guinep, and mango trees around the island.

While seafood and provisions were plentiful, we also consumed large amounts of salt in corned beef, shad, and red herring, as well as white flour and sugar. We did not have refrigeration, so regular salt, which was plentiful and inexpensive, was the main method we used for curing and preserving certain foods to stop toxins or bacteria from developing.

After a day at sea, I remember Dad cleaning his catch of eel, shark, and octopus. He would cut the eels down the center, cover them with salt, and hang them on a nail outside the kitchen door. After hanging there for a few days, the skin of the eels would begin to tighten more and more each day, until the skin could be pulled off easily. I never liked seeing the eels hanging from the nail, but I still picked little pieces off to eat during the drying process as I passed by. Shark and octopus were eaten pretty quickly, so there was no need for them to be cured.

On Sundays, we ate pork from the pigs we raised, which were fed fruits and vegetables, or grain-fed chickens we raised, or beef we purchased from the community butcher. One of our traditional dishes was ducana. This was by far my favorite dish because it was made with plenty of shredded coconut, sweet potatoes, sugar, flour, and spices all wrapped in banana leaves. It was a delicious dish Mom always prepared on Sundays and special occasions like a baptism or church confirmation.

In the Caribbean, we would strive to keep our African heritage alive and still practice our own culture. How we dressed, moved, and danced was emphasized. We loved to dress in native clothing and dance to calypso and reggae music. My father liked to dance, and from time to time, he would put on the radio and sing and dance to calypso music. His favorite dance was the merengue, and occasionally he'd have one of my sisters do the dance steps with him.

On weekends, we could hear the blaring sounds of steelpans, drums, jazz musicians, piano players, reggae, and calypso music coming from Salmon's Juke Joint, an adult night club around the corner from our house. This kept the energy and vibrancy of the island culture alive.

The cultural practices were prevalent at all times. Sailing events, which were held annually at the end of April, brought many sailing vessels and sailors to the island to play sports like cricket and soccer.

As mentioned, travel by foot was the preferred mode of transportation in my neighborhood, and on rare occasions, we would ride a donkey. The various neighborhoods were interwoven by narrow, twisting alleyways. My small neighborhood had lots of nooks, crannies, and alleyways that were used as short cuts to quickly and easily get to another part of the village, visiting friends, and traveling to the beach. Since we lived only ten minutes away from the sea, going to the beach was my favorite pastime.

I enjoyed weaving through alleyways until the white, glistening sands and delicate date trees at Green Bay Beach appeared. It was called Green Bay because it was located in that village. There was Green Bay School, Green Bay Church, and Green Bay Beach. We always knew when we arrived at Green Bay Beach because that was where all the children in the neighborhood went to cool off during the hot, sweltering summer months.

As a child, I often ran to the beach for refuge. Mom said the sea water had curative values. Walking and wading in the water always calmed my nerves. Whenever I needed to clear my head and find inspiration, I ran to the beach. At the beach, I found peace and tranquility. I liked to look at huge ships as they passed by. I wondered how far they had travelled and how much farther they had to go as they glided beyond my peripheral vision and out of sight. I respected the power of this body of water and was intrigued by its vastness. I often looked and wondered what it might be like beyond the horizon.

Some of our other cultural practices included hair braiding, hair straightening, and ear piercing. I didn't enjoy getting my hair combed and braided because it was painful to me. Not only was my hair red, which they said was from being in the hot broiling Caribbean sun, but it was tightly curled. My sister had no sympathy for me when she pulled and tugged at my hair during the braiding process. The only beauty parlor in the neighborhood was owned by Miss Pearle who would use a pressing comb to straighten my hair, which lessened the pulling and tugging.

When I was seven years old, my older sister, who was not a beautician, tried to press my hair with the pressing comb. It was a frightening experience because the pressing comb was over heated from the coals in the coal pot and dipped in a container of hair grease as she proceeded to run the hot comb through my hair. I could see the excess smoke and smell the scent of my hair burning from the overheated comb. In addition, she almost burned the flesh off the top of my right ear.

In the same year, the same sister pierced both of my ears. She first used white thread to thread a sewing needle, sterilized the needle with alcohol, and placed ice on one earlobe at a time to numb the lobe before piercing it with the needle. She then left the white thread to hang loose in my earlobes. The thread was lubricated with yellow salt butter to allow it to be pulled back and forth through the earlobe until it was healed. Needless to say, the initial puncture of the earlobe was very painful.

My family did not celebrate birthdays or Halloween. We always went to church on Easter and held an annual harvest, a big holiday on the island.

Carnival was and continues to be an important annual cultural affair. Carnival is a celebration of the emancipation of slavery. We celebrated with sports and other cultural events, such as limbo dancing, crabbing, and children playing and emulating the king and queen competition. This is an extensive event that is very exciting and held at the end of July for a ten-day period. It is a festival of colorful costumes, beauty pageants, talent shows, music, and parades.

J'ouvert Morning is a special event that precedes the carnival festivities where people congregate as early as five o'clock in the morning to walk and dance behind the brass and steel bands.

Mom was very busy during the annual carnival as she always made special ice cream and cakes, ginger beer, and greased breads to sell.

In addition to the many practices, rituals, and celebrations, the islanders were generally very religious. My parents believed that a family that prayed together stayed together. They believed in God as the creator and supreme ruler of all and instilled in us the truth of a Higher Source greater than us who would guide and protect us. In addition, they taught we must do our part through inspired action and staying connected to the church.

My parents were well-known and respected in the community. Every Saturday, Dad helped get us ready for church on Sunday, polished our shoes, and made sure my brothers had haircuts.

My parents took us to church every Sunday and insisted we return during the weekdays for choir practice and youth services. They taught us to live by the Ten Commandments as well as to focus on Jesus' Golden Rule, *"Do unto others as you'd have them do unto you."* Each Sunday as a family, we walked about a half of a mile to attend Green Bay Moravian Church. Most Sundays after church, we walked together as a family to visit our relatives or to collect donations to be delivered to the church.

Each night before we went to bed, Mom got down on her knees and asked God to take care of her children. That was her way of asking for help and support and instilling hope and faith in us. She always emphasized that there was a greater power over and protecting us. We would all get down on our knees every night to say our prayers, a practice I still engage in today.

Educational Aspirations

While my parents were not very educated, they believed in and valued education. Having an education was also considered a status symbol. My father never went to school and could not read. He was not able to sign his signature or print his name, and signed with an X. My mother left school in the fifth grade. Mom knew the value of having an education and believed that education was your passport to a better life. She knew that this would be a ticket to freedom. As much as she could, she sent her children, especially her daughters, to the best schools she could afford and believed in preparing us to be self-sufficient, productive adults.

My formative school years began at five years old in kindergarten at the Weston's Kindergarten School where we learned social skills and pre-reading skills. This was essential preparation for developing good interpersonal relationships.

In the first grade, I attended Otters School in the corporal-punishment-ruled British colonial system. Every morning before classes began, we stood in a straight line in the broiling hot sun turning both palms of our hands upward while our nails were inspected. If a speck of dirt were found under our nails, we'd turn our hands over to receive about three whacks with a wooden ruler across the knuckles. This was to encourage good hygiene practices, which would be helpful in our lives.

In school, I did not like the way of taking attendance because we had no privacy and everything was done in the open. When we got to our class, all the students stood up to greet the teacher until she said, "Good morning class, you may sit down." From the roll book, she called our names in alphabetical order and we would say, "Present please." Our notebooks had pictures of our Queen Elizabeth wearing her crown filled with diamonds and white pearls around her neck.

By the second grade I realized that, even though I liked to read, I didn't always comprehend all I was reading. I felt ashamed to ask my teacher for help. No one helped me. I started to doodle, drawing boxes and people's faces.

In the third grade, I became precocious and quite a talker. I enjoyed school because I liked learning. I liked spelling, reading, penmanship, and sports. I did not like arithmetic but still did well enough in that subject. I was not a quick learner, but I often knew the answers and would raise my hand a lot. However, I noticed that the teacher would call on other kids before calling on me. This made me feel less liked by my teacher.

I was punished a lot for either talking too much or chewing gum. In this one-room school house, I walked slowly to receive the punishment, which was either to stand on a bench in front of the entire school, go up to the head master's desk on the stage in front of the entire school, receive a few whacks across the knuckles, or be hit across the back with a thick, leather strap by the head mistress. These were very oppressive, embarrassing, and humiliating methods of punishment that could destroy anyone's self-esteem.

In fourth grade, the subject was geography. Miss Alexander spoke very fast with a Barbudan accent. She wrote in big letters on the black board, and for this I was grateful. It was hard to see and read smaller writing on the black board. Miss Alexander located America on the globe, which was a familiar word to me. She told us that many dreams could be realized in America. That tweaked my interest.

By grade five, I still talked a lot and felt compelled to speak out against what I considered injustices I witnessed in the classroom. I felt that certain students seemed to get preferential treatment from the teacher when others did not. Because I spoke out, again I was punished. By now my self-esteem was being more impacted, and I began to speak up less, becoming more introverted. I felt it was not safe to share my thoughts and beliefs because I could be reprimanded for doing so. Over time, I felt the use of my voice and my confidence level waning.

CHAPTER 4

My Childhood Dream of Going to America

I had already heard about America before Miss Alexander pointed it out on the globe in geography class. My longing for America began after observing the Westons, who had moved from America to our island. Mr. Weston was just returning home with his wife after having lived in England and America.

Everything they did seemed very different from the way we did things: the way they spoke, looked, dressed, and how they carried themselves. They were well-travelled, sophisticated, and educated. They were on a mission to travel from village to village on the island, encouraging children to want more, to set goals, and to follow through with their educational aspirations, which could only help to build good self-esteem among them.

Mr. Weston was a handsome man about fifty but looked and behaved older than his age. He had long sideburns and short, fine, *coolie* hair, which meant his hair was not tightly curled. His silvery-gray beard cascaded down his tall skinny frame part way to his slightly bulging belly.

Mr. Weston was always neatly dressed. He often wore a full cream-beige suit with a watch chain in his pocket, which he used to tell the time. Sometimes he wore navy blue pants, a beige cardigan over a long-sleeved white shirt and blue tie. Yet, other times he dressed as if he were a king—in full African regalia.

On Saturday afternoons, he took leisurely walks while little girls played hopscotch and jump rope and the little boys played cricket on unpaved dirt roads. Always curiously amazed by his presence, I watched as he would gingerly stroll along, whistling and swinging a natural wooden walking stick. He would step cautiously over dips and cracks in the dirt road and occasionally use his stick for support.

With friendly cordial laughter, he greeted everyone, even children—bowing, nodding, smiling, and shaking hands as he yanked, "Hello little ones, how are you? What's your name? How is your family?"

Mr. Weston also liked to whistle and would sometimes sing songs, like "If I Had a Hammer," "Leaving on a Jet Plane," and calypso songs to the children. One afternoon, as he bowed his head to say goodbye to my sister, the purple kufi he wore that particular day, which matched his loose-fitting dashiki pants, fell off his head, exposing the bald horseshoe-shaped spot in the crown of his head and his short, matted woolen locks. I remember wondering if he were disguised as Father Christmas. Why else would his beard be so long and silvery gray?

Mrs. Weston was a small-statured woman with a strong African presence. She had clean skin, full lips, and wore African clothes with head wraps in matching cloth. She had a Miriam Makeba look about her. She had taught African dance classes in America and was now teaching women and children in the neighborhood.

It was hard to guess her exact age, but Mrs. Weston looked younger than my mom. Maybe her life had been easier. Her well-groomed, small boxed braids, partially covered by her head wrap, were accentuated by her hazel eyes and golden-brown skin, which were usually shielded from the often-sweltering hot sun by a red parasol. Everyone was taken with her style and countenance.

Mr. and Mrs. Weston were dedicated to exploring, researching, and sharing information about those who came before us and those currently fighting for civil rights and freedom for African Americans and all of humanity—people like Marcus Garvey, Dr. Martin Luther King Jr., and Malcolm X. The events happening in America were in the form of nonviolent marches and protests against the inequalities of their democratic system.

The Westons continued to give back to the community by opening a private school for kindergarteners through grade four, where the students had African dance classes and studied African American history. The Westons also addressed the needs of people who were interested in serving in our tourism industry. They encouraged and helped people to apply for and pursue admission into hotel management schools in preparation for working in this type of employment.

I wanted to emulate their lifestyle. They would tell us stories of the tall buildings in America that looked like mountains. It was a place where you could do and be anything you want. People in America could have their own mansions, which are really beautiful houses with a large kitchen, electricity, running water, bathrooms, and great big back yards. This was called the *American Dream*.

I began to yearn even more for America. I created visuals from Mr. Weston's description of America, the "Land of the free, the home of the brave," which kept me excited about the possibility of one day living like people in America. I could get the education in whatever area I liked: sketching or sewing fashions or maybe teaching. Listening to the Westons inspired me to dream big, keep hope alive, and aspire to be the best I could be in whatever I chose.

I became better able to understand my mom's intense desire to go to St. Thomas to procure work and relocate my younger brother and me to begin a better life. Mom wanted more for her children than what was available on my island. She wanted a more sophisticated environment in which to rear her children. She could foresee the upcoming deterioration of our island and was determined to rescue and offer us better opportunities through education and exposure. She had a vision for her offspring that could better prepare them for their future. Everyone knew that St. Thomas was a portal to get to the United States.

Mom was intuitive, adventurous, ambitious, and a woman of faith. She allowed the power of faith to work in her life. She used to say, "Faith without works is dead." So, she devised and began implementing a plan to gradually relocate her remaining children to St. Thomas. The two oldest daughters had already left home and were living in St. Thomas and the U.S., and my third older sister and an older brother were still at home.

When my oldest brother turned seventeen years old, my parents sent him to St. Thomas, USVI, to live with my maternal uncle. He traveled by boat in the middle of the night during a hurricane. Needless to say, my parents couldn't wait to hear he had indeed arrived safely, although the boat had drifted a bit in the high winds.

Thus began the gradual pilgrimage of the remaining siblings off our native island of Antigua.

After my brother had been living in St. Thomas for a while and had gotten married, my mom decided to go there to live with him and his wife until she could find a job. Through my brother's associations and friends, Mom found work pretty quickly with Mrs. Ella, who bonded her as her housekeeper. Bonding from your employer would allow you to stay longer in St. Thomas in order to work, save money, and procure residency. Mom worked hard, sent money back home to help take care of us, and saved enough to rent a one-bedroom apartment.

I didn't quite understand why Mom was away for so long because no one explained that she had gone to St. Thomas to eventually send for my younger brother and me. I just remembered her leaving one day without saying a word to me. I asked my sister where Mom was and she just said, "No worry, me go tek care of you and little brother."

Dad said Mom went overseas to get some well needed rest. She said she would be gone for two weeks, but a month later she had not come back.

My sister then told me that Mom had gone to St. Thomas to visit my brother and his wife to find work so that she could send for us. Knowing Mom's plan didn't stop my pining over her absence—I felt such a sense of loss, separation, and abandonment that I acted out. I was beginning to be a little defiant; I started visiting neighbor's houses, which is not what I would have done if Mom had been home. For example, I went to my classmate Gracelyn's house to play, and sometimes I stayed for dinner or until it got dark before I went home. Other times, I would go to Miss Maize's house to watch her black and white television.

Luckily, the strict guidelines Mom set for us put me back on track quickly. I didn't want to disappoint her by behaving badly while she was away. I just wanted her back home.

I remember there was no stirring at night or smell of kerosene oil from flambos burning brightly under pitch black skies, when the stars refused to surrender their light. I missed the glimmer of the faraway look in her eyes of wanting more out of life. There was no earnest humming along with the radio as George Beverly Shea sang, "The Old, Old Story." I missed the smell of mouthwatering aromas from Mom's cooking and the taste of our nightly meals. I missed the squish-squash sounds of her washing at night in the white enamel basin with brown common soap that lathered the clothes while pressing, rubbing, pulling, and tugging with strong calloused hands. Many times, the sound of the wet clothes was in rhythm with the melody of "The Old, Old Story:" *I love to tell the story, and it will be my theme in glory, to tell the old, old story of Jesus and his love.*

Everyone wants what is best for their family. Immigrants dream too. Like every other human being, they want to feel equal and free in the world.

It was a necessary transition for Mom to leave home and start the process of rescuing her children from our small island. Her plan was to get the older children out first and then the younger ones. She would send for my two oldest sisters first, one at a time, who lived in Mom's one-bedroom apartment with her until they found jobs and were able to move into their own apartment. My third oldest sister and my older brother, who would remain in Antigua to care for my younger brother and me until we left, would then have their turn to leave for St. Thomas.

However, my older brother remained in Antigua with my father when my third oldest sister left for St. Thomas. She only stayed with us in St. Thomas for a couple of weeks before leaving for the U.S. to stay with her Antiguan boyfriend who was already there.

Mom loved to write letters, so she would often communicate with my older sister to check on our well-being and things happening on the island. She told my sister the date she would be coming home.

Mom Returned Home

We all excitedly waited outside on the gallery in our front yard the day Mom arrived in a big black four-door car. I did not recognize that healthy, vibrant looking woman and wondered if she were my real mother. Gone was that old woman singing and squinting while wiping sweaty brows and lifting 100-pound bags of white flour in a hot, steamy bakery shop. I could hardly believe that was my real mother because she looked rested, fresh, and relaxed.

"Mom, is that really you"? I asked. Her big grin revealed a mouth full of beautiful white teeth, deep dimples in her cheeks, dancing in her eyes, and a contagious smile, which I returned. "Mom, is that really you"? I repeated.

Suddenly she reached for me with a big hug, and I relaxed into her strong arms. Her soft patchouli scent infiltrated the space, and her breasts protruded firmly under her maxi jump suit. She looked younger and more vibrant than ever. My mom looked pretty to me, like Mrs. Weston. This made me happy. If my Mom could look this different after going to St. Thomas, my desire to leave home increased even more. That day she brought several parcels of food and clothes to us, and for the first time that night Mom made Kraft Macaroni & Cheese with chicken for dinner. This was a memorable moment with my mother. After dinner, she sat at the table in the drawing room and began to read her Bible.

The joy of being with Mom and having her back at home on the island did not last long because before I knew it, she had left me again for the second time after having been home for less than five weeks. I was sad and disappointed because I thought she was home to stay. This time I was told that Mom had secured work with Mrs. Ella, a native of St. Thomas, who hired her on a work bond. Unless she returned by a certain date, she would forfeit her time and would not be able to re-enter St. Thomas. My older brother hurriedly took Mom to the airport to fly back to St. Thomas.

"You Muda done gone," Dad said with a nonchalant look on his face.

After Mom left this time, I didn't know what to do with myself. Mostly, I continued to hang out with my new friends. Every day when I got home from school, I dropped my books on the food safe counter and ran back outside to play. I stopped going to church on Sundays and spent more time at my friends' houses. Sometimes I would go to the ocean and imagine what it would be like to live in America and have other opportunities.

Now that Mom had a job with Mrs. Ella, her priority was to begin the process of securing green cards and ultimately obtaining American residency for her children and herself. Dad was not interested in leaving his beloved island in the sun.

Before it was time for my younger brother and me to leave Antigua for St. Thomas, Mom wrote letters asking for our release from school. I had just passed my exam to transfer to Princess Margaret School, which was the best school on the island. The school was named after Princess Margaret, the daughter of Queen Elizabeth. I wanted to attend that school, but I also understood that my goal of pursuing my dream of getting a better education would begin in St. Thomas.

After returning to St. Thomas, Mom was relentless in contacting and communicating with the consulate of Antigua and Barbuda. Mom's efforts were not in vain because soon enough my younger brother and I took our first flight to St. Thomas. The idea of going on an airplane was foreign to me, but the thought of going to be with Mom gave me comfort. I knew nothing about how an airplane worked except what I had seen on Miss Maize's TV. The thought of getting on an airplane made me feel afraid because I did not know who would steer it, what to expect, or how to behave. Even though I was going to be with Mom in the Virgin Islands, I was already beginning to feel misplaced or out of place. I was glad my little brother was traveling with me.

On the way to the airport, I felt neither happy nor sad, but because of my sweaty, clammy, hands, I knew I was nervous. I sat back into the soft, velour seats of Big Brother's car, closed my eyes, and tried to calm my nerves. I thought about my island paradise, the mangoes, the sour sops, and sugar apples all falling from the trees, and how I wouldn't be there to pick them.

Upon boarding the plane, we were greeted by a tall, slim lady who knew my name. She was dressed in a white short-sleeved blouse with pockets, tucked into a navy-blue hobble skirt. The matching navy blue, British West Indian Airline hat, neatly covered the crown of her straight, shoulder-length red hair. As if she were somehow in charge of us, she took me by the hand and escorted us to two seats in the front of a fifteen-seater plane. There was a lady seated in the back of the plane holding a baby in her arms. The baby kept crying, which made me nervous.

As the plane lifted off the runway, my head felt hollow, and I tried to put both forefingers in my ears to ease the clogging. The nice lady smiled at me, then she pinned a silver BWIA toy pin with red wings on the dress I was wearing. The nice lady handed blankets to everyone. I placed one over my brother and pulled my soft, navy-blue blanket up to my neck.

Comforted by her kindness, I dozed and dreamt about our dog, Tarzan, floating in thin air and flying alongside us outside the plane. I tried to reach him, but I was jolted and awakened by the shaking and bouncing from the strong turbulence against the airplane. I was frightened and nervous but felt calmer after the nice lady made a quick announcement that everything was all right but to please fasten our seatbelts. The nice lady served egg salad sandwiches with Fanta sweet drinks, but I had no appetite. I sat back in my seat and thought about leaving home, my school, and my friends, and the beginning of my new life.

Another jolt startled me, but this time it was a couple of hours later, and we were landing in the Virgin Islands. The nice lady asked me to wait for her so she could take us directly to our mother.

Exiting the airplane, we walked towards the arrival signs. I noticed a woman waving at me from the arrival gate ahead of us. I knew it was Mom. I knew she would be there waiting for me, and for the first time in a long time I felt excited and happy.

Mom welcomed me with a broad smile that flashed from her smooth, round face, revealing her strong white teeth like un-cracked cowrie shells strung closely together.

I felt proud to have such a beautiful mom dressed in a stylish, dropped-waist floral cotton frock and black patent leather pumps, with her memorable tightly curled locks intact. I reached up and gave her a big hug and a kiss. We embraced for such a long time that I was beginning to feel awkward and started to squirm.

Mom immediately took us to meet Mrs. Ella, the woman who had bonded her and had taken her to the airport to pick us up. A cheerful voice chimed, "These must be the two little ones."

"Oh yes, these are my daughter and son," Mom proudly responded.

"What a pretty little girl and handsome son," Mrs. Ella said while holding me at arm's length.

"Thank you, Ella," Mom replied with an unfamiliar look of shyness on her face.

"You are the spitting image of your mother," Mrs. Ella added.

"Sweetie, what do you say to Mrs. Ella"? Mom quickly asked.

"Thank you, Mrs. Ella," I said.

"You're a good, girl," she responded, opening her arms, beckoning me to enter. Mrs. Ella gave me such a big bear hug. It was so tight that I could hardly breathe as my face squashed against her fleshy chest. "You're such a sweet little girl," she cooed.

Mrs. Ella was a mulatto and a native of St. Thomas. She was a short, light-skinned lady with long black hair, flowing down her back in a single plat.

As we walked toward the customs area located in the center of an old dreary, windowless room, Mrs. Ella went to retrieve her car to take us home. There were several people ahead of us. There were children and families coming to St. Thomas, connecting with their relatives. Some were leaving their island for the first time like me, I imagined. When it was our turn, we walked briskly behind Mom to the immigration officer behind the counter. Mom showed him a medium-sized piece of white paper with something written on it.

The tall, dark officer looked directly at me, "Is this child in school?"

"Yes sir," Mom quickly responded.

"Who is her bonder?" He continued staring directly at me.

"She's on the account of my work bond, Sir," Mom replied.

"Who is your bonder?" He probed, piercing the document as if looking to find something wrong.

"Mrs. Ella Castel," Mom replied, unraveling an additional piece of paper, showing that she was employed by her, and we were on her bond.

Still looking directly at me he asked, "How old are you?"

"Nine years old," I replied proudly.

"Good girl," he responded, stamping the white paper Mom gave him. "I will allow these children to stay here as long as you are bonded by Mrs. Ella Castel, and the bond must be renewed every school year," he stated, handing the stamped paper back to Mom.

"Thank you, Sir," she replied, as she slowly and carefully folded the documents, placing them into her brown straw bag and leading us out of the dark, dreary room.

We met Mrs. Ella at the back side of the airport as she drove up in a green Volkswagen to take us to her home in French Town. She lived in a big white house surrounded with a black wrought iron fence on Bradford Road. I felt excited and glad because I had never seen a lady driving a car before. It was then I decided that when I was grown, I would buy and drive my own car.

Driving through French Town gave me a familiar feeling of still being at home in Antigua, enjoying the broiling hot sun, fresh breeze, buoyant trees, and white-powder sand beaches.

Mrs. Ella had the most beautiful house I had ever seen. There was a bookshelf from wall to wall filled with all types of books. I wondered if she had read them all. In her bright yellow kitchen, we ate butter cookies and drank homemade ginger beer while we watched a show on her Zenith color television. We became caught up in the color TV because we did not know they existed. We only had a black and white TV that Mom sent back home from St. Thomas.

Soon they started talking and making plans for our future. I asked to be excused to use the latrine; Mrs. Ella called it the bathroom. She had a lavish bathroom with a tub, a sink with hot and cold-running water, and a toilet with a septic tank attached to it that you could flush by pulling on a rope. Having electricity and an indoor bathroom was a luxury. I knew of no one on my island with a bathroom in their house. Our bathroom was located outside in our back yard.

Soon after we arrived in St. Thomas, my brother and I were enrolled in Seventh Day Adventist school. He was placed in the fifth grade, and I was placed in the sixth grade. With much pride, my brother and I wore our school uniforms. I wore my white shirt, navy blue pleated skirt, and black tie, and my brother wore his white shirt, navy blue pants, and black tie, which Mom washed in a blue solution, starched, and ironed each night. It made me feel very special, and I loved to watch Mom take the time to methodically prepare our clothes for school. She would press the shirt collar, the upper back, the lower back, the sides, and finally the sleeves. I felt clean and pretty.

Each day, we walked about one mile to town to attend the Seventh Day Adventist school. By half past eight o'clock a.m., before classes began, the entire school body of about fifty students would boldly chant in unison the twenty-third Psalm, "The Lord is my Shepherd, I shall not want . . .," and sing the Lord's prayer, "Our Father who art in heaven . . .." These practices were designed to ground us with a religious connection.

Living in St. Thomas was a step up from how we lived on our island. This island was more commercial. We had electricity in the small apartment, but no running water or indoor bathroom. There was a pail in an adjacent room to our apartment that we used as our bathroom at night. The pail was taken to the outhouse in the backyard to be picked up later that day by the sanitation department. There was also a well in the yard where we could get fresh water without having to walk to a public pipe. Across the street in the unpainted cement house lived a little black girl about my age who had my complexion. She was visiting her grandmother, so I tried to befriend her. Being a shy and quiet child, I didn't make friends easily. However, I took a risk to reach out to her. I smiled as I hung outside the bedroom window one day trying to get her attention, "Psst, psst, psst, psst," I beckoned, but she ignored me and looked the other way. I felt so hurt; so, I rolled my eyes, sucked my teeth, and pulled down the window curtain. She was not friendly and acted like she thought she was better than me.

I was sitting outside on the stoop greasing my hair with petroleum jelly when I heard a shrill, *Yankee* voice from her window asking, "What's wrong with your hair? It's so rough and nappy." Laughing, she twisted a few strands of her stiff, medium-length hair and said, "I have good, fine hair, see!" She climbed onto her windowsill, showing off her blue corduroy, red-checkered cotton blouse, clean white socks, and new black and white shoes.

My face felt flushed and hot as I put my hands on my hips, rolled my eyes, put my head up in the air and said, "Chewps." She laughed at how I spoke, how I looked, and told me that I was ugly. I couldn't understand why someone who looked like me would call me ugly.

I began to feel ashamed that I was not from the U. S. I felt ashamed that I wore flour-bag dresses—crocus-bag skirts that Mom made—and ashamed a little black girl thought I was ugly and she was better than I. Needless to say, my confidence level was badly impacted.

MY CHILDHOOD DREAM OF GOING TO AMERICA

The day she left to go back to the States it was pouring rain, and I prayed that a flood would come and drown *she*; that's when I started to talk like a St. Thomean.

It was difficult adjusting to my new life in St. Thomas. I became more conscious of how I looked and spoke. I spoke with an Antiguan creole accent and felt embarrassed about my dialect, who I thought I was, and where I came from.

Every morning, Mom made our breakfast and sent us off to school before she went to work. We grew accustomed to the snap, crackle, pop sounds of Kellogg's Rice Krispies, floating in Pet evaporated milk as well as our favorite dinner of fried chicken with macaroni and cheese. We were fortunate to have a hot plate in the small apartment on which Mom prepared our meals.

Because of my accent, I was always afraid I would be ridiculed, bullied, or provoked to a physical fight at school. We were called names, like *alien* and *garrot*. These names were given to people who were not born in St. Thomas. I felt stigmatized and slightly unwelcomed, so I mostly stayed inside the house after school and waited for Mom to get home from work.

I was happy to be with my mother, but I really missed my school back home. I missed the cakes, breads, sweets, and ginger beer drinks I could easily buy in town.

As far as I knew, things were going well as I became more accepted by my classmates. On Sunday afternoons after church, Mom, my brother, and I would walk down Main Street to window shop. We walked in the park and smelled the beautiful flowers; we looked into the jewelry stores, clothing stores, and perfume and beauty shops as if we were tourists visiting the island. This was the first time I felt I had my mother's total attention and didn't mind sharing her with my baby brother. I felt loved by my mother and brother. Mostly, my dream of seeing my mother looking beautiful like other mothers came true.

By the time my brother and I were beginning to settle into our new school, our new environment, and were feeling accepted and comfortable enough to make new friends, Mom began to say that she didn't feel well. I noticed she was not eating or sleeping well. I began to worry about her because she grew tired and weary very quickly. I knew something was terribly wrong when Mom no longer prepared our nightly meals. Instead, my brother and I ate canned Campbell ravioli or spaghetti in tomato sauce. I didn't mind so much because I loved the sweet and tangy flavor of the sauce.

Though Mom wasn't feeling her best, she continued to work for Mrs. Ella in order to provide for us, to continue pursuing our green card documentation, and to keep us in school. To me, this was great because that meant that I would have my school bond as long as Mom was alive and worked for Mrs. Ella.

I often came home from school, and Mom was still in bed and had not gone to work. I began making dinner for the three of us and made sure we had breakfast before going to school. I prayed a lot for God to heal my Mom. The fear of losing her terrified me. I recalled joking with Mom, asking if she were to die would she scare us.

She smiled and said, "Don't worry baby, I wouldn't scare you."

I was not prepared for what was next to come. My second oldest sister also grew increasingly alarmed and took my mother to the doctor. No one apprised me of her diagnosis or prognosis, but I noticed that she was becoming weaker and weaker. Shortly after the doctor's visit, Mom announced that we'd be going back to Antigua for her to get some needed rest.

I didn't really mind. I felt happy because I would see my friend Lillian again and maybe end up at Princess Margaret Secondary School. I had previously taken and passed the entrance exam to attend that school. I could begin memorizing the catechism for the following year when I would be of age and ready for confirmation. I also knew that when Mom got better, my school bond could be reactivated once we returned to St. Thomas and Mom could return to work for Mrs. Ella.

It was a bright sunny day toward the end of December 1970, when we returned to Antigua. Mom had just had her 58th birthday, but it was not celebrated because it was not customary for us to celebrate birthdays. Not only did our house look smaller, but the circumference of our yard was significantly smaller. Returning to Antigua was a bittersweet experience.

"She com' bak from de States," the gallery women said. I was shaken when I first heard the gallery women gossiping about me and my family.

"Dem say somebody put jumbee 'pon she," whispered Eunice.

"No, 'mon, me no believe in dem kind a t'ing day," she retorted. "She is a Christian woman," she added.

"Poor t'ing," Gladys said.

My father somehow believed that someone had done something to Mom because two nights a week he allowed a woman to come into our house and sprinkle white powder in the corners. He also had someone else to come and give her an herbal bush bath. They said it would drive the jumbee and keep any evil spirits away. They also burned incense which made the house smell terrible.

After returning to Antigua, I was enrolled in Princess Margaret Secondary School. In the British school system, this was a notable secondary school for which you had to complete both Form 1 and Form 2 as well to qualify for consideration. I was proud to attend such a prestigious school.

After school, I became Mom's helper. I fetched her water and made and fed her pumpkin soup. I placed moist rags on her forehead and rubbed her feet while she lay on her back. I took care of her as best I could. Sometimes, however, I wanted to go outside and play, so every chance I got, I sneaked out of the house to play cowboys and Indians with my brother. I liked being an Indian. One day Mom was coughing up phlegm, and I rushed to hold the bowl for her to spit. I felt nauseous, as if I were going to throw up. From the look in her eyes, I believed she was hurt from my reaction. I felt embarrassed and ashamed because I was scornful of my own mother.

As time passed, Mom grew more tired and sick. When she came home from seeing the doctor, people stood outside with dirty laughs and upturned, lips, shaking their heads whispering, "Me can't believe she done lost all dat weight, she lookin' like a "marga dawg." No one knew what was wrong with my Mom. It was hard to not feel angry hearing these kinds of statements. I was struck with fear when I realized that Mom was too weak to go to church that Sunday. I felt a tinge of sadness in my chest, but I didn't cry.

Time passed and Mom's spirit dwindled. She was not her lively self. I comforted her and continued to help around the house as best I could. Except for my father, baby brother, my other brother and me, all of my siblings were in St. Thomas or the States. Mom did not want to send for my sisters in the States because of their status. She was aware of the hardship it would present for them to leave Antigua and to get back to the States.

Mom began to lose her appetite and did not want to eat. It was difficult to ignore the gossip in the neighborhood. "Dem a wait 'pon she to dead," they said.

The atmosphere was often long and dreary, like a drawn-out nightmare with no end. It felt like we were waiting for something, but I didn't know for what we were waiting. There was a deep-seated feeling of helplessness that permeated the air like smoke casting a paralysis over my family. My third older sister took a chance and came home from the States. As soon as she got home, she called Mr. Eric and immediately took Mom to the hospital. Mr. Erick was the only man in the neighborhood with a car service. He was the one who used his car as a taxi to get her to the hospital. We paid him about $7. The emergency room staff wanted to send Mom back home, but after seeing a doctor, she was admitted to the hospital.

After Mom was taken to the hospital, I began to feel sadder. I had done the best I could to take care of her and never considered she would die. I felt helpless and did not know what to do. I prayed again and asked God to make Mom well again.

It wasn't much longer before Mom's condition grew worse. She could not swallow the pills given by the nurse and was beginning to lose control of her bowels. Mom asked my sister to tell my oldest brother who had come home to bring her one cup of fresh milk. My brother was confused by her request but found a way to get exactly one cup of milk to our mother. He put it in a bottle and brought it to her. She drank all of it and seemed satisfied and contented. However, we found it strange that Mom asked for only one cup of milk to be brought to her by her firstborn son. We never found out what that meant.

The night before Mom died, I had a dream. In my dream, I cut school so I could visit her in the hospital. I swiftly ran up the steep cement and graveled hill to the hospital. When I got to her room, she hid her face because she was sad. This made me sad too. At that moment, I wondered what her thoughts and feelings were. I remembered Mom as brave. When I heard her sobbing, I hugged her and we cried together. At that moment, someone called my name.

It was my sister shaking me out of sleep, "Gal, you too old to pee the bed," she scolded and continued shaking me out of my sleep. I was almost ten years old, and I felt embarrassed and ashamed that I would still periodically wet the bed. "Get up and take off the wet night gown," she insisted. Our mother's pink, polyester laced night gown my sister had worn to bed got soggy wet, and it was my fault.

My heavy flour-bag fabric gown was soiled with cold sweat and urine. I should have gotten up, reached for the white pail under the bed, urinated, then gone back to bed. I struggled to wake up, but not quickly enough to avoid the guilt and shame I felt as my cold, soggy night gown rubbed against my soft skin. These shivers of guilt and shame were emotions that would entrap me for years to come.

CHAPTER 5

Mourning

Mom was still in the hospital, but it just seemed like she had gone away again. However, I worried that she may not return this time, though I constantly prayed, "God please heal my Mom. Do not let her die."

About a week later, one morning seemed very different from other mornings. About 6:30 a.m., the rain prevented the sun from showing her face. I didn't hear the rooster crowing, and I didn't hear Big Church bell ringing, but as usual, third sister greased and plaited my hair and laid out my green pleated jumper and beige blouse uniform for me to proceed to Princess Margaret School.

To my surprise, Big Brother pulled up in a burgundy truck that was badly in need of a paint job and delivered the dreaded news, which felt like an impending storm with a devastating end. His knees seemed to wobble in slow motion as he made his way to the foot of the gallery. With a dried-up tear-stained face, eyes ablaze with blood, he whispered and squeaked out, "Mama Fernie is dead."

In that moment, my body felt weak, my knees were shaking, my palms were sweating, and my mouth felt as dry as a desert. I was shocked and immediately denied it. I did not believe it. I just could not believe it. I was left, confused, numb, helpless, alone, and lost in the world because my sweet, beautiful mother was dead. From the moment of Big Brother's arrival with the news, a shadow was cast over my world, and for me, my tropical paradise lost its flavor.

Instead of going to school, I ran to the hospital. When I got to Mom's room, her body laid wrapped in a purple, cotton sheet knotted at the neck, waist, wrists, and ankles. Loud screams escaped my lungs, rushing through my lips as I ran and ran and ran, away from the hospital until I was out of breath. I did not want anyone to know I had gone there by myself because children were not allowed in the hospital alone. Even though I didn't see her face, I knew from the shape of the body and the energy in the quiet, sterile room, that it was she, and I would never see her again. I wanted to believe that at the moment of her death, Mom was at peace.

I couldn't believe—I just couldn't believe it was happening to me. I knew she was sick, but I didn't know she was going to die. It was only a week prior when my sister and I visited her in the hospital, and she seemed to be getting better. It was shocking to believe that one week later my Mom was dead and gone. They said she died because the hospital didn't have enough equipment to save her life.

"This was such a shame," I thought.

Cousin Conce said, "No me chile, your Mama no gone, she's just away safe in de arms of Jesus."

That night I could not go to sleep. I wanted them to keep the lights on because I was afraid of seeing Mom. There was an old superstition: if you saw someone in a dream after they died, your own death would soon be eminent. I became afraid of my own mortality after I dreamt that I heard Mom's beautiful voice singing, "The Old, Old Story" as she was washing and cooking and just being my mom again. I was also afraid to look in the mirror because I feared I would see her reflection. These old superstitions haunted me.

The next day, early in the morning, cousin Conce came and hurriedly took Baby Brother and me to her house in the country. She said, "All dis ya a grown folk's biznezz."

I was glad she did, but I still felt alone with a numb and helpless heart.

For the next few days, I walked around in a daze. My third sister had not yet returned to the States and was waiting for other family members to come home.

My sister told us that Mom's death certificate stated that she died from heart failure that was related to plaque buildup resulting in hardening of the arteries.

Mom's Funeral

Though Mom's body had remained in Mr. Strafe's funeral home for seven days, allowing time for other family members to arrive on the island, my oldest sister, who lived in the

States, could not attend the funeral because of documentation complications. It would have been a big risk for her to come home to the funeral and take a chance on her immigration status being discovered. I can only imagine how disappointed and alone she must have felt.

Finally, the day had come for the funeral and the burial. My family was all together, but I didn't want to go to the funeral because this would mean that it was real, and Mom wouldn't be returning home.

It was customary for the hearse to bring the body to the house for viewing before heading to the church for the service and burial. After which, people would disperse and go their own way. Our family had gathered at our house waiting for the hearse to bring Mom. Dad was getting anxious when the hearse was late to arrive. He kept walking into the middle of the street, looking up and down in anticipation of the hearse's arrival. Finally, after seeming like an eternity, the hearse arrived with Mom. Her casket was too large to fit in our house or on our gallery, so we placed it in our yard in front of the gallery.

When the big black hearse turned the corner heading to our house, the pomp and circumstance began; the Big Church bell rang to signal the funeral ceremony was on the way, and the people in the neighborhood began lining Parliament Street to get the last glimpse of my Mom at our house before the funeral.

I wanted to scream at them, "Get away from us!" but I had no voice.

They stood there in the broiling hot sun, some without shoes in raggedy clothes standing around as if it were a state affair. Confused, I wondered why the same people who stoned our house, breaking and shattering the glass in our front door and windows, gave us evil looks, and even threw human feces on our walkway, came to her funeral supposedly to pay their respects.

Mr. Strafe, the best funeral director on the island, chose to attend Mom's funeral. He did not drive the hearse that day but chose to wear his top hat and long-tailed coat suit instead, to show the respect and honor for the life of my mother.

Gladiolus, tulips, lilies, and wide sprigs of exotic ferns created a pathway to where she was displayed. The strong scent of resin from the pitch-pine coffin mixed with the odor of bouquets aroused my sense of smell, giving me chills of loneliness, making me feel weak.

For the funeral, I wore my best outfit: an orange, green, and black knit dress, the one which third sister brought to me when she came home from America. I never wore it again. Dad wore Mom's favorite black hat, and he didn't care if he were laughed at. With a face full of pain, he swore to wear it until he too, should die. Somehow, Dad must have known they would meet again.

When it was time for the family to view the body, I stood there stoic, spacey, and stiff, until Big Brother's wife wrapped her right arm around my waist. "Com', say bye to you mother," she said soothingly, walking with me to the front.

With wobbly legs and borrowed strength, I made my way to her, but midway my sister-in-law broke down and I fell to my knees. The smooth pitch-pine coffin glistened in the broiling hot sun, and it seemed surreal that the figure inside—adorned in a pink and white satin floral bonnet which covered her Nubian locks—nestled in soft white cushion was my mother. That person in the casket did not look like my mom. She was stiff and still. Her face had gray and blue undertones in her skin. Her eyes shut tightly, her dark and thin lips were closed tightly, and her cheekbones were now hollow.

Mom, Mom, please open your eyes, I thought while wanting to reach out and touch her, but I couldn't. With silent screams I shouted, *Mom, open your eyes*! I closed my eyes and tried to imagine her dimpled cheeks and dancing eyes that always made me smile.

During a slow procession after the viewing, people walked alongside and behind the hearse on route to the church. I could hear them whispering, "Strafe done a good job 'pon she. He mek she looks fresh like she sleeping." "Strafe had 'nuf respect for the Mistress."

I felt guilty, sad, disappointed, and angry because I never got the chance to say goodbye to Mom, which left my heart full of sorrow. Numbness had set in. I could not cry at the funeral. I was concentrating on holding myself together. I thought I had to keep my composure. Pastor Knight prayed, the choir sang her favorite song, "I surrender all . . . all to Thee my Blessed Savior, I surrender all." Though many people had words to say, I could not recall what they were saying because it seemed like they were all talking at the same time, and it was too much for me to grasp.

Then they took her outside and put her in a freshly dug hole on the northeast corner in the church yard. Bowing their heads, everyone held hands forming a circle around the freshly dug grave while Pastor Knight, his wife, and other choir members sang as they marched to the graveyard. Two burly men came and used pieces of rope to lower the casket into the grave. The pastor began to pray as the men shoveled dirt on Mom's casket. The sound made me shudder from my core. Big Brother, who had made a huge white cross adorned with flowers, laid it at her head so everyone could see when they passed by.

My father did not want to leave her and had to be escorted out of the graveyard. I could not stop worrying and obsessing about what was to happen next. I was hoping that I would soon awake from this nightmare, but it was not to be.

The next morning when Big Church bell rang and the sun rose, I was overtaken with fresh feelings of grief. I grew more introverted and developed a mask to hide the pain inside and did not express my real feelings.

My memory of events after the funeral that night was blurred because I was overwhelmed with my own emotions. The following afternoon, I heard the gallery women talking and gossiping about us.

"Dem put she 'way good "mon. Dem mus' hav' money", Gladys said taking a bite of the ripe banana she just peeled.

"Me no like dat floral robe dem put 'pon she. Dem should da dress she in a pretty frock", Eunice responded after taking a sip of her soursop juice.

"Me no see not'in' wrong wit' how dem dress she," Mildred commented.

"She casket had glass in the front so you can see she face w'en it shuts down. Dem mus' hav' plenty money," Gladys repeated, throwing the banana peel in a brown paper bag in the corner.

"Dat no mean dem hav' plenty money," Eunice concluded, smacking her lips from the last mouthful of soursop juice.

This is what my Mom wanted to get us away from: the gossipy mentality of an unsophisticated environment. After the funeral, nobody in the family said a word about what had happened. No one said a word. We were all left with our thoughts to form our own conclusions—except for the gaping hole and blaring fact that Mom was missing. It was as if nothing had happened. We did have one constant reminder because Dad wore black for a very long time.

I believe Dad wore Mom's hat as a way to keep her close to him because his side of the bed was empty. At night, he took off the hat and laid it next to him on her pillow. I believe that when he awoke early the next morning, he must have put the hat back on his head because whenever I saw him, he was wearing it.

Having a death in the family at such an early age was traumatizing. It felt as if things got really quiet, and it felt like there was a deep, dark secret. I thought this was a family secret and not something to be discussed.

Verbal expression from my parents or anyone in my family was not habitual. My parents were very private and discreet, and as a child, I was not privy to their conversations. We were a generation that didn't communicate with each other about traumatic issues. As a result, I was left feeling responsible for Mom's death.

I became bombarded by a series of dreams. I dreamt I was alone on Margins Bay, but I didn't remember how I got there. It was a beautiful sunny day and the water was unusually blue with silver streaks glistening. I decided to go into the water, welcoming its embrace. Suddenly the sky got dreary, and the sun went under the now dark clouds. I felt as though I was suffocating and obviously making sounds when my third sister shook me out of sleep. Again, my night gown was drenched from my sweat.

Were my nightmares related to my trying to understand or figure out why Mom died? Did I think that my family was being punished for something that caused Mom to die? Had she overworked herself to provide for the family and not paid enough attention to her own health? Had I done something wrong and God was punishing me? Had Mom chosen to die and leave her family?

I did not want to accept the fact that no one had to be blamed, and we had to get on with our lives. I just knew that when Mom died, I felt a piece of me died also.

I became afraid that Mom would return in spirit and frighten us. I was afraid to go to sleep or sleep in Mom's room. I was consumed with fearful thoughts and had allowed guilt and shame to overtake me. I wondered if my heart were frozen because I often felt cold to the point of shivering.

I became very angry and blamed God for taking my mom away from us. "She loved Him so, why would He do this to her and us," I wondered. I felt guilty for questioning God's decision and for having those questions and thoughts. I lost all desire to pray.

Dad was determined to continue Mom's ritual of going to church, but I would always sit in the back of the church where the door was kept closed and I could not see Mom's grave.

After Mom's passing, my life was in a state of confusion. I continued to feel afraid, alone, unloved, insecure, and unsure about my life. My family members who lived elsewhere had now dispersed and moved back into their own lives. My second sister and my oldest brother had returned to St. Thomas, and my third sister somehow was able to return to the States.

After Mom's death, things got worse. There was a skeleton in my closet. I was that little black girl whose mother had left, and I no longer belonged anywhere. As far as I was concerned, I was the only motherless child I knew, and I was not sure how I would make it through all those unsettling changes.

I wished for a way to voice and express myself, yet I couldn't utter a word. This is when I needed my family's support and comfort, but I knew my family was not the talking kind, so I kept my feelings bottled up inside. I had no one to grieve with or talk with about Mom's passing, so I learned to grieve alone and not share my feelings with others.

After my mother died, I was filled with anger, mistrust, and despair. I felt angry and resentful that I didn't have the benefit of my mother's love in my life. I resented not having my mom like other girls. I wanted to be someone's daughter, to experience the feeling of a mother's love. Passing children playing with their mothers made me sad, and I found myself yearning secretly to spend just one more day with Mom.

I missed the love of my mother. I wished I could resurrect the dead. I missed Mom more and more every day. I longed for someone to take care of me. It's a longing that never goes away.

During those uncertain weeks, my life seemed to be on hold, and I didn't know what the plan would be for my future. My fear increased, I continued to blame God, and I did not want to go to church. I began to act out in school again in search of attention from my teachers and other students. No one seemed to have known about Mom's death because no one said anything. I eventually got suspended from school for talking back to the teacher.

This was a defining moment in my life. Things had changed and decisions had to be made. Indirectly one day, I heard my Dad talking about the future of my brother and me. I hoped that we were both going to live with my oldest sister who lived in the States. Though I felt excited and happy about the possibility of this happening, I knew it would be difficult because we had no documentation.

I felt it would be easier to reactivate my younger brother's and my school bonds in St. Thomas, which would allow us time to finish high school and to procure our green cards. Green card procurement was a process Mom began in St. Thomas, but it ended after she became ill and died.

A couple of months after Mom died, my oldest sister took a chance and came home to Antigua to see what she could do to get my younger brother and me out of Antigua, because this was Mom's dream. This was a big risk because she could have been detained in Antigua and not allowed to return to the United States. I don't know how she arranged the visit, but I was so happy to see her. I felt very grateful for the love, compassion, and responsibility my sister showed as the eldest daughter.

My sister immediately began researching what it would take to get us back to St. Thomas. One beautiful sunny day, Sister took my brother and me into town to get our photographs taken so we could apply for and receive our British passports, which would allow us to return to St. Thomas. I was very happy to be with my youngest brother and oldest sister and to wear my new red dress that my sister brought from the States.

It was the most joyous day I had experienced since Mom's passing. We spent quality time with Big Sister eating curry chicken with peas and rice, hog maws from Auntie Marie, a street vendor, and drinking ginger beer in town. My big sister was able to spend enough time with us in Antigua to prepare Baby Brother and me for a plane ride to return to St. Thomas.

We were excited and ready to begin our new life with my intention of attending and graduating from high school, establishing residency, and moving to the United States to pursue higher education.

Return to St. Thomas

I returned to a new and different life in St. Thomas. I was scheduled to live with my second sister and her boyfriend, and Baby Brother would live with my oldest brother and his wife.

Adjusting to my new life was difficult, and it took me a long time. Being twelve years old and living without Mom was sad and lonely. My sister had only two bedrooms, so I had to share one bedroom with my niece and nephew. From the moment I moved in with my sister and her family, my life as an immigrant began all over again.

When Mom passed, my second sister became a full-time employee of Mrs. Ella. Because we were already in the school system from Mom's work bond with Mrs. Ella, we qualified for an independent school bond that would allow us to stay in St. Thomas until we graduated from high school. After graduating from high school, our school bonds would end, and we would have to return to our native island of Antigua.

For the next five years, I had to entertain the reality that I would be deported back to my island after high school graduation. It was an albatross around my neck. As a result, I became more and more fearful, distrustful of people, and lived with my own secret of being an immigrant. I lived with a big secret that stopped me from using my voice for fear of being discovered, but, though I stopped going to church during my rebellious state, I always prayed and believed that God would make a way. I believed it!

While living with my sister, I was old enough to have chores and help with my four-year-old nephew and two-year-old niece. My chores included: washing clothes, cleaning the house, and cooking. I had a full schedule of chores and schoolwork, which aided in my becoming more introverted and marginalized for fear of people knowing too much about me. I stayed pretty close to home after school.

While doing the washing, I often thought about Mom standing inside the kitchen door doing the washing. In our backyard, we had a stone heap and two parallel clotheslines running from the east to the west above the heap. I often thought about how great Mom was at doing the laundry, and I would try to emulate her.

Mom had a particular method of washing the white clothes. First, she'd wash the white garments, usually shirts, towels, sheets, and pillowcases; she then soaked them in Clorox bleach. Next, she dissolved a cake of Reckitt's Crown Blue in the rinsing water to brighten the wash. It clearly seemed that Dad's and my brother's shirts came out whiter after soaking in the blue water. Finally, she added prepared arrowroot starch in another container of water. The starch served as a stiffener and made it easier for ironing the clothes.

It was a magical experience for me. After the final rinse, Mom hung the shirts, sheets, and pillowcases on the line, and sometimes my sister hung the colored clothes on the additional line in the back of the house. It was important to keep an eye out for rain because you never knew when rain would come. And if rain threatened to come, I was ready to run outside and help unpin the clothes from the line before they got wet.

One Saturday morning after doing the wash and hanging clothes on the line, I felt something running in streams down my face. The dam had broken and all my pent-up feelings came tumbling out as George Beverly Shea was singing, "How Great Thou Art."

I was grateful for my sister taking me in, but I missed my mom. I had the same dream that Mom had for me—to stay focused on getting to the United States and pursuing a higher education. I had to keep plowing through all of my sadness, fears, and distrust of people.

At Charlotte Amalie High School, we had to wear a uniform with a necktie and black shoes. Unlike other schools that I attended where we went home for lunch at noon and returned to school by one o'clock, we did not have to go home for lunch because lunch was served in school. If we finished lunch early, we could go to the library and study, or we could go to our next class early. In high school, I focused on secretarial and business skills, *i.e.*, stenography and typing, which would prepare me for a job once I got to the States. I typed 90 words per minute and took 120 words of shorthand per minute. I was the fastest typist in my class.

Two years after moving back to St. Thomas, my sister and her boyfriend, with whom I lived, got married, and I was one of her bridesmaids. I was excited to see my dad after two years when he attended the wedding and gave my sister away. Dad did not like St. Thomas and chose to return home after the wedding where he continued going out to sea and making fish pots and being with another older brother who also remained in Antigua.

Because my brother-in-law had obtained his green card through his mother, a resident of St. Thomas, my sister could now get her green card through her husband. They explained that through the immigration law you could bring your family in when you got your green card. This was called *a chain migration*. We were all happy because my sister could be in the position to be able to apply for my green card or maybe to adopt me.

Unfortunately, we learned because I was now fourteen years old, I would be too old for my sister and her husband to adopt me. As a result, I continued to feel disconnected and misplaced. I felt like I didn't belong anywhere or to anybody, but I held onto my dream and Mom's dream for me of becoming independent and self-sufficient.

For most of my high school years, I felt anxious, but I was more anxious in my senior year because my school bond would end and I would be deported back to Antigua. I knew I would not be allowed to stay even one day after my school bond had expired, and I was constantly worried about what would become of me. I knew I had two of my older sisters in the States with whom I could possibility live, so that gave me some hope.

For almost two years on Friday afternoons after school and Saturdays, I went to help clean Mrs. Ella's home. I worked hard and took pride in my work because I wanted to do at least half as good a job as my mother did and my sister was doing. I liked going to Mrs. Ella's house because she had many interesting books, and to me that meant she was smart. I was totally inspired even more to get my high school diploma and college degree. I believed it would be my ticket to open doors for me in the future.

As a junior in high school, I won the title of Miss Easter Bunny. This was an annual fashion show and pageant that occurred for high school juniors. I felt brave and confident enough to participate in the pageant and fashion show and was sponsored by the Oyster Shell Boutique in Corn Alley, who provided my clothing and accessories for the fashion show. However, I was responsible for my own talent.

I had been inspired by Mr. Weston who talked about Dr. Martin Luther King Jr.'s legacy and his "I Have a Dream" speech, so I knew that I wanted to recite his speech. It was a hit and my confidence level soared. I knew I would need confidence to move on with the next phase of my life after graduation.

Six months before graduating from high school, I was still not sure of my future. I had heard my sisters were working on a plan for me to escape the island, which made me hopeful, but there was a delay for reasons unknown to me and graduation was getting closer. Deep inside my heart, I believed things would work out for me as I tried hard to pull up on the faith that my mother had displayed. However, when two days had passed since graduation day, I was still not sure of the plan for me until that night when the immigration authorities pounded on my sister's door.

PART III

MY PERSONAL ODYSSEY IN AMERICA

CHAPTER 6

A Cultural Melting Pot

On the night I arrived in the United States, I did not use my name for fear of being discovered and deported back to Antigua. Thereafter, I had all intentions of using my own name. If I didn't use my name, then I would be invisible, I thought. I believed I would be seen as a fraud. Besides, I knew that in order for me to get a job so that I could contribute to the household and make my own way, I needed to use my name.

I did this because I wanted to tell the truth and did not want to carry the shame of being dishonest and not authentic.

Even though I had employment in the United States, I still had no papers—other than my social security card from St. Thomas. I still didn't know how I would get a green card or permanent residency, but I was hopeful and prayerful that somehow a way would be made for me to get all I needed to survive. I felt it was important to collect anything that had my name on it to show I lived in America.

As soon as I received my first paycheck from my job, I quickly opened a checking account in my own name. From that moment onward, I kept every receipt and any correspondence that I received. I felt there was a force guiding me to accumulate these pieces of paper because they would be pertinent in procuring what I needed for residency later and to prove that I was who I said I was. Getting legal residency was vital to my success, and I believed it would allow me to come out of the shadows and be a productive human being in American society.

I continued to attend Bright Light Church where no one ever asked about my immigration or legal status, but I was still afraid to trust anyone for fear of becoming exposed to the authorities. I was very careful not to divulge too much information about myself. I lived with constant anxiety about being deported.

I kept myself imprisoned except for going out for the bare necessities, work, and church. Though I felt some security in the church, I was guarded and didn't allow myself to make friends and socialize easily.

By not allowing myself to make friends, I continued to be aloof and guarded. This impacted my ability to communicate my feelings in social situations and in forming trusting, healthy, authentic relationships. By living this way, I knew I was thwarting my opportunities to develop my social and interpersonal relationship skills. I knew eventually I would have to break this pattern of fear I was inflicting upon myself, and I believed that Bright Light Church was the place where I could tap into my spiritual reservoir for strength, belief, power, support, and the spiritual guidance I sought.

While at Bright Light Church, instead of expressing my feelings and thoughts to others, I began to write poetry. This gave me an outlet to express my inner most feelings in private, though I prayed that through my poetry writing, I would eventually be able to communicate as freely outwardly.

Prayer

As I continued to make my way in America, it became clear that I would have to use all the tools in my toolkit to keep me focused and on track to cope with whatever I may encounter on my journey. Attending Bright Light Church was the main tool upon which I relied.

Seeking divine intervention, I developed a daily spiritual practice of praying and attending prayer meetings regularly. Praying was the center of my life. I prayed when I arose in the morning, and I prayed before going to bed at night. It was imperative to pray in order to stay on my journey. Prayer was my time to communicate with God and listen for guidance that came in the form of a quiet voice delivering a message. I had to trust the messages I heard because I was developing my faith practice of belief.

I was taught that the power of belief and focus would bring things to manifestation: *What we think about we bring about* (Law of Attraction). I believed if I stopped praying, I might lose my way. I prayed consistently to develop and strengthen my faith muscle to have it support me throughout my life's journey.

In an effort to be proactive in my growth process, I even joined the junior choir in hopes of raising my confidence level. However, I still continued to experience the fear of assimilating into the American society and found it scary and emotionally debilitating to me.

My first Christmas was exciting. My younger brother, my two sisters, their children and I all gathered at my oldest sister's house for dinner. My sister's house was beautifully decorated with a white artificial Christmas tree with colorful blinking lights. *How wonderful,* I thought, as we sang carols and opened presents under the tree. I was happy to receive a beautiful wool sweater as a gift. I helped my sister prepare Christmas dinner, which consisted of curried goat, a ham, peas and rice, macaroni and cheese, turkey with cornmeal stuffing, and cranberry sauce from the can. Before dinner, it began to snow lightly. Though it was just a dusting of snow, I was very excited to see it for the first time.

My sister had told me that in America it gets cold in the winter and snow falls from the sky. I had never seen snow, but I knew it was white and cold. That following winter, I had my first major snow experience. It was beautiful and calming as it fell from the sky. People came together riding sleighs and sleds in the park, and children made snowmen and threw snowballs. What a wonderful and exciting experience. Unfortunately, after a day or two, the snow was dirty and piled up in multiple mounds in front of people's homes. That was not very pretty or clean, and it took a long time to melt.

Not long after that first Christmas dinner in America with my family, it became clear to me there were serious issues between my sisters. I was not privy to the particular issues, yet I felt myself being caught in the middle of them, though I did not want to choose, take sides, or have confrontations with my sisters. The discord between them saddened me.

In early spring the following year, my third sister announced she was getting married. It was exciting to witness another wedding in our family. I assisted with the pomp and circumstance. It was a small gathering made up of friends of the bride and groom and our family. Soon after, sister announced she was pregnant. Since they had only one bedroom, I knew they would need to create space for the baby's crib in the living room where I slept on the couch.

Shortly before the baby arrived, I moved upstairs to stay with my oldest sister, her three sons, my youngest brother, and her husband. It was difficult adjusting to being in my oldest sister's home because the loud noises of four boys were often deafening. They played the radio and the television and practiced their new karate moves with sounds. It was difficult for me to find my quiet time to pray and do my morning rituals in private. Even though it felt a little cramped and over-crowded, I made the best of it and felt grateful I had somewhere warm to stay until I could get my own apartment.

To get away from the noise and loudness at home, I began to spend more of my free time at Bright Light Church visiting with Mrs. Winters, who lived on the top floor in the same building of the church where Pastor Bradly had his office.

Mrs. Winters was the church secretary, and sometimes after work, I would stop by the church to help her with the church's bookkeeping. I enjoyed serving by adding and recording the collection monies and tithes given by the congregants. Often, Pastor Bradly was in his office studying the Bible and preparing for his upcoming sermon. Apart from choir practice, Tuesday and Friday night services, I began to spend Saturday afternoons at church, helping the church mothers sell cakes and pies to raise money for the church building fund.

After three months of being in my sister's home, I began to feel like a liability. I did not want to be burdensome to anyone. I tried to stay out of the way as much as I could by spending more time in the church, but I knew I needed more space to spread my wings as well as give them their space. I needed to get my own apartment. I had already begun to save money towards that end. It would soon be time to leave my sister's home and make a life for myself.

After praying earnestly for God to grant me the desires of my heart and believing the desires would be manifested, I came home from work one day and noticed that several apartments were available in my sister's building. I went into the management office and inquired about a one-bedroom apartment, but it was beyond my budget. Fortunately, a studio apartment was also vacant on the first floor in the same building. The rent was $90 per month and required no security deposit. A week later, I moved into my own new apartment where I lived for the next twelve years without bars on my one large window, not knowing that it was potentially unsafe.

Acculturation

When I came to America, I stepped into a brand
new world and became a part of a minority;
I was consumed by "isms," shaken by barrages
of inquisitions and intrusions of who I am
and what I am not.

When I came to America, the people were
nosy, inquisitive, curious, and proud—
all up in my business and sometimes very loud;
They wanted to know about me,
To know all here and now: "How old are you?"
"Where do you come from?"

When I came to America, I repeated myself often
when asked: "What are you saying?"
"Where are you going?"
"Where do you live?"
"What are you doing now?"

When I came to America, people seemed bossy,
They had a way, as if to say, "This is how we do it here,
So, do it the way we do it, or you're not welcome here."

Americans are great at making you feel, you have to
assimilate, you have to measure up, you have to fit in,
As if being your own individual self is a mortal sin.

When I came to America, the struggle was great and
I wanted to know, "To what degree must I assimilate?"

Emotional Eating

When I first came to America, I did not eat out in restaurants. I did not have to eat there because I cooked my own Caribbean dishes at home. I felt proud that I brought a little bit of my culture with me.

I found solace in food and became an emotional eater. I ate all the time, even when I wasn't hungry. My social lifestyle was pretty much reclusive, and I rewarded myself every Sunday night with a pint of Haagen-Dazs ice cream after church. The ice cream was very comforting as it reminded me of the ice cream Mom made for us at home. Over time, I began eating out at various restaurants and did not stick to cooking my West Indian dishes.

Because West Indian dishes take more time to prepare, my scheduling didn't afford me the time needed to do so often. My weekly itinerary included: working 9–5 on M-F, church services 4–6 x weekly (often late night), Sunday school, and attending college.

As a result, I began eating fast foods, Chinese food, and the breakfasts and dinners prepared by the church kitchen staff. I equated much of my new habit of eating out to my emotional state. Food became my comforter when I needed a *hug*.

Now that I had my own apartment, I could have many quiet moments of privacy in my own home. I often reflected on how far I had come: from that red tightly-curly-haired, dark complexioned, flat-nosed little girl, running around barefoot, catching crabs at Mangrove and playing on the beach, enjoying the freedom of her tropical lifestyle, to now living in America.

I continued with my regular schedule of going to work, going to Bright Light Church, and sharing the Pentecostal church doctrine, but I became a little fanatical. I believed the teachings and biases of the church and judged anyone who was not ready or willing to commit their life to the Creator God. I had become a zealous, self-righteous, overbearing new convert, who would go out into the community, recruiting members to join our church and receive Christ as their personal savior.

Though the church had many rules, I was an obedient member and tried my best to live according to the rules of the church. For example, they had a strict dress code. Men wore suits and ties; women wore their dresses and skirts well below the knees and were not allowed to wear short sleeve dresses or blouses, pants, lipstick, nor any form of makeup on their face. Though I wore my hair in boxed braids on a daily basis, I wore a wig to church because women were not allowed to wear their hair braided.

Though I came to view the rules of the church as excessive, I had become a loyal, passionate member of the church and had committed my life to serving God. I was more outgoing in the church and enjoyed sharing and dramatizing my poems.

Nothing to Give to Jesus
I have nothing to give to Jesus
For the amazing grace He gave

How He suffered for salvation
That the world through Him might be saved.

I have nothing to give to Jesus
Though his precious love I possess
Was it not for my Lord, Jesus,
My soul wouldn't be at rest.

Should I give Him all my earnings
When the tide comes rolling in?
Or should I just forget about Him
Though He washed away my sins?

I cannot think of what I did
For Him to love me so
For His love is so unchanging
To Him my life I owe,
So, I give Him myself instead.

As a part of the outreach ministry in the church, I began to go out into the various neighborhoods to do missionary work with people we met on the streets. Sometimes we went to people's homes and to various community programs to minister to them.

Even though I became *saved* in the church, I still felt guarded and afraid. I still had difficulty trusting others and making new friends because the fears about my immigration status remained prevalent in my mind.

Time passed, and one day in the fall of 1979, we received a telegram from my sister in St. Thomas stating that our father had died. They said he died from old age, but I believed he died from sadness and grief. I couldn't help remembering how sad Dad looked at Mom's funeral. His face showed a man who had a broken heart, was grief-stricken, and lost.

My third sister commented, "Dad is at peace now and out of his misery."

They said that Dad had grown old and had no one to care for him back on the island. I felt a familiar sadness about Dad's death and began to feel guilty about his dying alone. Soon after receiving the news, my family began to make arrangements and to decide who would go to Antigua. We agreed that my two sisters and I would go to Dad's funeral. None of us had legal documentation, but we were willing and took the risk.

That deep-seated fear of deportation was still very prevalent.

It was a hot day in November 1979 when we gathered once again at our home on Parliament Street in Grays Farm. This time it was Dad's funeral, and in his memory, I wrote a poem about the brave, strong father I remembered. Mr. Strafe brought Dad's body in the hearse and placed his varnished, pine-box coffin, on our gallery where it fit with space to spare.

To my surprise, when they opened the coffin, I couldn't believe that was my father. He looked gaunt, and his previously strapping body had shriveled up. His cheeks were sunken, and his complexion was extra dark and discolored. Gone was that strong, tall, strapping man I knew as my dad.

The people in the neighborhood stood in the streets, shaking their heads in sadness because "Massa Lynch" was gone.

After a slow procession to Green Bay Church, Mr. Strafe's associates laid his coffin in the center isle of the church while Mrs. White sang a solo, "Abide with Me." I then followed with my poem.

I did not cry because I wanted to appear strong and brave, but Dad's death brought back all those feelings of loss and grief once again. I had to find a way to rid myself or minimize the impact of those losses that were just a part of life.

One week after Dad's funeral, all my siblings left to return to their homes. My two sisters and I left on a Saturday night at twelve o'clock midnight to fly back to Puerto Rico en route to the States and landed at JFK early Sunday morning about six o'clock. As we were landing, I secretly thanked God for a safe flight and that we had all made it back to America safely.

When I returned to my apartment, I experienced an overwhelming sense of sadness, grief, and loss again. My loss was multifaceted. Not only did I lose my mother and father but coming to America as an undocumented immigrant represented a loss of my country, family, and sense of self. All these losses impacted my confidence and overall self-esteem.

The next day, when I returned to work at the Jackie Robinson Management Corporation, Mrs. Winters welcomed me back with a big hug. I was happy to be back at work, but the shock of how my father looked in that pinewood coffin stayed with me for quite a long while. Except for Mrs. Winters, I did not share my grief with anyone. I did not explain where I had been or what had taken place.

Being an Undocumented Immigrant

The experience of undocumented immigrants in the United States is plagued by trauma, fear, stress, marginalization, unhappiness, loneliness, anxiety, and lack of authenticity. Our integrity is compromised as we're forced to play small and hide our light under a bushel, darkening an already dimmed world.

Though America is a cultural melting pot of documented and undocumented immigrants, the acculturation process may not be an easy transition. There are many obstacles to overcome before becoming documented while keeping the secret long enough to allow time to put affairs in order. Still there are millions of undocumented immigrants in the U.S. willing to do what it takes to remain here and become legal and voiced.

The fear of deportation had a tremendous impact on me. I cringed, hyperventilated, and had nightmares about anyone in an official uniform as it triggered memories of that night when I escaped from my island to enter America in the wee hours of the morning. The emotional impact of being chased, sought out, and unable to speak traumatized me in my dreams. It created anxiety about being deported, and I wondered how much time I had left in the States, and how much longer it might take before they caught up with me.

At some point, I understood this was PTSD, having worked at the VA and other populations with this condition. I knew that

PTSD has symptoms that linger, sometimes through a lifetime, without treatment. PTSD doesn't stop just because you gain documented papers or become a citizen. It helped to know that post-traumatic stress disorder could be managed, and it was a matter of staying busy, focused, and understanding that things may not be as bad as I imagined them to be.

Today for undocumented immigrants, the impact is worse, especially on the children. I wonder if they ever get rid of PTSD. Again, I lived in constant anxiety and kept myself imprisoned except for the need to go out for the bare necessities, like work, church, and going to the laundromat almost a block away. I was always looking over my shoulder. As I was coming from food shopping one day with a bag of groceries, I saw several men wearing suits and ties walking swiftly behind me. I became so afraid they may work for immigration that I dropped the bag of groceries again and ran home.

Being an undocumented immigrant can impact life in a myriad of ways. For example, not having health care coverage can affect overall health and well-being. An undocumented immigrant is prone to physical ailments, accidents, disorders, and emotional issues, just like anyone else.

As an undocumented immigrant, people must find their own way because nothing is done for them. When a person is undocumented, the system forces them to hide who they are, preventing them from living an authentic lifestyle.

It took all of my courage and energy to survive in America. Being undocumented, I was secretive and did not go out of my way to share my thoughts with anyone. I was unvoiced because

I didn't want to answer any questions for fear of exposing myself. I was afraid to be myself and didn't feel safe enough in my environment to grow in healthy ways.

Still today, being an undocumented immigrant has impacted my life in so many traumatizing ways.

Here are some of my anxiety triggers and situations:
1. When I see someone dressed in an authoritative uniform
2. As a social worker, having to go to court with or for my clients
3. Being stopped by a traffic cop
4. Renewing my driver's license or car registration
5. Applying for a passport
6. Arriving on my home island or returning to an airport in America and going through customs
7. Filling out official documents
8. Unidentifiable phone numbers on caller ID
9. A knock at the door when I'm not expecting company
10. Being afraid to take pictures or share too much information
11. Afraid to post on social media sites

My Dialect/Accent

Being an undocumented black immigrant also impacted my life in many ways in terms of interpersonal relationships, friendships, and communication.

As a native Antiguan, I spoke with a dialect. Initiating discussion or interacting with others was hard for me because

I did not want to be laughed at for the way I spoke. Because I was reclusive and had no real friends outside of church, I needed to fill my time with something other than the routine of going to work and church. I was becoming concerned the isolation was eroding away my well-being. Still I was afraid of being asked questions about my background and status. After I moved into my apartment, I bought a sewing machine and learned how to make my clothes.

I had learned how to sew as a child by putting pieces of scraps together to make a quilt. It boosted my confidence that I could cut and sew an outfit at night and wear it to work the next day. I enjoyed the attention and compliments I received from co-workers, my church family, and others. It felt good to be praised. I felt proud that I was creative and artistic enough to make my own clothes. It made me feel self-sufficient.

Family Disconnection

My relationship with my third sister became more problematic. I did not want to take sides, and I did not know how to communicate appropriately between my sisters. After I got my apartment, my third sister never visited me, and whenever I visited her, she became upset because I refused to share with her the details of my conversations with my oldest sister. This led to several arguments that were painful and upsetting to me. I began to feel abused and beaten up by my third sister and did not want to be the victim of her anger. Because these visits were uncomfortable, I eventually stopped visiting her home.

After Dad died, new and unpleasant news began to spread within my family. The rift between my two sisters widened when it was rumored that there were issues about our family inheritance. This issue became a new wedge in our family that kept us from communicating. No one wanted to talk about the issue of inheritance and kept it inside as a family secret. Over time, the relationship between my sisters and my relationship with my sisters became more strained. Though my sisters and I lived in the same building, there were long periods of no contact between us.

Because my immediate family support system was in short supply, it was important for me to try to make some friends other than Mrs. Winters. The thought of this petrified me.

An Embarrassing Moment

After being in my own apartment for a while, I felt secure in expanding and wanted to get another job. My goal was to continue working in my current position, then find an additional job. The two jobs would afford me the opportunity to support myself and go to college.

In addition to notifying my previous placement office, I decided to regularly check the employment listing of several newspapers like the *Daily News*, the *Amsterdam News* and *The Post* newspapers.

I was thrilled when I found a listing for a job as a data entry worker at Metropolitan Life Insurance Company at night. After contacting the personnel office, I was given an interview a few days later.

Going on this job interview is the story of one of my most embarrassing moments.

In preparation for my interview for the job in a big insurance company on the Upper East Side, I picked out my lavender scooped-neck, tulip-sleeve blouse and my purple maxi-wrap skirt that was the best outfit I owned. The skirt was cute, with a narrow sash around the waist.

There were ten people sitting in the room. They asked me all kinds of questions, like what is my greatest weakness? Where did I see myself in five years? To the best of my ability, I answered every question. The interview was very long, but filled with promise. When I finally got up, I realized that my skirt did not come up with me; the skirt had dropped down to my feet. The men looked away, pretending they didn't see me. I was so embarrassed. I thought, it's a good thing my panties didn't have any holes in them.

Fortunately for me, I got the job. I was told to report for work Tuesday the following week. Things were going well now and I was very grateful.

My work hours and tour of duty at Metropolitan Life Insurance Company were from 4–12 p.m. at night. I was happy, anxious, and nervous about working in Manhattan. I had to take the train daily. The fare to get on the train was a token, which was 25 cents one way. It was a hardship to take the subway to work the night shift. However, I soon became accustomed to the routine and began to make friends. The program and process departments were located on the 12th floor. The room in which we worked was very large, outfitted with desktop computers and chairs for the workers. There were separate cubicles for managers. It held about one hundred workers. It was a rigid, strict environment; we took turns taking our breaks, and we ate lunch and dinner together.

As fate would have it, I met a woman named Margie one night at work, just before we took our dinner break. Her cubicle, in this large open room at Metropolitan Life Insurance Company, was right next to mine. We were breaking for dinner when she invited me to have dinner with her and I said yes. This was the beginning of my venturing out and trusting maybe I could feel safe if I made one new friend.

Margie was twenty years old. Her parents were from Italy, but she was born in America. She was about my age and height. We quickly became fast friends. I was taken with and impressed by Margie because she was smart and a good worker, easily making her nightly quota of one thousand data entries. She walked and moved around the work area with confidence, as if she were comfortable in her own skin. Her shoulder length blonde hair pulled back into a ponytail revealed her full, round face and cheery personality. I remember thinking how much more mature she seemed than me. I too wanted to be as sociable, confident, and mature as she seemed to be. She wore pants, a blouse, makeup, and had her own apartment in Manhattan. I identified with Margie because I, too, had my own apartment in Brooklyn.

I was also taken with Margie because we were both open to sharing and accepting each other's cultural diversities. This began my process of allowing a few more people into my life.

Because riding the train to work at night became very tedious, I needed to find work closer to home. I began to look for work in Brooklyn.

Having worked at the Metropolitan Life Insurance Company for a little over a year, I decided to apply for a position at Long Island University. This would make it easier for me to apply for admittance to college later. I still didn't have any papers but moved through life in my new culture on sheer faith and the continued belief that I would not be discovered and would succeed at achieving my dreams. I was hired for a full-time day job as a receptionist in the Continuing Education Department at Long Island University.

Excited about having a day job, I was pleased to have a work schedule from 9–5. This would free up my time to take classes at LIU in the CE program and possibly attend school full time. I resigned from my other two jobs, only worked at LIU, and registered to take courses in the Continuing Education program.

I began to spend time in the library and started reading books on psychology, sociology, Black History, and personality development.

After I started working at LIU, I somehow lost contact with Margie. I devoted more time to writing and dramatizing my poems in church. By spending most of my time at work and in the church, I had little or no interaction with my family. I began to feel my family did not care about me, and I continued to spend most of my spare time alone. At times, I didn't mind being alone because alone, no one got close enough to hurt me.

A CULTURAL MELTING POT

Thank God I had my own apartment in which I could escape and hide. That is where I felt safest because I hoped no one would come looking for me there. This was my safe haven.

CHAPTER 7

What I Did to Accomplish My Dream

My hopes and dreams were to do something impactful with my life. Because I believed an education was a way to find freedom and create my own journey in life, I knew going to college was my highest priority. I was a conscientious student and believed I could succeed. Success to me meant pursuing my goals.

In my heart, I dreamt of living in and owning a brick house with a green grass lawn and white picket fence in America. I also dreamt of buying and driving my own car someday.

The words I recited that night at the Easter Bunny Pageant from Dr. Martin Luther King's "I Have a Dream" speech, "Free at last, free at last, thank God Almighty I'm free at last," felt as if they were my own words. In my mind, I wanted freedom and liberation, not deportation.

After working for a few months in the Continuing Education Department at Long Island University, I decided to apply for college only to discover I would be given a college entrance examination for proper placement. After taking the examination, I learned that I needed to take remedial courses before I would be considered for matriculation. These courses were in math, science, physics, and English because I did not score well in those areas.

At the moment of hearing the news I would have to take remedial classes, it felt like a bubble burst inside me. I was shocked, surprised, and disappointed to know I had scored so poorly on the college examination. This did not help my self-esteem and made me feel less smart than American students. I came to the United States feeling very confident about my accomplishments in high school.

How could that be? I asked myself.

For a while, I kept my feelings secret and continued to write poetry. Then one day, I decided to share my feelings with Mrs. Winters. She explained to me that here in America all students entering a new school are given an entrance examination that determines the grade in which they will be placed. I accepted her explanation that helped me not feel so bad.

Upon completion of these remedial classes with a passing grade of C or better, I would be eligible to move on to matriculation status. Needless to say, I completed the assigned classes with ease and moved on to full matriculation status. Even though I didn't think I needed to take a course in remedial English, I knew I had a dialect and assumed they knew best. I can see now how it helped me with sentence structure, subject-verb agreement, and tenses.

After working in the Continuing Education Department for a few weeks, a position became available in the Psychology Department for a secretary. I requested a transfer from the Continuing Education Department to the Psychology Department because it would afford me the opportunity to attend classes at night and on weekends.

As a full-time employee in the Psychology Department, I would be eligible to take six college credits tuition free per semester, but any additional credits could be through obtaining educational loans and grants. As a full-time secretary in the Department of Psychology, I was able to take up to twenty-two credits per semester. Now, I could comfortably devote my life to church, school, and work.

As an undergraduate student, I had to make a decision about my major and minor classes. Now that I was working in the Department of Psychology at Long Island University, it made sense to take most of my classes in psychology.

I liked helping people and thought I would one day open a school for adolescent girls who felt abandoned and unloved like me, who had difficulty adjusting in a new environment. I also wanted to make a contribution to the world.

As an undergraduate student in college, I became curious about Black history, and because there were no Black study programs in my college at that time, I spent time in the library reading books in addition to attending workshops on the Black experience in America. After reading Maulana

Karenga's book, *Introduction to Black Studies; The African Origin of Civilization: Myth or Reality* by Cheikh Anta Diop; *Africans and Their History,* by Joseph E. Harris; *Stolen Legacy,* by George G. M. James; and *African Religions and Philosophy* by John S. Mbiti, I was inspired to continue seeking for knowledge about myself and my history.

A Nation of Immigrants
America is a nation of immigrants. It is like a pot or container filled with people from various cultures, races, religions, and beliefs, seeking freedom and working on some level for unity. America is known as a place where opportunities are plentiful and is governed by the Constitution, a set of guidelines and amendments under the law by which people live. The constitution is supposed to give equal protection and the right to liberty and justice for all.

Everyone from every culture wants the same things. Apart from our basic needs for survival, parents want better lives for their children and families, happiness, comfort, acceptance, and the interconnectedness of people, for the greater good of all.

However, many families who immigrate to America in search of a better life are undocumented and don't have the freedoms to openly pursue their dreams until they become documented. Thus begins their journey of becoming documented in America to be able to openly take advantage of all the opportunities offered. My entire family had to deal with immigration issues.

Stories abound of the various ways an immigrant may seek to gain legal status. It is common for immigrants to become creative in ways to become legalized. Some people married citizens, obtained legal status through their parents, a sibling, or other family members, and some people never changed their status and remained undocumented.

After a period of time, if an undocumented immigrant married a U.S. citizen to become legal and the marriage didn't last for whatever reasons, the undocumented person continued to maintain their permanent residency.

Being undocumented can cause a person to feel less than a whole human being. Everything seems to say, "You don't have a right to be here." People can feel diminished, unwelcomed, and displaced. There are a lot of situations which scare undocumented immigrants and make them feel as if they don't have intelligence.

I did not see any undocumented immigrants in my community who had the right to vote or a driver's license. It was as if their civil rights and human rights were being violated. They dared not think of breaking the law. No undocumented immigrants I knew had committed a crime. They only wanted to work hard and become a legal member of American society.

Though I came from a family of immigrants, I did not want to accept I had no rights. I believed I had a right to an education, so I went to school. I believed that education was my ticket to freedom. I believed if I worked hard and got an education, I would be free, I would fit in, and I would be accepted. I took advantage of all I considered to be my rights.

College Graduate

In the spring of 1982, I received my Bachelor of Arts degree in Psychology from LIU.

Graduating from high school was a big deal to me, and I was the first in my family to attend and to graduate from college. Mrs. Winters attended my college graduation, but I resented that no one from my nuclear family celebrated me and my accomplishments. When I saw Mrs. Winters in the audience, it made me feel good that *someone* came on my behalf.

I continued to attend Bright Light Church and enjoyed the occasional visits to and from other churches. This was a highlight for me. I enjoyed the guest choirs and guest speakers. This was usually on Sunday morning or evening. After being on the Junior Missionary Board in Bright Light Church, I became interested in field work and visiting other churches in the neighborhood.

In the spring of 1983, Mother Jessie Turner was the featured speaker at the annual Women's Day, which was held on the fourth Sunday at Bright Light Church during the month of May. This is how I met Mother Turner, who was the regional manager of the women's missionary boards in our church district. Because Mother Turner was born in Mississippi during a time when birth certificates were often not kept, neither she nor anyone in the church knew her real age. However, she was old enough to be considered the senior missionary and church mother of Kelly Temple Church of God in Christ in Manhattan.

She spoke under the anointing of the Holy Spirit about the story of Ruth. I was inspired by her words. Mother Turner visited as the speaker at Bright Light frequently, and I would make sure I was present and looked forward to hearing her speak. Bright Light was very strict and rigid about church members visiting other churches, which made me more curious about visiting other churches with Mother Turner. This meant that the church did not want young converts to visit other churches because they feared them leaving and joining other congregations. I did not like this rule.

One Sunday afternoon, to my surprise, Mother Turner asked me to dramatize one of my poems before she spoke. She was impressed by my writing poetry and said it fit right into her topic. She told me about the joyous choir in her church and the wonderful work the young people were doing there. I felt conflicted, knowing that Bright Light frowned upon its members visiting other churches. However, after getting permission from my pastor, I did begin to travel as Mother Turner's guest on her speaking engagements to various churches where I often dramatized my poems. Since we both lived in Brooklyn, there was usually a church member who would give us a ride, so we wouldn't have to take the train home.

After these events, we'd go and get something to eat— Salisbury steak with mashed potatoes and string beans, or baked turkey or chicken with yellow rice and beans, topped off with ice cream for dessert.

For the next few months, we were able to develop a close mother and daughter relationship. I missed my mother desperately and was always looking to find her. Mother Turner did not have a daughter and welcomed me as her goddaughter.

During this time, I continued to express my feelings and thoughts through poetry. While I continued to visit various churches and dramatized my poetry, I believed I was destined to have a deeper calling on my life.

Philosophy and Spirituality
As a child, I was always curious about the nature of the Universe and had many questions about the purpose of life like: *Who am I? Why am I here?* and *Where am I going?*

At LIU, undergraduate students were allowed to take graduate courses. At the end of my junior year, I applied and was accepted into the Guidance and Counseling graduate program and was allowed to take classes toward a Master of Science degree. I believed that having my master's degree could afford me the option to work part-time as a guidance counselor in the public schools if I desired.

I took philosophy courses and poetry classes as electives. I enjoyed the works of poets like Gibran, Browning, Keats, Chaucer, and Frost. I was also drawn to philosophers, such as Plato, Descartes, Hume, Confucius, and Yates, and I continued to explore various forms of philosophy as I searched for some clarity about my spiritual life.

In the fall of 1982, the same year I received my BA in Psychology from LIU, I received my Master of Science degree in Guidance and Counseling from LIU, Brooklyn Campus.

To develop my understanding of my history, I continued reading Black History books, which included: *Ancient African Kingdoms,* by Margaret Shinnie; *They Came Before Columbus:*

The African Presence in Ancient America, by Ivan Van Sertima; *No Longer at Ease,* by Chinua Achebe; *Egypt to the End of the Old Kingdom* by Cyril Aldred; and *Amistad I: Writings on Black History and Culture,* Edited by John A. Williams and Charles F. Harris.

Seeking Soul

While in the church, I wanted to know more about the Soul. There was always a thirst for spiritual knowledge and guidance inside me. I felt I was no longer getting my needs met in the church. Even though they talked about Soul in the church, it was not clear that I was a Soul that had a body and not the other way around. I felt my Soul was calling for more knowledge and guidance. So, after college graduation, I began the journey to search for peace and stability in my life. I wanted to be happy and practice the steps of exercising faith.

I began to research more about the Soul and sought resources in the community. One day as I wandered into one of the new age bookstores, I bought *The Seat of the Soul,* by Gary Zukav. Reading it made a big impression on me; it changed my life. I felt a deeper calling to know more about the part of me that was divine. I listened to new age music and continued to buy new age books about soul, such as: *"Discovering Your Soul's Purpose,* by Mark Thurston; *The Road Less Travelled: A New Psychology of Love, Traditional Values, and Spiritual Growth* by M. Scott Peck, M.D.; and *The Life of the Soul,* by Samuel H. Miller.

From an early age, I realized I had a different perspective and curiosity than many of my family and friends about the metaphysical dimensions of existence.

Search for Higher Learning

I loved God and Jesus, and when I got *saved*, I made a commitment to serve God for the rest of my life. I was eager to seek knowledge and grow spiritually. Though I intended to continue my graduate study in psychology, I wanted to study the *Word of God* and sought out resources that could be a good fit for me.

Mrs. Winters encouraged me to consider attending a Bible college instead of a parochial school for higher learning.

A year before graduating from Long Island University, I began to research various graduate programs, including Bible colleges. I applied to study at Fuller Theological Seminary in Pasadena, California. I also applied for admission to the master's program in social work as well as Union Theological Seminary at Columbia University in Manhattan, New York.

I chose to apply to Fuller Theological Seminary because they offered degree programs that would meet my needs in preparation for the ministry or further education and spiritual enrichment. I wanted to attend Fuller because they attempted to integrate psychology and theology in theory, research, and practice.

At that time, I was willing and prepared to move to California in pursuit of a higher education because I believed the graduate programs in psychology or theology would be a good fit for me. Though Columbia University was my first choice, I believed that either school would provide the special training to assist me on my journey to spiritual and emotional wholeness.

I remember the excitement I felt when I received an invitation for consideration at both schools.

After a second interview with the admissions committee at Fuller Theological Seminary, I was not chosen among the final twelve applicants. Needless to say, I not only felt disappointed and rejected, but it bruised my pride and self-esteem. I was overjoyed, however, when I received the correspondence from the Dean of Students that I was accepted to the Columbia University School of Social Work.

I was also granted a scholarship for my first year of learning. This was my opportunity to get not only an Ivy League college education and subsequently a decent paying job, but more importantly, I would be able to serve others and share love and support with them. I would still be working at LIU and travelling by the A, 2, and 6 trains after work to attend my classes in Manhattan.

I was awed by the campus of Columbia University and its blue school color. I was taken by the huge buildings. When I attended my first clinical practice class, I was thrilled that my dream of getting a higher education was indeed becoming a reality. I was happy I was enrolled at Columbia University and was excited to meet other students from different parts of the country who also wanted to help others, as I did.

As time passed and the excitement of the newness wore off, I felt more alone, unloved, and insecure. I became more and more reclusive as I steadily marginalized myself after one of my sisters threatened, during a heated argument, to report me to the authorities. I couldn't understand why she would do that when she knew of my fear of being deported.

What had I done to her for her to hate me so and to frighten me with such a threat?

Now my fears were compounded by the thought of being discovered as well as being reported to immigration by a family member. This created a chasm between my sister and me for many years.

I mostly avoided any kind of confrontation with my sister because it was frightening and threatening. I did not want to give her the satisfaction of knowing that I was afraid she would follow through on her threats. We did not speak for more than six years, though we encountered each other in the hallways of the apartment building we both lived in. During those chaotic times, I felt more and more disconnected from my family.

Soon after I started attending Columbia University, I became even more afraid I could be discovered and deported before completing my course of study. Though I was excited about my curriculum that included personality development, clinical practice, and field work, I had low self-esteem and I felt I lacked courage. I began to feel I was not smart enough and resisted asserting myself in class. Sometimes I was filled with self-doubt and anxiety. Poor self-esteem and doubt were taking a toll on me.

My first-year fieldwork placement was at a psychiatric hospital in Long Island, New York. For my second-year fieldwork assignment, I was placed at the Veteran's Administration Mental Hygiene Clinic in Brooklyn, New York.

Because I continued to feel angry and sad, I decided to seek out a psychiatrist. I was tormented with emotions for which I had no name; I was experiencing feelings of sadness that pervaded my mood, attitude, and daily habits. I needed outside support to help me sort things out. I believed therapy would help me to stay on track and focus on my dreams and goals. Not only was I angry at my family and believed they did not care about me, but I still felt angry and rejected that I did not get into Fuller Theological Seminary.

During a workshop at Columbia University one day, I decided to share with my clinical practice professor some of the sadness, irritability, and fear-based thoughts I was experiencing. After checking with me about my preferences, she referred me to a black, female psychiatrist in New York City. I was motivated to meet her because I had not seen many black, female psychiatrists in the facilities where I did my fieldwork assignments.

The following Friday, I was invited for a consultation after work. I was given a series of psychological and psychosocial assessments in which she asked me questions about my thoughts, feelings, and behaviors to see what diagnostic criteria I met, based on the *Diagnostic Statistical Manual* (DSM).

We agreed that talk therapy would be the best treatment to help me focus on my negative thoughts, patterns, and behaviors. Though we discussed medication, the doctor agreed it was not indicated at that time. On a long-term basis, I met with her weekly for psychotherapy to tackle my many issues. Fascinated about seeing a black, female psychiatrist, I was inspired to maybe one day open my own private practice.

I was given a diagnosis of dysthymic disorder, a type of depression that lasts a long time. It is also known as persistent depressive disorder (PPD) and is a mood disorder which starts very early in childhood and is characterized by a chronic course through adolescence or early adulthood. While the person's mood is generally low, their depression is usually mild or moderate, rather than severe.

Although it was hard for me to accept such a diagnosis, I could not deny the reality of it. However, with acceptance of the diagnosis, I had a better understanding of my persistent sadness. I immediately felt some relief because there was possibly a physiological cause for my sadness as opposed to my just being stuck in fear and grief. I was now more open to explore and understand some of the root causes of my sadness and began to work on developing better coping skills.

Among the books my psychiatrist recommended to me were: *Necessary Losses: The Loves, Illusions, Dependencies, and Impossible Expectations that All of Us Have to Give Up in Order to Grow*, by Judith Viorst; *Self-Reliance*, by Ralph Waldo Emerson; *I Know Why the Caged Bird Sings*, by Maya Angelou; *Jonathan Livingston Seagull*, by Richard Bach; *The Bluest Eye*, by Toni Morrison; and *The Mis-Education of the Negro*, by Carter G. Woodson.

To help me interpret and process my many dreams that added to my confusion, fears, and sadness, my psychiatrist suggested I purchase a journal to begin recording my dreams. I kept the journal next to my bed. One night, I had a dream that started with a drizzling rain as I was driving to work. It rained continuously for five days. It seemed as though I was going along the FDR Drive in New York City. Before I knew it, the FDR Drive became flooded and merged with the East River. All of a sudden, I was out of my car and swimming in the river.

In another dream, I was on the B44 bus going to work. When my stop arrived and I started to disembark, I discovered I was naked.

My therapist helped me to understand that my dreams of feeling exposed and vulnerable were indicative of my emotional state at the time. This helped release some of my fears.

As a graduate student at Columbia University, I was among the foreign students targeted for a new amnesty program and was found eligible for the program.

I was interviewed and assisted by a male and a female lawyer, together and separately, and through the amnesty proceedings, I was fortunate to qualify. I received a green card in 1984. At the time I received my green card, I believed I was blessed, and some may say lucky, that it occurred at the time it did, when it was easier for one to become legal.

A green card is the very basic legal document for legal residence in the United States. Having a green card was proof I was legal here. Having a card was valuable. Having a green card meant I could go to the grocery store without looking over my shoulder to see who was watching me.

It meant not worrying my voice would trigger attention from others and give away that I was not from here. Having a green card made me feel that I belonged here, yet I was still not happy. I was not happy because I was still disconnected from my family. I could not shake the anger and disappointment I felt from not feeling loved and wanted by my family.

It was a two-by-two green card, laminated in hard plastic, with my personal information on it. This was an ID card, which all immigrants were required by law to carry at all times. With my green card, I could sign up for driving lessons and I did. I did not pass the test the first time but was successful on the second time around. I was grateful that my sister had helped me to perfect my driving and parking while attending high school in St. Thomas. However, I did not carry my green card with me and chose to leave it locked up in my apartment with other important documents, for fear of losing it.

Often, I thought about Mom and how much she struggled to get my younger brother and me green cards. I always believed that someone was watching over me; I believed we had good fortune.

After I received my green card, I hoped I could breathe more easily because I was now put in the category of a documented immigrant, but I was still plagued by the fear of being deported. I just didn't feel safe, but knew I had to acculturate into a new and different culture.

In the spring of 1985, I graduated from Columbia University with a master's degree in Social Work and became certified as a licensed clinical social worker that same year.

After graduation from Columbia University, I was fortunate to be offered a social work position at the VA hospital in Brooklyn, NY. I felt proud of myself that I was now a civil servant. I believed I was blessed and still had the option of taking either the bus or train to get to work because my work was now in Brooklyn. My tour of duty was 8 a.m. to 5 p.m. every day, with an hour for lunch.

It was an exciting day when I started working at the Veterans Administration hospital, especially since I had my own office. I was assigned a clinical supervisor, who quickly assigned two patients to me, and who met with me on a weekly basis for supervision. I was overjoyed when I met with my patients for our private sessions in my office. I felt very proud of what I had accomplished and thanked God that the American dream my Mom wanted for me and I wanted for myself was coming true.

After working at the VA for two years, I bought my first car. I felt very proud of myself and my accomplishment. Having a car would be helpful because it would be less of a hassle to get around. I am proud to say I purchased my first car in America with cash, and I was able to take it home right away.

Private Psychotherapy Practice

I seemed to have had an insatiable desire to explore the many passions I had. As a clinician, I loved listening to others and helping them out of their dilemmas. One of my passions was to have my own private practice. Soon after graduation from Columbia University in social work, I moved out of my one-bedroom apartment into a larger apartment, where I shared all expenses with a housemate and was able to have my private psychotherapeutic practice.

I saw clients two nights a week after work and on weekends. This satisfied my great desire to help people find their way as I was finding my way.

To keep up with my many passions, I created space in my schedule to continue developing my skills in sewing, which soon led to my pursuing courses in fashion design at the Fashion Institute of Technology in New York City. Because I was an entrepreneur by nature, I could readily pursue my passion for fashion. I would make an outfit at night to wear to work the next day. I loved wearing beautiful clothes. I enjoyed how the different patterns and textures looked against my ebony complexion.

As a way of saving money, I purchased a stronger performing sewing machine. Creating paper patterns of my own clothes, I made new garments with beautiful fabrics, which ultimately resulted in designing and sketching fashions and displaying those fashions in shows. I was beginning to come out of hiding a little more, which boosted my confidence.

Unfortunately, after participating in a fashion show where my designer wedding gowns and garments were modelled, all my fashions were stolen from my car. Needless to say, after that invasion of my privacy, my lack of trust issues resurfaced, and I retreated back into myself.

Becoming a Citizen

To me, becoming a citizen meant I would be abandoning my culture. Even though I dreamt of becoming an American citizen, I did not want to lose my culture. I was conflicted, but I felt I had plenty of time to make the decision to pursue citizenship. Interestingly enough, I didn't have as much time as I thought. One day, not long after procuring my green card, I arrived home from work and discovered my green card was missing from where it was hidden.

As previously stated, rather than keeping my green card on my person at all times, I thought it would be safer to leave my card at home. I was wrong. Only my housekeeper and the superintendent of the building had access to my apartment, but I could not prove anything. This generated more fear and anxiety because I had no proof to show that I belonged here. A green card is a precious commodity.

It was now 1991, and I had to quickly change my thinking about abandoning my culture to find a way to fuse the two cultures. I needed to become a citizen and deal with other emotions later, like being afraid that I would be denied citizenship. I had to act immediately.

I contacted the lawyers who could advise me of my next steps for obtaining citizenship from the Amnesty program at Columbia University. They advised me to seek naturalized citizenship right away. I had to take a written test, learn the constitution, and to pledge to know and obey the laws of the United States of America.

In June of 1992, I became naturalized. Yes, I gave up my island rights and became an American citizen, but naturalization for me was no celebration party. They gave me a test of the constitution that sad, complex day to prove I believed the pledge I was saying as my life changed forever.

Five hundred people took an oath with me, pledging allegiance to the flag in a new country, land of freedom and liberty. The melodious sound of their voices was in unison as the song, "God Bless America" burst from speakers in the ceiling of the room while people with jovial, excited, worn faces, stood ready to become citizens of the United States of America.

Hundreds of people that day pledged allegiance to the red, white, and blue flag, chanting and singing, "Land of the free and home of the brave," and "We're free!"

I did not feel happy. No, naturalization was no celebration for me. The fear of deportation still crippled me. Though I knew I should have been happy, I still felt no relief from being afraid, unhappy, traumatized, and stigmatized by having been an undocumented immigrant. Though my legal status had changed, my emotional state of fear persisted.

Because I had limited or no contact with my family, there was never anyone from my family to celebrate me or my accomplishments. They weren't aware of what was happening in my life. I still felt totally unloved, insecure, angry, and sad. I couldn't even celebrate myself. I found it hard to find joy in this accomplishment. I yearned for the support of my family and still built up resistance and anger against them. I needed to feel that they cared. I wanted to connect with my family and feel safe enough to know that they supported me in my endeavors.

Leaving Bright Light

When I attended Bible classes in Bright Light Church, I asked many questions. Mostly, I was not satisfied with the answers and wanted more information. After being a member of Bright Light Church for a few years, I did not feel inspired by the messages and became dissatisfied with the oppressive, dogmatic views. I had a hunger for knowledge that my church was not able to address.

I was taught I would go to hell if I didn't make decisions for my life based on the restrictive doctrines of the church. Being encumbered by the rigid, patriarchal rules in the church, I wanted more freedom in my life.

I had been in this church for more than fifteen years but felt that my Soul was not being fed at Bright Light. I was becoming confused and disillusioned about the concepts of God and church. I wanted a church that had a more upwardly mobile and a more sophisticated congregation. Thus, I left Bright Light Church in the summer of 1988. It was time to spread my wings and take flight.

It was imperative I stay on my spiritual quest of Soul work, so I joined Kelly Temple, Church of God in Christ, Mother Turner's church that same year, hoping to find the in-depth self-knowledge I was seeking. I really wanted to find out what my purpose was for being here on Earth. I wanted to know more about my Soul on a deeper level. I had questions about dying, reincarnation, heaven versus hell, who, when, and what to love. I believed there was more to my existence, and I was determined to find answers to my questions.

Whole

I wanted a higher consciousness in order to live my life from a higher perspective. I wanted to become awakened and to connect to my true divine self. I wanted to experience divine oneness. I believed: *The Divine is you and you are the Divine.* I wanted to feel whole. I was caught up in a cycle of negative thoughts, and I knew that I had to find a way to become whole.

Freedom and wholeness are elements of the Divine. Becoming whole and feeling free means recognizing our divinity and being aware we are one with the Divine and everything there is.

However, at the time I could only imagine there was some sort of consciousness that transcended my current state.

The third Sunday in the summer of 1988, when I joined Kelly Temple in hopes of finding answers to my questions, I felt happy. I became a little nervous when the pastor invited all new members to come forward and introduce themselves to the whole congregation. I went forward and introduced myself and felt welcomed.

Shortly after joining Kelly Temple, I was baptized in water and began to grow more spiritually. I was also able to share some of my gifts. I wrote, directed, and produced a play about the "Five Talents," and as a junior missionary, I started the first church newspaper called, *Focus*.

I found it more exciting at Kelly Temple because they had a larger group of young people my age, and I quickly joined the junior choir. Even though I joined the junior choir at Kelly Temple and started to associate with more people, my own resistance to trust and communicate my feelings made it hard for me to develop lasting relationships with anyone.

However, I continued to write and dramatize my poetry at Kelly Temple and other churches Mother Turner and I visited. I joined the junior missionary board and the Young People

Willing Worker's Group, which afforded me the opportunity to teach Sunday school and occasionally deliver a speech from a verse or chapter in the Bible. The young people in my new church were very active in the church and often attended events outside. We visited other churches where we sang as the guest choir and in addition, we invited other churches to visit us.

I continued reading books on Black History as well as other books, such as: *Deceptions and Myths of the Bible,* by Lloyd M. Graham; *The Spiritual Seeker's Guide,* by Steven S. Sadleir; *The Community of Self,* by Dr. Na'im Akbar; *When God Was a Woman,* by Merlin Stone; *Heal Your Body: The Mental Causes for Physical Illness and the Metaphysical Way to Overcome Them,* by Louise L. Hay; *The Healing Power Within,* by Ann Wigmore; and *My Mother My Self: A Daughter's Search for Identity,* by Nancy Friday.

After spending a couple of years at Kelly Temple, I still felt unfulfilled in my quest for knowledge on my spiritual path. I did not like how the church vehemently denied or rejected other people's way of worshipping God. I felt stifled. I did not feel any better after church services. I thought seriously about leaving Kelly Temple church and looked for the best time to do so.

Leaving the church was a gradual occurrence. I stopped attending weeknight services and Sunday school, but continued to attend Bible classes. I still had many questions that couldn't seem to be answered by the Bible class teachers, so I became consumed with religious doubts and began to feel more confused about what I believed. As a result, almost two years after joining Kelly Temple, I decided to leave the Church of God in Christ doctrine.

Losing My Way

Initially, I missed the various rituals in the church, like tarry services that were held bi-monthly, where the entire congregation prayed from midnight to six o'clock the following morning. I was always amazed after tarry services how refreshed and energized the congregation felt as the church mothers prepared breakfast. The smells of fat back and biscuits with the aroma of black coffee were inviting. That is when I first drank hot brewed coffee, black.

After leaving the church, my spiritual practice of prayer began to suffer, and there were times when I felt I had lost my way. I kept reading the Bible and other philosophical books to help me grow.

I began taking on vices that I hadn't done before. I developed a taste for caffeine and black coffee and drank it during the day, taking regular coffee breaks at work. I began smoking Marlboro cigarettes. I smoked in my office, on my job, and in my car on my way to and from work. Though I did not enjoy the taste or odor of cigarettes, I continued to smoke them.

When a co-worker offered me a Virginia Slims cigarette, I gladly accepted because I did not want to say no, which was indicative of being a people pleaser. I shortly realized I did not want to take on practices that could be damaging to my health, so I began giving up those unhealthy vices. When I left the church doctrine, I thought I was doing the right thing, yet deep inside I felt ashamed and guilty about leaving the church.

Over time, my connection to the church was completely severed as I isolated myself and disconnected from everyone in the church. Not only did I close my heart to the outside world, but I worried that I might get disconnected from God because I had left the church. I was caught up in a mindset of fear and misdirection.

Since I no longer attended church on Sundays or during the week, sometimes I did not know what to do with myself. Most of my days were spent at home where I felt alone and sad while thinking of the events going on at any particular time during the church services.

There were times when I felt confused about what I believed and felt my faith and courage had waned. So much so that eventually I began to doubt my ability to succeed at my endeavors.

I said I had faith, but I didn't know if I still believed. I needed to turn my doubts into beliefs. I prayed and asked God to help my unbelief.

Leaving the religious institution of the church doctrine was a big transition, but I knew deep inside there was something more. I wanted to find my own path to God through other means of searching, apart from the church teachings. I began to seek out other resources and groups in the community for support. I believed I needed group support to help me stay focused and to strengthen my self-confidence and self-esteem.

When I left the church, my intention was to learn more and explore the nature of my Soul on a deeper level.

I began to revisit my time of taking various workshops on spirituality in the mid-80s and continued my work as a clinical social worker, while I explored the Soul as a way to deepen my search. I wanted to understand the illusion of separation between the physical and non-physical, or metaphysical. I was seeking more spiritual fulfillment.

As a young social worker, a civil servant, I was on a quest to find freedom and find myself. The quest to find my way turned out to be the actual journey of my life to find spiritual fulfillment. This began the emotional, spiritual journey on which I am still unfolding and becoming.

One day I had an interesting experience as I was walking to a store that had metaphysical items and jewelry. A Caucasian woman exiting the store gifted me with a single earring with an ornament of an angel on it. Though I was surprised, I received the gift as an omen of being on the right track for seeking spiritual enlightenment. At the time, I did not research what an angel symbolized, but I believed it had something to do with my protection. I kept that gift in my purse.

For the next few years, I attended meditations and ritual ceremonies at different locations but was careful not to commit to any belief systems or become a member of any organization.

Not only did I desire to understand me, but I wanted to understand my divine self and knowledge about the state of my Soul. I was very curious about the nature of the world and my place in it.

I loved God and vowed to live my life serving Him, but I didn't know what my purpose was for being here. I believed there was more to my existence and I wanted more for my life. I believed there was a bigger purpose.

After leaving the church, I continued to read books on Black History, spirituality, and psychology, like: *Before the Mayflower*, by Lerone Bennett; *From Columbus to Castro: The History of the Caribbean, 1492-1969*, by Eric Williams; *The Psychology of the Afro-American: A Humanistic Approach*, by Albert H. Jenkins; *Faces at the Bottom of the Well: The Permanence of Racism*, by Derrick Bell; and *The Destruction of Black Civilization*, by Chancellor Williams.

As a way of strengthening my connection to Spirit, I learned how to listen for divine inspiration and intervention through meditation. I meditated and communicated with Spirit twice a day. I spoke and wrote positive affirmations daily to keep me uplifted, and I was always grateful for all of my blessings.

I shared my interest in African spiritual teachings with my psychiatrist, and she referred me for a spiritual reading to a healer and guide, Priestess Ayofeme, who lived in lower Manhattan. I wanted to know about steps to become more spiritual. Again, as far back as I could remember, I had an interest in the mystical, spiritual. and philosophical realms of life.

Priestess Ayofeme, who was highly recommended to me, is a Priestess in the Yoruba religion and believes in honoring her ancestors and her African heritage.

This was my first spiritual reading, and I didn't think of much else that day. I had many questions in my mind. I didn't know what to expect. I arrived at the brownstone house about 5:30 p.m. I was welcomed with a big smile by a black woman wearing a yellow dress and an African printed cloth, which is called a *gele'*, tied on her head. This gave me pride in my

Caribbean, African culture. She was very calm, relaxed, and soft-spoken as she invited me inside.

She shared that she studied African spirituality, which is rooted in feminism, as well as the practices of Yoruba cosmology, which is the definitive compendium of African History. She explained that African spiritualism embraces a perspective that encourages happiness. These ideas resonated with me because I had grown tired of the dogmatically reinforced ideas of sinfulness, shame, and heaven-or-hell that were reinforced in the church.

Before ending the session, Priestess Ayofeme, handed me a booklist of resources she recommended for reading, including: *Jambalaya: The Natural Woman's Book*, by Luisah Teish; *African Spirituality: Forms, Meanings, and Expressions*, by Jacob K. Olexpona; *Metu Neter, Volume 1*, by Ra Un Nefer Amen; *The Book of Coming Forth by Day*, by Maulana Karenga; and other books and resources on mysticism and African spirituality.

I left this session very excited with booklist in hand.

During the reading, among the things Priestess Ayofeme told me was that Mom's diet contributed greatly to her death.

I was aware that Mom's diet consisted of white sugar, white flour, and other processed foods, and that possibly, a lack of rest and burnout impacted her health as well. This information prompted me to pay more attention to my nutritional intake and learn more about healthy eating. I borrowed a *Natural Living* tape library series on basic nutrition from the local library.

Moreover, I became aware that I needed to watch what I ate for fear I would die of the same illness, atherosclerosis, as Mom. Knowledge is power, so I set out to adopt a better way of eating. I began to visit various health food stores and cut down on portion size.

In 1988, I left the VA Hospital and accepted a position as a team supervisor in New York City working with the mentally ill and substance abusers. The job entailed going out into a certain catchment area where we fed them food and offered resources and services. The goal was to clean up certain areas, such as the streets and subway stations, by finding housing and placement for homeless persons, people suffering from mental illness, and folks abusing chemicals. My tour of duty was from 8:30 a.m. to 6:30 p.m. with a one-hour lunch break. I accepted this position because it was a promotion and was a developmental step as a professional clinician. In addition to supervising other workers, I was responsible for record keeping and completing daily documentations.

Because of my grueling schedule at work, I began to feel burned out, so in 1990, I applied for a clinical social work position at Manhattan Children's Psychiatric Center and was hired to work in the adolescent day program with immigrant youths and families from various cultures. As the primary therapist, I provided individual psychotherapy and group work daily from 8:30 a.m. to 4:30 p.m. I continued to attend therapy, which was designed to help me find peace. However, I still struggled with self-doubts, insecurities, poor self-esteem, and anxiety. With my therapist's encouragement, I delved deeper into what was familiar: my God Source. I wanted to live my life differently.

I continued to read books on philosophy and Black History, like: *When God Was A Woman,* by Merlin Stone; *The Gnostic Gospels,* by Elaine Pagels; *Many Lives, Many Masters,* by Brian L. Weiss, MD; *Radical Spirituality,* by Dick Sutphen; *Cinderella & Her Sisters: The Envied and the Envying,* by Ann & Barry Ulanov; *The Prophet,* by Kahlil Gibran; and *Understanding an Afrocentric World View: Introduction to an Optimal Psychology,* by Linda James Myers, PhD.

Reading Dr. Meyer's book motivated me to examine my current worldview in contrast with the optimal human psychology offered in her book.

An Afrocentric Worldview

According to Dr. Myers, *Afrocentric* refers to a worldview centered in Africa as the historical point of generation. I was inspired by her work and perspective of the world.

Dr. Meyers postulated (1) self-knowledge is the basis for all knowledge and (2) the process by which one can achieve goals is through human and spiritual networks. She pointed out the idea of seeing the world in a holistic way and assumes the unity of spirit and matter, as oneness.

As I continued to read, I became more eager and interested in the exploration of African spirituality and self-knowledge.

In November of 1990, I was excited to meet Dr. Linda James Myers, a black female psychologist and associate professor at Ohio State University, at a conference in New York City. I was especially ecstatic to meet the author in person and thank her for her contribution.

Being inspired by her work and perspective of the world, her book, *Understanding an Afrocentric World View*, shaped my worldview and helped transform my thinking. Her book helped me share my perspective. It gave me a different base for increasing my knowledge of self.

Because I had a master's degree in guidance and counseling, I sought a part-time job to lead a support group on death and dying in an after-school program. The group was made up of children between the ages of five and ten. I enjoyed leading the group. The sad stories from children who had lost loved ones at such a young age brought up old memories and sadness for me, but I was able to suppress my feelings of sadness for the benefit of supporting the children so they could better cope with their grief. While the group was successful, the program in the school was not funded for the following semester.

After working with the children, I realized I needed to continue to seek out workshops, retreats, etc., on handling my own grief. I wanted to take the steps needed to give me comfort, peace, acceptance, and recovery from the pain of grief.

In 1991, I was invited to attend a dream weaver's retreat in Colorado where I rediscovered journaling. Writing about what I was feeling was a helpful tool. On the last day of the retreat, I confronted God and told Him everything I could remember that had happened to me. I told Him how afraid, grief-stricken, unhappy, and sad I had been. I told Him how angry I felt at Him for allowing so many sad things to happen to me. After I had wept and purged every angry emotion I felt, I listened for His response and heard nothing. Though I heard nothing, I later came to acknowledge and accept that God was always there; He never left me. I could not have made it had He abandoned me.

At the dream retreat, I learned to let go and not be too attached to anything as life is fluid and must be free. I also understood and accepted my share of the responsibility for feeling incomplete. As a result of attending this holistic retreat, I decided to expand my private practice to focus on death and dying with children coping with grief and loss. I believed that helping them would help me.

That same year, 1991, I joined the faculty at the College of New Rochelle in the Bronx, New York, where I taught clinical family practice to adults and continuing education students. In 1992, I was hired as an adjunct professor at the college of New Rochelle.

I continued to gain weight around my waist and my thighs. I continued to have difficulty sleeping and often had low energy. I was surprised to learn from my esthetician that she believed the hair growth under my chin was due to possible imbalanced hormones and poor eating habits.

This assessment reminded me of my meeting with Priestess Ayofeme, when I became totally aware that I needed to watch my nutritional intake. I was embarrassed about my poor body image, so I joined the gym at the YWCA and began to focus on strength training. In a very short while, I began to lose weight and tone my body.

I had been curious since childhood about pertinent questions like: *Who am I? Who are we really? Where did we come from?* and *Why are we here?* In 1994, I applied for a PhD in metaphysics with a focus on spirituality in hopes of finding some answers to my childhood questions.

Metaphysics is the science that systematically investigates the nature of all existence and the nature of the Universe. It is the science that deals with matters above and beyond the physical and material planes of existence.

I chose metaphysics as a way to understand and interpret life on the physical, mental, emotional, and spiritual planes as it goes beyond the visible to the invisible realms. I believed I would find answers, and thus, find peace.

It would take another eleven years before I was able to complete the program.

CHAPTER 8

Ditching the Confines of Fear and Grief

Though I had achieved several academic milestones, I was still not content. I couldn't seem to appreciate that I was good enough and sing my own praises. All I knew was that I had reached a point of being tired of all the emotional residuals of my parents' deaths and other losses I had incurred. I was tired of feeling sick, afraid, lonely, angry, resentful, stubborn, abandoned, unloved, unsupported by family, embarrassed, and just tired of being without my authentic voice.

I wanted to heal my emotional state and raise my confidence level, which had both been badly impacted by the perpetual feelings of loss, grief, and mourning. This challenge would be monumental to get myself aligned, but I was totally open to do whatever it took to be balanced, happy, and whole. By now, I had been in the states for about nineteen years. I had spent several years as a psychotherapeutic practitioner but desired to pursue a life-dream for creative self-expression through the performing arts. I wanted to feel accepted and valued so, somehow, I thought this endeavor could convince me I mattered and was good enough, especially if I succeeded in developing my craft and landing good management. Thus, began my continued journey of finding and releasing my authentic voice and freeing my truth.

Because I had been dramatizing my poems at various churches and private community settings, I was invited to several theatrical performances where I was introduced to psychodrama. I joined a psychodrama group in Brooklyn and soon met a group of actors in the community where I fell in love with the stage.

These psychodrama techniques were most helpful in providing tools to tap into and change lingering unresolved issues, which I used in my private practice. Needless to say, the exercises used became a work in progress for my clients and me as we worked toward understanding and coping with situations through role playing, to develop skills for survival in life.

I began auditioning for roles in community theatre and landed a role as a witch in the Witches Brew Productions company. I fell in love with acting and decided to pursue this endeavor.

In 1992, I decided to pursue acting as a craft, which would eventually lead me to move to Los Angeles, California to try my hand at acting, but I needed to do more preparation before embarking upon such an endeavor.

I found myself in voice, diction, and speech classes trying to change my language, accent, and dialect, so that I could speak *proper standard English*. Voice and diction were required to pursue my goal of acting.

Taking acting classes at HB Studios in New York City was very helpful in boosting my self-esteem and in assisting me in decision-making. After attending several classes and auditioning for the theatre, I sought representation at a talent agency that signed me.

As a result, I was able to procure extra work on soap operas, but because I thought I still had a very pronounced Caribbean accent, I was constantly trying to change my way of speaking in hopes of procuring more work on soap operas.

Needless to say, I gained more confidence, but there were still disappointing pitfalls along the way. One incident that stands out for me happened after joining the African Repertory Theatre Group and having my first Off-Broadway stage performance. We had a photo spread of the cast in the local newspaper.

I was delighted they shared a photo of me and another actor. However, I was shocked they had switched our names. They had placed my name next to her photo and her name next to my photo. I felt they had taken away my identity. The following day, I decided to contact the newspaper and inform them of the error. To my dismay, they refused to correct the misprint.

The other actor, who was fair-skinned, had my American sounding last name attached to her photo, and I, who was dark-skinned, had her African sounding last name attached to my photo. Again, I was left feeling unvoiced.

From this experience, I felt confused, like I was unjustly treated and life was not always fair. This injustice brought me the fortitude to pick myself up and continue to pursue my endeavors, to not let this break my spirit. I was on a mission to no longer feel victimized. I had to stay persistent and consistent in attaining my goals. I would not be discouraged to the point of giving up. I was a survivor.

In 1994, I moved again to another apartment in Brooklyn where I began writing a play with my writing partner. I was determined to stay the course and pursue the acting business, which afforded me the opportunity to receive my AFTRA card and be considered and paid for more work on television soap operas. I felt fortunate I was now a naturalized citizen and was eager to find more work in this industry.

I continued to work as a clinical social worker for another four years in Manhattan as I watched several turnovers and changes among the clinical staff of the hospital. Most of my co-workers had left and had been replaced by new staff.

In addition, the stress of traveling from Brooklyn to Manhattan by both bus and train was wearing on me, and upon my request, I was transferred to the new Brooklyn Children's Psychiatric Hospital to continue working as a clinical social worker.

After being there for about one year, I became stressed and burned out from the emotional toll the job had taken on me. I was ready for a change that would free me to create and perform in the acting industry. Thus, the time came for my talent agency to find opportunities for me to go to Los Angeles to try my acting endeavor.

Meanwhile, I still had not found love with a mate but believed that as soon as I could open my heart to receive and give love, a mate would come my way. I had work to do to attract someone who would be compatible with me.

One day in 1993, an associate of mine told me about a psychic reader whom she thought could be helpful to me to ascertain that I was on the right track for finding peace and love in my life: a life where I could have more impact on directing my path of choice, hope, beliefs, and faith. Needless to say, I did go for a reading and was given great hope for obtaining my heart's desire of finding and giving love and being very happy. So, because the psychic came highly recommended for the accuracy of her long-term prophecies, I believed they would come true. However, I hoped it wouldn't be too far into the future before I would find love. I continued my self-improvement journey in preparation of being as ready as I could be to receive love in my life.

Among the things she predicted was my success as an actor in the future. She foresaw my traveling to Los Angeles, California and joked she couldn't wait to come visit and enjoy my pool, and we both laughed.

In 1997, Tomorrow Talent Agency, located in New York City, sponsored a group of selected talents to attend an annual convention in Los Angeles for consideration of relocating to pursue our acting dreams. I excitedly attended the convention.

After receiving several awards for modeling, commercials, and monologues on this sponsored trip, I returned home convinced I wanted to try my hand at acting. I continued to prepare monetarily to relocate to LA in pursuit of an acting career. Though I was still concerned my Caribbean accent might impede my progress in the acting industry, I was determined to not let that stop me.

I would need to complete my remaining two-year stint at the College of New Rochelle, where I was an adjunct professor in the social work department. For the next two years, I saved a substantial amount of money, quit my job, and in the winter of 1999, I set out for Los Angeles, California because I believed I had a chance of making it as an actor.

I was thrilled with excitement when I saw the Hollywood sign after arriving in Los Angeles. I could not believe the many gated communities with huge beautiful, mansions, the rampant array of birds of paradise flowers that lined people's yards, the silky leaves of the bougainvillea plants, and the six-lane freeways that were always congested with traffic. The tropical breezes in Los Angeles reminded me of home and gave me a warm feeling of *having arrived.*

I continued to take many voice, diction, and language classes to sound more like an American until one day in my acting class, my teacher asked me to use my native dialect in an assigned scene. The scene was received very well, and other students began to ask me if I would teach them to speak my dialect. The teacher encouraged me to be who I really am and insisted that I use my native tongue more often. What an esteem builder that was, when all the time I did not think I would be received well because I am not from America.

This inspired me to want to accept who I am and to stop trying to conform to others' ways of being, to appreciate my own gifts and talents.

Social Work in Los Angeles

Though I went to Los Angeles with enough money to last for at least eighteen months, I knew I needed to supplement my finances. Therefore, I applied and was hired as a clinical social worker in the pediatric department at Kaiser Permanente Hospital. My initial schedule consisted of working a 9–5 job, acting classes four times a week, and participation in community theatre and stage plays. These performances fed my enthusiasm while I worked diligently to cultivate my craft and acclimate myself to a new environment and lifestyle.

Exploring the community, I joined the public library where I borrowed books on honing my craft as well as stage and screen playwriting and producing.

I was gifted the book, *The Artist Way: A Spiritual Path to Higher Creativity,* by Julia Cameron and began doing *Morning Pages* exercises, writing at least three pages of long hand, stream-of-consciousness writing done first thing in the morning. This exercise helped me gain self-confidence in harnessing my creative talents and skills.

After three years with this scheduling and no real leads for parts after procuring an agent, I began to really look at the Los Angeles culture and the industry. I had to accept that the acting industry focused on youths to promote, unless you were older and had credentials, experiences, and developed skills.

I began to question my decision to be a beginning seeker of a career path in acting in LA at my age and experience level. I did feel some rejection, but not that I had failed; though there were instances when I would inadvertently sabotage a job by not thoroughly preparing for callbacks or letting fear and nerves take over, hampering me from a good audition. I was ready to move on to my next endeavor after having given myself five years to see if acting was a good match for me. I finally accepted that acting was not a good fit for me. However, I am so grateful to have had that exposure, which helped me become more assertive and a little more confident.

Soon after, I decided to register and enroll as a student at Los Angeles Community College with a focus on media arts. I wanted to know more about making and producing my own stage or screen plays.

However, I recalled from childhood that my comprehension, reading, listening, and following instructions needed some attention. So, I decided to try to discover what the deficit was all about. I made an appointment to be tested at the Learning Center at LACC and discovered that I had dyslexia, a learning disability that made letters seem to jump around on the page as well as hearing the opposite of what's being spoken, thus explaining a major mishap in one of my auditions.

On this occasion, I was asked to reenact a scene where I would *lean forward*, but I heard *lean backward*, and I awkwardly did so. Needless to say, I did not pass the audition, which made me doubt my abilities until I began to connect the dots from the diagnosis of being dyslexic. I did feel hampered by this disorder, which did indeed influence my decision to not pursue acting as a goal. The news motivated me to pay attention to details more closely and to stay focused more than ever.

However, I did attend one acting class on Saturdays while I continued to write poetry. I also joined a creative writing class and started writing a stage play.

As time passed, I remained in Los Angeles and felt more disconnected from my nuclear family. I was still afraid I would live a whole lifetime without the love and intimacy of my family. My sister and I had begun to communicate by telephone, and I was happy to know the bad blood experiences were finally beginning to heal. That was the only rekindled connection I had with my nuclear family at that time.

While on a trip to New Orleans from Los Angeles, I received a phone call from my nephew explaining that his mom had had a stroke, was unconscious, and was hospitalized. He asked if I would come home to New York to see about her. I immediately reached out to my oldest sister, who lived in Brooklyn, to see if she would be willing to support as well. She was willing.

Because my five-year commitment to being in Los Angeles was coming to a close, I decided to return to New York instead of extending my stay. I had to make the decision to give up my writing classes, but I had to make the adjustment and reach out to help my sister regain her health. It seemed to be the time to begin healing old wounds.

Why I Became a Social Worker

In 2003, I returned to Brooklyn and procured a job with Caribbean children and their families in a mental health program. Many of these families were immigrants, so I quickly identified with the population and was frustrated with the lack of resources and rights they were afforded.

Many of the youths in this program were emotionally disturbed and had difficulty adjusting to their new culture. Working with this population brought back many feelings of my own acculturation woes. Because of my empathetic and sympathetic concerns, I spent many hours encouraging them emotionally and psychologically to help them find peace and comfort. I wanted to help my clients avoid some of my own experiences of marginalization and feeling unwelcomed. Though I was still working on my own acculturation issues, I believed I could help them find their way.

I remembered I went into social work and studied psychology partly to figure out my life and partly to be an advocate for others. My aim was to help someone who could benefit from my support. As a social worker, I enjoyed listening to my clients and helping them figure out what to do in planning their lives.

While working in the Caribbean Mental Health Program in Brooklyn, I was introduced to the book and DVD, *The Secret*, by Rhonda Byrne, which I shared with some of my clients on a regular basis.

This resource reminded me that thoughts can influence feelings. It also reminded me of a lesson I was taught in church: whatever we do or think on frequently will grow and be reinforced.

Because I was working on my own issues of self-esteem, I found it imperative to help my clients and their families avoid some of the pitfalls I had experienced in acculturation into my new society. They were receptive to my support and implementation of the concepts of the Law of Attraction. I felt pleased to see that my sharing was helpful.

How I Saw Myself: *Still* Not Good Enough

As I was helping my clients to create a new life, I was still going through the same issues. I knew I still had work to do because my self-esteem was still not where I wanted it to be. *Not good enough* is how I saw myself. I believed no one loved me. I believed I did not matter and had no value as I experienced the shame of coming from an undeveloped homeland.

I still tended to hold onto the negative experiences from childhood. I felt resentful, isolated, and angry and sometimes blamed everyone for what was happening to me. For example, when I was a child, there were many times it rained a lot on the island, and students would be dismissed from school early. During those rainy days, parents came to the school to pick up their children and brought their raincoats and galoshes to walk them home. I always felt neglected and abandoned because no one ever came to get me. After the rain eased, I walked home without galoshes, often stepping into puddles of water that had filled the numerous potholes on the roads. By the time I got home, my clothes were wet and soggy, my shoes and socks dripping wet as well.

I saw myself as a victim and blamed everyone for my situation. At that point, I had convinced myself of my victimhood. I was not ready to let go and let anyone help me rationalize my thinking that no one cared. It was a perfect circle eight. I was caught up in a never-ending drama that plagued me like an ongoing nightmare.

Not only was I my own self-judge, but I was the jury as well. I personalized, internalized, and believed the criticisms, judgments, stories, and chatter I heard in my head. I judged myself by what I thought people thought of me. After I said or did something with others, I later replayed every detail in my mind over and over again when I was by myself. I would comb for mistakes I may have made or ways that I could have said something better or with more diplomacy. When I found what I called mistakes, I judged myself as not good or smart enough.

Self-blame was common in my reclusive state. Not only did I blame myself for my Mom's death, I blamed myself for not doing enough to help take care of her initially and letting her down. Somewhere in my young mind, I knew I had no control over her dying, but that didn't stop my self-blame.

I never saw myself without blame in some way. I blamed myself for everything—the way I grew up, for losing my family, for personalizing everything, and feeling it was all about me. I seemed to find every excuse in the book to retard my moving forward emotionally and ridding myself of old patterns—holding feelings of resentment and blame—which kept me physically and emotionally sick.

Fear

They say the definition of fear is: False Evidence Appearing Real. Whether it is so or not, fear has been a thorn in my flesh for many years.

My fears were multifaceted. Over the years, the trauma of my mother's death, grieving the loss of home, and the disintegration of my family caused me to develop a plethora of fears, including my fear of the unknown.

My fears, I believed, began with the injustices and abuse my family experienced when I was a child. The way we were treated in the neighborhood made me feel *less than*, as if something were wrong with me and my family.

Fear kept me silent.

Being an undocumented immigrant also contributed to my being unvoiced. Prior to coming to the States, I was told not to talk too much once I got there and to act like an American. However, my accent alone would indicate I was not from the States. I was afraid I would be found out and deported. I was unvoiced because I didn't want to answer any questions. I didn't want to divulge too much about myself.

Though my fears abounded, I persevered. Something within propelled me to push forward and not give up. I was determined to pursue my goals and dreams.

Mind Chatter

There was a continuous dialogue in my head I played over and over again. I was caught up in a loop of emotional symptoms that included mind chatter, old thoughts and feelings coming to the surface, needing to be healed.

I spent a significant amount of time thinking about things that should not have mattered to me. I spent a considerable amount of time in my head consumed by the need to know what people were saying about me. I sometimes wondered if other people spent a lot of time worrying about what others thought about them also.

Sometimes I wondered if the negative chatter in my mind had moved into my heart. Negative mind chatter, like *I didn't do it right* or *They'll know I'm not smart enough*, was always playing over and over in my head. The ocean of thoughts that ran through my mind was overwhelming at times. It began to develop a life story of its own.

I feared that others would see me and hear what I was thinking. I continued feeling afraid and insecure; fearful thoughts are not good thoughts. In many ways, I was standing in my own way. The voice in my head all the time was the involuntary thought process I didn't realize I had the power to stop. I did not realize I was enslaved by my mind, which was using the unvoiced negative thoughts to keep me bound.

My chitter-chatter, mind chatter, was running rampant. I often diminished or disparaged myself. Negative mind chatter sabotaged my movements and kept me small and unvoiced.

I began to see how I was contributing to my discomfort.

Playing into my own self-righteousness and victimhood mentality, I was caught up in a circle of self-lies that kept me spinning around and around. Running the same movie of blaming everyone and harboring my own guilt and resentment in my mind compromised my state of well-being.

I saw how I stood in my own way by allowing mind chatter to take over. I needed to remember the courage I had before I came to America. I needed to find courage again.

The stress of not living in integrity ravaged me, yet I swept it under the rug as a way to cope with my inner conflict of overthinking. I was good at living my life through everyone's eyes because I yearned to be liked. It was difficult to say no to others' requests. I was a people pleaser. I tried my best to please everyone. If they did not express satisfaction with me, I would be disappointed and would withdraw even more.

In 2004, I decided to reactivate and complete the Doctor of Philosophy in Metaphysics degree program. As a clinician, I wanted an alternative approach to my work. I wanted a whole-person approach of body, mind, and spirit in my practice. The true metaphysician is a teacher, a healer, and a counselor who espouses universal spirituality.

Some of the courses I took included: *Psychology, Religion, A Course in Miracles, Analysis of Death and Dying, Financial Success*, and a course in writing a dissertation. Among the many books I studied, I was particularly inspired by *A Course in Miracles*. It gave me some insights into my multifaceted way of being, and I became more curious to seek knowledge on an even higher spiritual level.

I was also inspired by the book *Return to Love*, by Marianne Williamson. This book sparked my desire to return to love. I didn't know what love was, but by reading this book, I was inspired and made a vow to find out what love was for me personally. Enrolling in the metaphysics course of study also helped me to find more patience, endurance, wisdom, courage, and humility.

As I moved along on my journey of shedding old practices, I began seriously looking at ditching my current nutritional practices for a different way of eating. I observed the increasing rate of obesity in people and the many illnesses related to diet in this country and I wondered how could they be feeling well. I thought, *What better way to serve than through enlightening others about creating and living a healthier lifestyle through diet and nutrition?*

Because my mother's death was related to diet and lifestyle, I always wanted to learn how to use food to prevent diet-related illnesses leading to early death. I also wanted to understand my own body and find ways to nourish and heal myself.

Self-Care

Because I have always struggled with my weight, when the opportunity presented itself in 2006 as a way to deepen my knowledge in this area, I enrolled in a nutrition program at the Institute for Integrative Nutrition (IIN) and became a certified health coach, which helped me to understand my body and how to nourish it on many levels.

At IIN, I learned about the energetics of food and how what you eat determines your health. I learned that everything is food and that we are nourished, to some extent, by life. I learned about the difference between primary and secondary foods.

Secondary foods, according to Joshua Rosenthal, founder of IIN and author of *The Energy Balanced Diet*, are what you put on your plate. Primary foods are the aspects of life that are not material but are fulfilling and nourishing. For example: happiness, peace, joy, and bliss.

In addition, I became aware of the technique of mindfulness. Mindfulness means being present and paying attention to what is happening in every moment. I decided to integrate mindfulness as a spiritual practice in my daily life. Mindfulness helped me in my eating practices, which helped in my weight control and digestion simply by masticating my food well so it would mix with the saliva in the mouth before swallowing.

The awareness of the need for self-care became paramount when I began daily practices that improved my well-being: 1) a hot towel scrub that left me feeling refreshed, relaxed, invigorated, and stimulated; 2) writing *Morning Pages* exercises; 3) practicing positive affirmations and visualizations; 4) preparing healthy, nutritious food to feed my body, mind, and soul; and 5) sharing these practices with my clients in my wellness business.

I became better able to manage and control my negative mind chatter through utilizing mindfulness and speaking positive affirmations daily.

Some of the other books and resources included: *Healing with Whole Foods*, by Paul Pitchford; *Food and Healing*, by Annemarie Colbin; *Nourishing Wisdom*, by Marc David; *The Self-healing Cookbook*, by Kristina Turner; and *The Alchemist*, by Paulo Coelho.

In 2006, while studying at the Institute for Integrative Nutrition, my download from the Divine was to *Create Whole*. I thought it was a name for my website or business, but it was a message for me, saying I needed to create wholeness in my life. I believed it was a message from my Soul to create and experience harmony in all areas of my being. Among my pursuits for wholeness, I needed to include a way to release doubts and fears as I continued my spiritual journey.

As a certified health coach, I began to coach individuals on creating a more wholesome lifestyle and volunteered to share health information to immigrant families whom I had encountered in the past. I wanted not only to see clients occasionally, but I wanted to create a space and environment where they could come for a period of time to retreat, relax, rejuvenate, and receive supportive inspirational guidance to kickstart and complete their wellness program.

After much discussion with my business partner, we researched areas that might be conducive for a healing retreat center, and we were led to South Carolina. We were invited by friends to explore the Low Country and were grateful to find the perfect space for our home-based retreat center. As a result, *Create Whole*™ *Wellness Services* was born in 2007.

Race Relations

Though I had to deal with my own issues of insecurity before coming to America, I did not know the severity of race relations in the American culture. At first, I did not understand this. I felt lost and out of my league. In college, I became more aware of race relations and began to attend workshops and read books about the Black experience.

I was introduced to the books, *Songs of Solomon*, by Toni Morrison; *Understanding Race, Ethnicity, & Power: The Key to Efficacy in Clinical Practice*, by Elaine Pinderhughes; *Women, Culture & Politics*, by Angela Davis; and *Black Women Writers: 1950-1980*, by Marie Evans, which were all eye-opening. Reading books like *The Dream Keeper and Other Poems*, by Langston Hughes; along with other works on Caribbean and American literature on race relations, were priceless in helping me to grasp the gravity of race relations with people of color in America at that time.

Moving from New York to the Low Country in South Carolina in 2007 was a major political transition. Not long after my arrival in South Carolina, I began to better understand race relations.

My American Politics

Though I always voted in the general elections after becoming a citizen, I did not get too involved in politics. However, in 2008 when a Black man ran for president, I was inspired to participate during the campaign, and I volunteered to help with voter registration in my local community. Throughout the 2008 campaign process, I was afraid to put the Obama campaign placards and signs in my yard because people had reported many signs were being removed. This was a blatant reminder of race relations.

On November 4, 2008, change came to America. When Barack Obama won the election, he said change had finally come to America. There were people talking everywhere about the long and complicated history of race relations in America. For the first time in its history, an African American man was elected president. To me, people were both elated and surprised. I still cannot express the pride I felt when he was elected. I did not believe I would see someone who looked like me become president of the United States. Out of happiness, pride, and joy, I physically jumped higher than I could have ever imagined.

These campaign posters and signs are now precious memorabilia that are kept in my home. I was hopeful because a black man inhabited the oval office, but I was still doubtful about improved race relations in our country.

As a naturalized citizen, I came to understand the powerful value of the vote. As a citizen and a registered voter, I vowed to always vote and work with community outreach in subsequent elections and have continued to do so.

My interest in politics reinforced my awareness of race relations in America. I did not expect the issues of race to be so severe. I became aware I was a part of the struggle for equal human rights for black people in America as well as immigrants' rights.

Why should people have to suffer because they were not born in America?

Every human being, including undocumented immigrants, has certain inalienable rights. Every human being has civil rights. Just because a person has a different immigration status doesn't mean they don't have the basic right for equal protection under the law. Their rights should be respected and not violated.

As a human being, every person should have the right to choose religion and the form of worship they want. It should not matter what their faith is, how they look, or where they come from.

Coming to America

Coming to America made me see
A whole different aspect of my story
I didn't have to ride in the back of no bus
Nor was I denied my right to vote,
But coming to America has made me see
How "isms" have bombarded and consumed me.

In my island country, everyone looked
talked, acted, and lived like me,
I was the majority, and never considered
myself a minority until I came to America.

In Antigua, I didn't worry 'bout the
fullness of my lips, the flatness of my nose,
Nor the sway in my hips,
Because everyone looked like me.

I wasn't ashamed of the way I dressed
The texture of my hair
Nor my language and dialect,
Everyone talked and dressed like me.

UNDOCUMENTED

Before I went to the U.S. Virgin Islands
I didn't fret 'bout the size of my breasts,
Shape of my legs, nor the glide in my step
I wasn't concerned about my brown eyes,
Dimples in my cheeks nor my broad smile
Until I met an American.

I didn't grow up on stocks or TV
Nor exposed to media negativity,
My island life was natural beauty
Sheltered with peace and tranquility.

Coming to America I now understand
My people were enslaved and plucked
From our homeland, to be bred and
raped and sold by violent hands.

Coming to America I have come to realize
The color of my skin is no safety net
It will not keep me from harm
Nor do I expect my children will be
given privileges unearned.

Coming to America I have come to know
The sordid history of Jim Crow
The exploitation of my ancestor's bodies
Denying them rights of humanity.

Coming to America I have come to embrace
The pride and honor of my African race
Coming from a culture of style and beauty
Clinging, I hold on tight to my dignity.

What does an immigrant look like?

This is what an immigrant looks like. An immigrant looks like me! Or you: immigrants come in all colors, shades and shapes.

We come from all parts of the globe and entered America in different ways. We came through and landed at different locations and ports. Some came from Africa and other European countries and were scattered about. Some came in by boat through Ellis Island, by train, airplane, or by climbing a wall or crossing a border. Undocumented immigrants have the right to be treated humanely.

We are not all drug dealers, terrorists, and criminals; neither are we all from Mexico. It has been reported that undocumented immigrants engage in less crime than their American or legal immigrant peers.

Though they have a right to their native language, immigrants are encouraged to learn and speak English as their primary language. Just because we speak differently doesn't mean natives are better than us. Just because we have different looks doesn't mean we are less than anyone.

While in St. Thomas, I was constantly confronted with probing questions: *Why don't you talk like me? You talk different than me. You're not from here, are you? Where are you from?* Those questions were not asked in a welcoming way. I felt a little scorned.

When I arrived in the States, there was a constant dance of words between *I* and *me*, *us* and *we*. In the States they say, *I don't come from here,* and on the island, we say, "*Me no come from here."* In the States they say *us;* in the islands we say *we.*

Why are people afraid of those who come from a different place? Of people who look different? Why do they think they're better than we are?

Often degraded, we are mocked and called names like coons, dogs, low IQ, not intelligent. Undocumented immigrants today live in a culture of cruelty. Oftentimes, we are denied proper medical care; we are castigated just because we want to be able to feed our children. We are trying to find a better life for our family and for ourselves.

Not every immigrant comes to America to attain the dream, but some come here because they are not safe in their homeland and are seeking asylum. Yet they are castigated just for running for their lives.

The undocumented immigrant's life has been mostly invisible. Again, undocumented immigrants are robbed of their human rights, especially those who don't know they have rights regardless of their status.

For many, their lives seem meaningless. They have no security or safety. They are often exploited, abused, degraded, taken advantage of economically, and threatened with deportation. They will often take jobs many Americans don't want, and many people will hire them for cheap labor. Unfortunately, their income often won't afford them the opportunity to provide the most nutritious foods, nor health insurance for their families; thus, they must depend on public assistance and emergency room service for medical care.

I believe there is something hypocritical about degrading someone yet taking advantage of them. My contribution to transforming the world started with putting my feet on American soil as an outsider who had to work on overcoming fear, shame, and isolation. Branded as uninvited, invisible, and an alien, there was no welcome mat laid out for me to live the American dream.

My life is the American immigrant story. Despite the fears and traumas encountered in the course of my odyssey, I still managed to attain a high level of education in this country. I have studied and engaged in practices and methodologies that transformed my life. I now write this book standing in my own power. I have gone from trauma to triumph and am destined to share my experiences, and I am confident that others can be inspired to do the same.

My life is the American story. My journey has been the story of an immigrant. I found out that there is power in telling my story. I understand the ability to use my voice is a gift. I speak truth to power when I own and use my own voice. No longer do I give any energy to hopelessness or helplessness, but I focus on the power of my voice.

They've called me dark and dirty, but I am neither dark nor dirty. I am what an immigrant looks like.

I, too, am an American, living the American dream because of the incredible opportunities that are afforded me in every sense. I have come here and enjoyed the freedoms of America. I am standing on the shoulders of many brave, adventurous, savvy immigrants who came to America full of promise. I ride on their backs.

I was one of those undocumented immigrants and this is my story. My story is a story of hope and freedom. I am the Caribbean American migrant story.

Who will care to save the children?

It's a travesty what's been done to the children of immigrant families. They're ripped away from their parents, pushed into cages in remote places onto cold, hard floors, with aluminum foil type bedding. The sanitary conditions could not possibly be healthy.

They are denied their best childhood experiences. Their dreams are stymied, and their passions thwarted because they are being held hostage and are caught up in an immigration crisis. These vulnerable children are filled with mental despair and grief which will be remembered by them for a lifetime. It's an outrage.

Families should remain together for emotional and psychological support that is imperative to the well-being of children, especially in their formative years of development. These children could be scarred emotionally for life. Because there is no comprehensive tracking system in place, many children may never see their families again and can suffer irreparable, long-term, negative effects.

To the migrant youth today I say:

Keep on moving and pushing forward while holding your head up high. Unite and continue to fight. Turn over every pebble or stone you find in your way. Don't give up. No one has the power to keep you from achieving your dreams. Never stop fighting for your right to freedom. Keep fighting for your rights as free human beings.

Taken Away

They've taken away their freedom
Robbed them of their human rights,
Nobody considers the impact
Immigration has on a child.

The immigrant child is vulnerable
Robbed of their privilege of choice,
Overwhelmed by poor conditions
They're silenced and have no voice.

Feeling lost and lonely
A whole life is displaced,
Much work is left to do
Young, innocent lives to save.

DACA

The Deferred Action on Childhood Arrivals (DACA), an American immigration policy, was started by President Obama. During his second term in office, he signed an executive order to help young people who were brought to America illegally by their parents. These young people are called *dreamers*. This immigration policy was designed to make it easier for dreamers to pursue their dreams, to be given a chance to become eligible for a work permit, to pay taxes, and to maybe granted a renewal period of deferred action, all without access to citizenship in America.

Watching the news often leaves me feeling sad. Having been an undocumented immigrant myself, I understand the stress and worry that the thousands of dreamers must be experiencing. The dreamers are caught in the middle of a moral crisis and feel unsure and upset about their future in America.

Children should not be used as bargaining chips. America is the only home the dreamers know.

The wounds inflicted on these undocumented immigrants are deep, and a bandage will not stop the bleeding from the calloused inhumane treatment they are given—not to mention having their civil rights violated. Immigrants want protection not persecution. They should be shielded from cruel strategies.

Today, these dreamers want a way to citizenship and to stay with their families. Currently, there are members of my immediate family who are impacted by this trauma.

I would support a comprehensive immigration policy that is welcoming and at the same time upholds the law. I want a pathway to citizenship or some form of deportation relief. I often wondered, *What could be better than every immigrant enjoying their human rights.*

Immigrant Rights Are Human Rights

Immigrant rights are human rights
Right to freedom and equal justice
Right to feel you belong wherever you are
Right to ask for what you want and receive a response
Right to live without fear
Right to live in peace
Right to practice spirituality and worship freely
Right to not be called names
Right to not be bullied
Right to love
Right to be happy
Right to justice
Right to due process

Migrant Contributions

Undocumented immigrants need the freedom and opportunity to obtain their dream of a better life in America. Immigrants who come here are generally not stagnant because they are motivated to begin their new life in America. These people are courageous, strong, and brave. They bring raw passion and determination to America when given the opportunity to achieve their goals.

Not only do they often work for below minimum wages and pour their wisdom and teaching into American children by working as nannies and caregivers, they are marginalized and live a shadowed life. Not only are undocumented immigrants often scapegoated and blamed for all types of circumstances, they maintain a level of determination that cannot be denied.

The contributions of immigrants to this country are necessary. They are not necessarily less skilled or less educated. Research shows that in many cases immigrants work harder and do as much for America as American citizens.

Citizenship is not just having a piece of paper that says a person is a citizen. It is belonging to a community where that person feels loved and cared for. It's having the opportunity to realize their family dreams. It takes a brave, brave person to make it in America today. I am proud of the immigrant part of my family. They have asserted themselves as part of various communities.

Sometimes the fears that had been a way of life for so long do not end when citizenship becomes reality. Though it's thirty years later, there are still ways in which I still don't feel safe or free in America.

If anyone were to ask me what I want, I would say I want the government to shorten the application process for immigrants and give residency to those who contribute to our society.

Immigration Policy
There is little in the American government policy that makes the undocumented immigrant feel welcome.

Currently, the United States has a complicated immigration law. The government knows they need to heal the broken immigration system, but it is so complex they don't know how to do it yet. However, if the politicians weren't so focused on discrediting others in order to win elections and engaging in infighting, perhaps they could resolve some of these complicated immigration matters.

For the undocumented immigrant families who come to the border today, the situation is horrendous. The child separation policy is non-stop terror and cruelty. There is insensitivity to immigrants, refugees, and people seeking asylum. To seek asylum in America today is grounds for fear and persecution. Asylum seekers, refugees, and undocumented immigrants have the right to liberty and personal security as well as the right to life and the pursuit of happiness.

I thought that America was open to those seeking refuge. I thought that America was the land of liberty.

What happened to my America?

What about the most recognizable phrase associated with the Statue of Liberty?

Give me your tired, your poor, your huddled masses yearning to breathe free . . .

What happened to America?

What Is America?

What is America? An idea, a concept of a nation?
An ideal, an experiment, or democratic perception?
What is America? A place, a tribe or a vision?
A feeling of pride, an honor, or an expectation?

What is America? A world where all are free
Saluting a flag, symbolizing justice and liberty?
What is America? A document with equal protection
Under the law, or a house divided in two
Where equal rights exist only for a few?

What is America? A free state where all voices
Can be heard, telling your story in your own words?
What is America? A community, a world of humanity
Where everyone should have equal rights to be happy?

What is America? A group of states united,
A ritualistic act or a conglomeration divided?
What is America? An experience or a journey,
A path, a lifestyle, a mental state or an odyssey?

What is America? A place where the sum is greater
than its parts, connecting, uniting body, mind and heart?
I wish somebody could tell me exactly,
What is America?

America is, and always will be, a diverse nation of immigrants. I foresee a renewed comprehensive immigration reform policy that represents our diversity and addresses the concerns of the diverse nation that we are. I foresee a humane, caring system that opens the doors to people who are seeking opportunities for the betterment of themselves and their family members.

I want a more empathetic immigration policy that reflects a more generous America. Through humanitarian efforts, we can also help prospective undocumented immigrants rebuild their lives that have been torn by political violence and religious persecution in their own countries. This could possibly minimize the influx of undocumented immigrants seeking safety in our country.

America is made up of all of us. The charge to keep America going is the responsibility of each of us. We're all in this together. We all must rise up and speak out about the atrocities undocumented immigrants have to endure today. We must stand up and promote freedom and liberty for all.

My Emotional and Spiritual Journey

Even though I had voted as an American citizen, my fears of deportation persisted. The fear of being an undocumented immigrant kept me from taking risks.

Before graduation from college, there were times when I chose not to participate in an event because of my legal status. The thought of taking risks filled me with anxiety and worry. After getting a green card, I was still afraid to take certain chances. Even after I became a naturalized citizen, I still felt hostage to the fears of deportation, assimilation, and acculturation.

I was anxious and worried about everything. I worried that bad things could happen. My fears manifested in various ways. I felt guilty because I allowed myself to succumb to such emotions as fear, anxiety, doubt, and shame.

I was lost in limbo. I had become somewhat bitter and knew I had to find a way to release myself from these lingering emotions. It was now the fall of 2010, and at that point, I was really tired of being resistant, angry, and unhappy. Because my life had been filled with obstacles, setbacks, and blessings, it was necessary to stay on course on this emotional, spiritual journey.

The turning point from fear to love was the end of my searching outside myself for validation, acceptance, approval, self-worth, love, success, and truth. I began to focus on the desires of my Soul.

I was neglecting the needs of my Soul by looking outside for the answers. *What have you done for your Soul lately?* I asked myself while looking into my eyes in the mirror.

I started to look at what was unique about me and what was going well in my life. I had begun my business and felt fortunate that I would not have to worry about finding a location to see clients because our home-based retreat space and wellness center was the perfect environment to develop my practice.

Energy Healing

In spring 2011, I was attuned as an Usui Reiki practitioner by Ifetayo White, RMT.

Reiki refers to a technique of natural healing that promotes stress reduction and deep relaxation. This technique uses simple laying on of hands, or not, and visualization with goals of improving the flow of life-force energy, which flows through all living things. An ancient form of healing art, Reiki was rediscovered by Dr. Mikao Usui and is seen as a natural technique of spiritual healing and empowerment.

Integrating Reiki into my business was exciting and helped to enrich my work. As a practitioner, I was able to harness my energy in order to help myself and others. I also began to develop marketing strategies to reach more clients.

At *CreateWhole Wellness Services* we believe that food is not only what you put in your mouth to eat, but everything you ingest, including your environment. Recognizing the importance of art, be it singing or dancing, we launched the first ever Low Country Parlor Jazz Series in 2012, a series designed to provide nourishment for the community and artists that ignites joy and happiness.

I know my business is making an impact in the world because of the positive responses and testimonials we have received.

My personal goal as a health coach is to walk my talk. I want to be clearer in my message, communicate my message for better wellness to our tribe consistently and more clearly, break through my fear of technology and internet marketing, come out to my full potential, and reach more people with my message.

My Masterheart

I have always written my feelings and thoughts in my journal, and writing has been therapeutic throughout my journey. My dream was to write a book sharing my own story and immigrant experience, which I had been working on as a stage play. I wanted to become a published author but had no idea how to be published and put my message out into the world. However, I continued to write.

I believed I had a transformational story and wisdom to share, yet sometimes I would doubt myself. *No one wants to hear your story*, I whispered to myself. I continued to procrastinate.

As I continued contemplating the needs of my Soul, I was still seeking to find the truth for myself so that I could courageously shine my light in the world. I believed truth was the food I needed to feed my Soul.

Energy Healing

In the fall of 2012, I also enrolled and became a Quantum Touch (QT) practitioner. QT, founded by Richard Gordon, is a powerful way to reduce pain and inflammation and promote healing. QT healing is a powerful hands-on or not energy healing method that accelerates the healing process and quickly reduces and eliminates pain without touching. The practitioner learns to amplify and focus their life-force energy and share love with people in a new and transformative way.

This is accomplished by linking breathing and body awareness techniques through the process of resonance and entrainment. I wanted to work on myself and continue to change my negative vibration to love vibration. I wanted to feel balanced. I wanted to be in alignment and harmony.

Reading the books, *Quantum-Touch 2.0, The New Human: Discovering and Becoming; Quantum Touch: The Power to Heal*, by Richard Gordon, and participating in the *Self-Created Health* workshop he facilitated, opened me up to embracing more life-force energy.

Transformational Author
By divine grace, in 2012 I was sent a link by a friend to check out Christine Kloser and the Transformational Author Program. I logged onto the calls and learned about the various transformational programs offered by her company.

As I continued to listen and learn more about the various programs, I felt a deep call inside my heart to be liberated from fear, confusion, and outdated information.

I wanted the spark of passion within me to come out. I wanted to develop the courage to be who I am. I wanted to stop preventing myself from moving forward. I needed to create more balance in my life so that I could fully express in the world.

Soulful Messenger
In the spring of 2013, I signed up for a five-day webinar, "Soulful

Messenger," led by Christine Kloser. Midway into the webinar through her coaching and guidance, she confirmed clearly what I believed: I had a message from my Soul that I needed to share with the world.

Though I was not clear about what my message would be, I felt a fire inside that needed to be expressed. I believed I was a Soul messenger because I wanted to share my authentic truth. Christine encouraged me to not limit what was possible for me. I recognized I was on Earth for the purpose of my Soul's growth and education.

At that moment, I established I was meant to be here and I am called to share my knowledge and experience. I believed I was a Soul messenger. I became engulfed in practicing affirmations and visualizations and began to condition my mind for success. Having meaningful goals helped to control my mind and stay focused.

I really began to think about what I wanted and my goals, which were to gain clarity, share my Soul's message, and continue to expand my wellness business. In order to realize my goals, I began to use visualization as a way of creating what I wanted. I imagined my business expanding and my story being shared. I began to look at different ways to thrive in my business. I wanted to have a message-based business.

I was grateful when an invitation to participate in a writing contest was offered, and I jumped at the opportunity.

Christine responded to my story and agreed that I had a powerful story to tell and encouraged me to keep writing. I was beyond excited to learn I was one of three scholarship winners chosen to participate in her six month "Get Your Book Done" program. I believed my dream of being a published author was about to become a reality.

Speak and Write

In the summer of 2013, I attended the "Speak and Write to Make Millions" conference in San Diego with Lisa Nichols, Susie Carder, my profit coach, and the Motivating the Masses team. I went to the conference because I wanted to learn how to stand up and speak my truth about my life story and about how God had blessed me. I wanted my voice to be heard.

I learned that the way to tell my story was to become vulnerable and to allow others to get to know me. Thus, I joined a woman's support group, which was helpful. I realized that the past was holding me hostage, and I had accepted untruths about myself. As I continued to write, I meditated, visualized, and imagined experiencing myself on the stage speaking to an audience.

After I attended this conference, I was convinced that I could no longer hide. It was imperative to get out and speak my truth by adding my voice to the mix and taking a stand. Yet, I still struggled with doubts.

Clear Heart Pendant

After returning home from the "Speak and Write" conference in San Diego, California, in 2013, my Reiki master teacher gave me a gift of a clear heart pendant. I believed the gift was a symbol to teach me about opening my heart. My desire has always been for balance and harmony within myself and to feel a spiritual connection between the mind, body, and spirit.

I knew it was a message about trusting the process and receiving and giving love to me. However, I did not know how to go about opening my heart and being aware of the importance of doing so. As a reminder of opening my heart, I carried the heart pendant in my purse everywhere I went and used it as a gratitude token—a reminder to open my heart.

In the fall of 2013, I signed up for the Transformational Author Master Heart Program (TAMP), which provided more support and inspiration. One of the benefits of this program was the opportunity to contribute a chapter to Christine Kloser's international best-selling transformational book series *Pebbles in the Pond*. I felt honored to have been selected to write a chapter which I contributed to *Wave Four* of the series.

During the Transformational Author Experience, it became clear that I needed to continue my writing as well as to fulfill my Soul's calling. Now I was ready to collaborate, cooperate, and work with others as a way of sharing my gifts.

In the spring of 2014, I attended the Transformational Author Breakthrough (TAB) conference where I received another emotional download to open my heart by: being willing to let people in, letting go of anger and mistrust, and loving myself so I could love others.

Breakthrough

The TAB conference is a three-day immersive retreat where we joined with Christine and the Masterheart community to fully prepare our mind, body, and soul to become a published author. At this retreat, I experienced a powerful defining moment where I knew I was ready to share my message and bring it out to the world.

At that point on my journey, I believed I was heading in the right direction and was ready to move forward from the stagnant, resistant feelings that kept me from expressing myself fully and from being authentically me. Fortunately for me, on the last day of the TAB retreat, my message was to *open your heart*. I was also told *I was to trust my process as I would be unfolding into who I am meant to be*, so I began to focus on what that meant.

After receiving the transparent heart pendant, I began seeking more ways to open my heart. I knew my anger was still related to feeling abandoned and not having family support in the grieving process. Recognizing this, I surrendered to take the journey through faith to open my heart and to let down my walls some.

I made the decision to get to know myself in a meaningful way. I wanted to see the good in myself and the miracle of life. I decided to increase my time for meditation. I decided to let go and move on. I knew *unfolding* had to do with spiritual evolvement, awakening, and expansion. I googled the definition of the word, did some reading on unfolding, then focused on what needed to be done to unfold as I continued to write, listen, and recite more affirmations.

Affirmations are words that have the power to transform your life because thoughts are things. There is energy in words.

My intention in doing affirmations was to activate a sense of fearlessness, courage, inner power, and strength to conquer any challenges I might face. The practice of affirmations helped me to doubt less and believe more. I used them for clearing and cleaning my thoughts. They helped me to create my life.

I started paying more attention to my breathing. When I feel anxious, frustrated, and stressed, I do breathing exercises. Deep breathing helps let more oxygen into my body. I believe that breath is life.

Over time, I noticed my heart began to open more, and I felt more balanced, harmonious, and less afraid. My message was becoming clearer, and I wanted to share it with others. I began to release all that had stopped me in the past and contributed another chapter to *Pebbles in the Pond: Wave Five*.

My life so far has been a quest for freedom. I acknowledge I am still closed and still afraid that people will not like and accept me, but I'm still a work in progress. I've been collecting tools all my life with the intention of developing, strengthening, and getting to know myself better. I'm on a constant quest to find freedom of mind.

Though I was still in grief and fearful, I knew I had to free myself from the confines of fear and grief to allow myself to experience freedom through faith. Inside, I knew I could rely on that source of power I was aware of from my upbringing. I knew I was not really alone, as long as I remembered and believed that the Creator would never leave me.

However, if my emotions intensified, I would consistently doodle square boxes when I felt sad, angry, depressed, and or oppressed. I needed help to pull me out of these emotional states. Doodling and drawing gave me an escape route because I found a quiet place to reside versus wallowing in my negative mind chatter.

Having years of psychotherapy and group therapy was helpful at times in staying on track. However, I found that I was not as open and forthcoming in a group setting because of my apprehension to talk about myself or talk too much. Being an immigrant, I had learned how to withhold information that could expose me.

I continued to meditate to go inward and visualize a greater level of peace and the dreams I wanted. When I meditate, it is important for me to be totally quiet and relax, shutting out everything around me. I learned that when I meditate, I am able to reach a greater level of peace.

Writing poetry was my way of expressing and letting my feelings out. As time passed, I developed better coping skills.

Turning Point

This turning point was my end of searching outside. I was now ready to move beyond the old doctrine of the church to something new. I was ready to move inward and trust my intuitive guidance.

I continued to grow on my journey, though I was not always consistent in my spiritual practices. I began to think about my life and how I always needed validation and approval of others. I chose to change that habit.

It was time to turn the corner. It was time to stop looking outside of myself for validation of self-worth, love, success, and truth and to focus on the desires of my Soul. I was neglecting the needs of my Soul, looking outside for the answers. Again, I asked myself, *What have you done for your Soul lately?* while looking into my eyes in the mirror.

I desired to gain knowledge and live from my spiritual self. I was determined to gain a better understanding of how the Universe worked. I continued to attend writing workshops and retreats, and in addition to my practice of meditation and prayer, I continued to write and recite positive spoken words and affirmations.

In 2015, I enrolled again in the TAMP program. I was convinced I was called to share my gift of writing this book with the world. I believed writing this book would free me from the grips and shackles of fear and grief and help me embrace the Soul, joy, and light I am.

As an alumnus of TAMP, I started to focus on writing this book. I hoped my book would inform, inspire, educate, and liberate any immigrant who felt immobilized by situations that diminished their lives and sense of well-being.

Accepting Compliments

It was difficult for me to accept a compliment and receive praise. For example, if I were complimented on my clothing, instead of saying, "Thanks," I would say something like, "This old thing?" If I were complimented by a visitor to my home, I would apologize for it not being clean enough. Instead of receiving the praise, I would instead apologize for it not being perfect.

Celebrating Accomplishments

I did not consider celebrating my accomplishments because I still did not know my worth or my value. I believed celebrating accomplishments was a form of self-praise, and self-praise was a form of arrogance or being cocky. I believed in the platitude: *self-praise is no recommendation.* I did not want to be seen as an arrogant or haughty person.

While sharing Thanksgiving with my extended family and friends in 2015, I experienced severe pain in my lower back and down my legs. I recalled that in 2012, I experienced a pinch in my lower back one day while working in my yard. I began to wonder if fear had anything to do with this physical manifestation, and I set out to ascertain what my back pain could be teaching me. I continued to meditate and commune with Spirit while listening for and believing the answer would be revealed as to what I needed to do to restore my physical health.

It is said: *Faith is the substance of things hoped for, the evidence of things not seen.* (Hebrews 11:1, KJV)

There were times, however, when my faith waned, and I needed to see the physical manifestations of what I was asking for.

As time went by, the pain worsened. After having explored many areas of relief, such as physical therapy, chiropractic, acupuncture, massage therapy, and so on, I finally decided to have major back surgery in 2016, and I spent one and a half years recovering. While in recovery, I spent much time thinking constructively and staying on my path toward wholeness.

Deconstructing Me

Becoming whole means recognizing our divinity and being aware we are one with the divine and everything there is.

Discovering and practicing steps that could take me from *fear* to *embracing and exercising faith* has helped me be grounded and successful in my ongoing journey of creating wholeness.

Trusting the Process

Trusting the process meant going with the flow of the Universe, trusting God and knowing God had my back. Even though I received the message to trust the process, I didn't know how to open my heart. At that time, I was still having trouble believing in myself. Not only did I not trust others, but I did not trust myself enough to rid myself of those negative emotions.

To open my heart meant I had to have a measure of trust, but trust was difficult for me. I was afraid to open my heart because I didn't know what I would find there. I did not think I would have enough strength to withstand the discovery.

Trust and Faith

> *Trust in God with all your heart and lean*
> *not unto your own understanding.*
> Proverbs 3: 5–6, NIV

As a child, I was taught to believe in God, a higher power. I believed I had faith and a measure of trust, but I was let down when Mom was sick. I prayed and asked God to heal my mom.

I promised I would always be a good girl and commit my life to Him, yet, Mom died anyway. The death of my mother and not grieving collectively with my family impacted me in many areas, but especially in this area of trust.

Though my faith and trust in God was always strong, sometimes, somehow, my faith waned as well as my trust in God. Somewhere along the way, fear had stolen my trust in myself and in others. Not only did I not trust others, I wondered if the real issue was fear of trusting me.

I was caught up in a plane of fears and had to find a way to release them, not embrace them. I still had to lean on the higher power for my needs and not blame God for Mom's passing.

I found it hard to trust anyone because my trust in people had continually waned. I struggled to keep my head up. Feeling detached from loved ones made me more prone to negative thoughts and angry outbursts. I trusted no one. There were many opportunities for expressing my thoughts and feelings through interpersonal relationships, yet I refused to take advantage because of fear and mistrust of others. I believed people would gather my information and use it as ammunition against me.

I did not trust people to keep my secret, and I grew wary of their questions and constant probing. *Where are you from? Where are you working? Where are you going? How old are you?* I did not tell anyone my age. I did not like it when anyone asked how old I was as I felt my privacy was intruded upon. I also did not like it when anyone asked why I spoke or looked the way I did. At first, I was sometimes amused at how often people tried to guess my actual age and complimented me on looking younger than they imagined me to be.

I observed that people in this country were more open with their emotions. If they are not satisfied with your service, they will let you know. Though I admired those qualities, I knew I had to be cautious with my secrets and believed I was doing the right thing by remaining in hiding. Over time, I became guarded and suspicious of everyone. I saw the world as a mean and scary place. I believed people didn't like me, and I kept people away by hiding behind my door of shame.

Who Was I?

I did not know who I was, but I knew I didn't like who I was being. I realized I was still doubtful and angry at the condition of my life. I also felt I had no privacy. I was still afraid and resistant. I needed to take time to figure out who I was. I felt helpless and powerless.

In order to find out who I was, I knew I needed to open my heart, to be willing to trust myself, and let people, including my family, into my life.

Closed Heart

Over the years, I held onto the fears and emotions that made it easy for me to close my heart. My heart had been closed for a long time, and I didn't know how to open it.

The negative mind chatter had taken over my heart with self-limiting fears and beliefs that kept me from moving forward.

Stricken with fear, I was afraid to show my heart. Fear and lack of trust brought about more loneliness, anger, shame, guilt, isolation, resentment, and insecurity.

I created a wall of protection around me so as to not let anyone get too close for fear of them learning my secrets. Always guarded, I did not allow anyone to hug me. As a result, I was afraid to open my heart for fear of letting someone in to discover my feelings of inadequacy. Meanwhile my anger and distrust were festering.

Fear of Rejection

Opening my heart meant living in a place of vulnerability and openness. I feared no one loved me. I believed I was unlovable because I thought I was not good enough. If they knew how little self-value I had, I thought they would not want to be my friend.

Opening my heart meant being willing to open myself up to other's scrutiny. It meant being willing to put myself out there. It meant to trust.

Fear of Judgment

I did not want to lend my voice to anyone because I was too afraid of their judgments. My fear of judgment was greater than my fear of rejection. I now know and see how I've been my own critic, as I judged myself constantly.

Fear of Losing Family

As time passed, I felt more disconnected from my family. Not feeling close connection to my family made me feel very alone. Feelings of estrangement were so severe I wondered if I could live a whole lifetime without the love and intimacy of my nuclear family. That thought made me even sadder.

Fear of Losing Myself
Not only did I fear losing my way but feared I would lose myself. Feeling sad and alone, I sometimes worried I was in a spiritual crisis and could lose my identity. I did not want to lose my identity, yet I continued to seek my sense of self-worth from others.

The Crossroad
It felt as though I was at a major crossroad in my life. Despite all that I had done and years spent in churches, I still felt very much alone. It felt like fear had captured and held me hostage as I continued to feel unhappy and unfulfilled. Though I had accomplished much in my life, I felt like something was missing. I was working as a health coach and could not understand why I was still unhappy.

Working as a health coach, I could not shake or release the fears I had experienced as an undocumented immigrant because the negative emotions persisted. Though I was now a U.S. citizen, I continued to marginalize myself. Consumed by a vicious cycle of negative thoughts like mind chatter, lack of confidence, impatience, apathy, and not really caring, I yearned for a way to become whole again.

PART IV

BREAKTHROUGHS IN AMERICA

CHAPTER 9

Turning Point

Again, I had reached a point of being truly tired of all the residuals of Mom's death and the emotions I felt after losing her. I was tired of feeling angry, resentful, stubborn, set, still afraid and impacted by the immigration saga, abandoned, unloved, unsupported by family, and embarrassed.

I wanted to feel light, unencumbered, and free, to be able to love and receive love and believe I deserved to be loved. I believed that self-love could nourish my body, mind, and spirit and that I could not be healed until I opened myself to love.

I had locked my heart away and hidden the key from myself. The result was a closed heart to love. I was afraid I didn't know how to love; I thought myself unworthy. I felt ashamed to admit I did not love myself and guilty that I could not love anyone.

I embarked upon opening my heart to let love in, to love, to forgive, and to follow my Soul's calling. This effort was arduous and a breakthrough happened.

Now, I was at a crossroad looking for something different and better. I was looking for love.

Searching for love meant opening my heart, which meant trusting. I knew I had to be open to trusting myself and to embrace love for myself, but any attempt was met with my own fears, which always stepped in while I hid behind the mask of apathy and resistance. I had a big life decision to make.

I had to work on releasing the mistrust, feelings of abandonment, isolation, and anger I had harbored because of the losses I had experienced. I had to trust God. I had to trust to feel secure.

As I continued attending retreats and workshops, listening to inspirational tapes, and staying focused on my spiritual regimen, my heart began to open slowly. I wanted to be the best me that I knew deep inside myself I could be.

Finding My Way: Moving From Fear to Faith
To find my way, I knew there were specific steps I would need to take to move from fear to faith. Sadness and depression had turned into anger.

Anger, grief, and fear imprisoned me. I was emotionally deprived and burned out, though I struggled to escape the wilderness of my ignorance. I felt angry at everyone in the world, and I ultimately closed off my heart and trusted no one. I did not realize that I used anger as a protective mechanism to cover up the pain I was experiencing. It was imperative, therefore, to dispel the anger and doubt that had ravaged me for so many years; the doubt and fear that captivated me limited my potential to be my fullest.

Doubt sabotaged my ability to launch forward in many ways. It hindered my ability to follow through on certain projects that involved others.

Sometimes my faith was so subjected to doubt that I questioned my ability to succeed at any task. I needed to forgive myself and others so that I could release and free myself from the past. I was prone to believe self-criticism and judgment and needed to learn compassion for self and for those whom I felt hurt me.

During one of the retreats I attended in 2014, I learned about *Ho'oponopono*, an ancient tool and technique that could be used to reach peace and happiness. I heard it was not just a technique, but a method of problem-solving that could help transform awareness and lives. Based on the premise that we are 100 percent responsible for our experiences—which come from our memories—we're also wholly responsible for healing whatever we experience in the world.

This healing system could be used as a form of prayer for forgiveness, reconciliation, and transformation. I had not heard of this prayer before and believed that it was God's way of encouraging me to keep going. *Why else would these words be available to me?* I asked myself.

This method of prayer is based on reflecting upon and repeating four statements:

- *I'm sorry.*
- *Please forgive me.*
- *Thank you.*
- *I love you.*

These statements are not just words; they move you into states of awareness and consciousness to meditate and reflect upon.

I had heard this method was a powerful way to connect with the Divine Source, and I wanted to work on my relationship with the divinity within.

Inspired by this new tool, I committed to practice listening to the words every night before bed and at other times. This technique became my mantra and prayer. When I reflected on the phrase, *I'm sorry*, it put me in a state of repentance. I began to feel sorry I had allowed the negative experiences in my life to torment me. Humbled and remorseful, I began to reflect on how I had carried the burden of my emotions and knew I had reached my moment to make a change and allow personal healing to take place.

Listening to various tapes and reading books on the techniques of Ho'oponopono, I began to feel a stirring inside my heart to open. I felt the chain around my heart loosening, and my heart becoming transparent like the clear heart pendant I carried in my purse. *Thank you*, I said to the nudge of transparency as it rose in my heart.

Then I began to get in touch with forgiveness for myself. Even though forgiveness can be immediate, it took a long time for me to achieve self-forgiveness. I asked for forgiveness so

I would be released from the problems I had manifested and was experiencing.

I had to forgive myself for all the negative thoughts I harbored over the years. I also forgave myself for manifesting this mindset in my life. I forgave myself for past inadequacies. I forgave myself for the things of which I had no knowledge. I forgave myself for my own ignorance.

I decided to forgive myself for not taking better care of me. I forgave myself for choosing less than myself. As I continued to forgive myself, my heart gradually began to open wider.

Bad Habits

I had a bad habit of sabotaging opportunities that were presented and opened to me. After reading the book, *The Greatest Salesman in the World* by Og Mandino, I was reminded that habits are temporary and can be changed in about twenty-one to thirty days.

I always knew and kept on believing there was a Source who could save me from this plight of sabotaging my ability to launch forward. I was on a mission to free myself.

Over time, I decided to seek courage because on the other side of my fears was courage. I wanted to develop courage to stand in my authenticity. I knew finding freedom and happiness would take courage. I saw courage as being brave enough to persevere in confronting life's many uncertainties. If I gained more courage, it would empower me to move forward. I believed it would take courage for me to be healed.

Katye Anna

During the spring of the 2015 Transformation Author's Breakthrough Experience, I met my spiritual teacher, Katye Anna Clark. I was inspired by her story. In her book, *Soul Love Never Ends*, she tells her story about the power of love and communication after death. In her book, *Conscious Construction of the Soul*, she teaches how to live a Soul-inspired life, the various stages of consciousness, and the journey of the Soul.

I wanted to live a Soul-directed life. I enrolled in her weekly Mind Mastery group and individual coaching sessions. Because she talked in a way familiar to me, I believed she understood me. She reinforced the consciousness shift on the planet in 2012, and I knew I would need to dig deeper. Inspired and excited to learn more, my search to understand and care for my Soul was expanding.

My teacher encouraged me to create a vision board to help me stay focused on my goals and desires as I worked toward reinventing myself. I continued reading new age and self-help books, meditating, and speaking positive affirmations.

Mirror Exercise

Every morning upon rising, I looked in the mirror into my eyes and said, "I love you," "You're worthy," "You are enough." This exercise helped me stay focused on myself as a beautiful Soul. Speaking these words also helped improve my confidence.

> **What are your spiritual practices?**

My Affirmations Exercise

Because I had trouble accepting compliments, I began to pay attention to the complimentary words spoken to me instead of dwelling on the negative mind chatter I often entertained and believed about myself. I dug up old letters and cards I received from others along my journey that were inspiring and showed love and support for me.

As I wrote these words in my journal, I realized these complimentary words could be quotations, messages, verses, and phrases of affirmations. I wrote these affirmations on index cards and posted them on my walls and read them daily.

Here is my list of affirmations:
- *You are a POWERFUL woman.*
- *You are someone I ENJOY spending time with.*
- *You are AMAZING.*
- *People don't care how much you know until they know how much you CARE.*
- *You are an INSPIRATION.*
- *Working with you has been REFRESHING and UPLIFTING.*
- *Keep BELIEVING as you do.*
- *You are a JOYFUL Woman.*
- *Keep on SHINING.*
- *You are BEAUTIFUL.*
- *I've always felt very fortunate to be your FRIEND.*
- *You have a MAGNIFICENT HEART.*

Contemplating the messages in these words, I realized and clearly saw I was being supported by the Universe all this while, through the beautiful souls I met. Now I am able to listen and accept compliments and praise from others.

While working with Katye Anna, I continued to meditate and to explore more about the chakra system. *Chakra* is a Sanskrit word, which means vortex or circle. Chakras are spinning centers of energy that receive and emanate the flow of light that descends from God. Chakras are major centers of spiritual power in the human body. Certain recurring emotions and fears can be held as stale energy in our chakras. Clearing the stale energy can help to balance our emotional state of mind.

In Mind Mastery class, I began to gain clarity about the levels of consciousness. Consciousness is how we perceive our world. There are many states of consciousness in God. We're all born into divine consciousness. I came to understand the mind is a powerful machine, programmed to operate on different levels.

The conscious mind is aware, creative, and used every day. It operates on limited beliefs and experiences. The subconscious mind consists of our past and holds deep, long-term memories.

In his book, *The Biology of Belief,* Dr. Bruce Lipton points out that our programming occurs from the time we are born until the age of seven. This programming, which we learn from our parents, guardians, and schools, becomes our behaviors.

As I continued to evolve, it became clear I needed to reprogram my subconscious mind. I thought about my family and recognized how, for the most of my life, I acted from my subconscious. I saw how my beliefs and behaviors were a printout of my subconscious mind. I had to acknowledge that I was programmed to behave a certain way. I needed a transformation in consciousness.

Instead of watching television, I listened to subliminal tapes during the day and sometimes at night before going to bed. I enjoyed healing melodies and nature sounds, all of which helped me release old patterns.

I continued to awaken my spiritual senses and cleared my energy and consciousness of conditioning from the past. I became clearer about the programs and beliefs I wanted to transform.

During that time, I started talking to my heart by looking into the eyes of that little girl and saying, *I am a child of love. I allow you to love me.* Looking back on some of the old, outdated beliefs I held, I realized that allowing others to truly see me was not easy.

Slowly, I began to see why I was not getting my desires met and why I just couldn't feel happy. My subconscious mind prevented me from moving forward. I had to reprogram my subconscious thoughts and take responsibility for my life to learn how to be a conscious human being.

Dimensions

I felt there was a quiet, subtle part of me that was all-knowing. I felt this part of me was different from my personality, and I wanted to gain a better understanding of my being. I was operating from a dimension where my operating system ran on limited, old, outdated beliefs. I understood clearly that I was standing in my own way because I was not fully conscious.

During my class, I was reminded that we are all energy. We are more than our body, mind, and life experiences. All our thoughts, feelings, and beliefs have a certain frequency. Working with Katye Anna confirmed my long-held sense that there are dimensions other than the one in which I was living.

Dimensions are levels of consciousness that vibrate at certain frequencies. The third dimension is what I saw of my life, but that seeing was a limited state of consciousness. I wanted to vibrate on a higher level.

Katye Anna talked about the 2012 paradigm shift of consciousness into the fifth dimension. I recalled and began to make the connection between the paradigm shift and the time I received a clear *pendant heart* from my Reiki master teacher with the message to open my heart. I realized that I, too, was going through and experiencing a shift in consciousness. The 2012 energetic shift was the same as a spiritual awakening.

To be awakened is to be conscious. This shift of consciousness is known as the beginning of ascension. It is a path we can choose to move into higher dimensions. As humans, we can choose to shift gradually and ascend to these higher dimensions. When we choose to evolve higher and merge with our higher selves, we are opening up our hearts and expanding to reunite with God, Source, Universal Consciousness, and all levels and layers of our authentic selves.

Visualization

Using the method of visualization, I began clearing and grounding my seven main chakras. As I continued to meditate and focus on my chakras, I started to ground my energy into Earth. Grounding is important to stay connected to Mother Earth. To ground myself, I spent time in my yard walking without shoes, hugging trees, and being mindful of the grass under my feet. I began to feel more centered. I began to see the light of each chakra. I noticed my heart opened more, and I felt more balanced, harmonious, and less afraid.

As I continued to meditate and focus on my chakras, I saw how all my wounds were self-inflicted. I began to look at the words I thought about and believed about myself. I saw how I had allowed the past to hold me hostage.

I saw clearly how words blended with beliefs can create reality. I chose to stop blaming others and vowed to set healthier boundaries in my relationships. I no longer wanted to be held hostage or prisoner to my past experiences. As I continued clearing, cleaning my energetic fields, and paying more attention to my dreams, I kept a journal on my nightstand to record my dreams.

One night during meditation, I had an experience where I merged with an all-consuming light. I saw where my Soul connected with Source energy and at that moment, I realized I was a part of Source. At that moment, I realized who I was.

I was energy. I was love. I was light.

It was then I saw clearly how blessed I was, and I committed to embracing who I was becoming.

Embracing the Freedom of Faith

Fear had been a part of my life as long as I could remember. I wanted to be fearless, so I decided to embrace the freedom of faith. To me, embracing the freedom of faith meant releasing all fears. Ditching the confines of grief also meant releasing all fears. Fear and faith cannot co-exist because faith cancels fear.

Faith eradicates fear. Ditching fear indicates a process of moving toward living in total faith. As I continued my spiritual practice of forgiving, I could feel inner confidence and faith inside.

Getting out of my own way required faith. Not sabotaging my movements through fear requires faith and courage. Getting out of my own way also required a measure of surrender.

Surrender meant I stopped feeling the need to be caretaker of everything. During my deep state of surrender, it felt as though I was plowing and crawling my way out to clarity and freedom. Surrender meant letting go of all the things holding me back from freedom and trusting the inner force that says: *Take a chance and watch it work*. To surrender is to unfold gradually and live by faith.

When I realized that courage leads to confidence, I became more inspired. My intention was to release fears and replace them with faith and courage. As I continued to practice forgiving others and myself for a myriad of things, I watched my faith increase.

When I stopped working so hard to show I was confident or good enough, I gained the courage and empowerment to move forward. It takes courage to want to be healed.

For years, I wrestled to trust myself enough to let go of fear. My mind was controlled by fear. It was imperative to find a way to move out of that mindset. My challenge and task were to let go of my fears, let in love, and live in love. I was convinced I had carried around the sadness in my life for too long.

As I continued to chant the phrases to my new tool, Ho'oponopono, I became more open to seeing myself as I was. I realized I could not control anything, so I decided to stop trying and to let things flow while trusting that everything would always work out for my greater good.

I had to become aware of what was holding me back. I had to decide if I wanted these beliefs to continue to control my life or not. Instead of looking at what I was not doing or getting done, I turned it around and began to look at what was actually being done. I began to focus on what I wanted and why I wanted the things I wanted. My priority was to feel happy so that I could be who I really was.

Not only was it necessary for me to let go of my need to control but also to let go of the feelings of resentment, shame, guilt, and regret. I needed to accept the truth that I couldn't change the past.

I began to let go of and release things over which I had no control. For example, I have no control over what others say or do. I'd been carrying the baggage of my affected, damaged life—writing and saying the same things repeatedly, carrying the same baggage and singing the same old song. I had not given up struggling, fighting, and reliving the moments of a time gone by.

I finally realized that when I was holding onto blame and pointing fingers, it was my way of trying to control the situation. I eventually accepted that I didn't need to be in control.

Family Love
Not feeling loved or cared for by my family impacted my confidence level. I did not value myself because I did not know my worth. I needed to see my family in a different light. I needed to know, love, and respect my family for the beautiful beings they had become. I realized we had all come such a long way. It was time for us to tell each other how we really felt about each other. It was time for us to show our love for each other.

Family Reunion
In 2014, the death my mother's brother, my last living uncle, made me acknowledge the fact the recovery from my sometimes debilitating grief was not complete. All the old emotions after Mom's and Dad's deaths, which I thought were healed, came flowing to the surface again.

It was hard for me to accept that I had not completely recovered from grief. I had not let my family into my life or heart all this time. My family was still dispersed through different parts of the world, and I had no real contact with most of them. I take full responsibility for my part in not reaching out to others to help mend the divide.

I was so caught up in my own lingering grief that I hadn't stopped to consider my siblings could have endured some of the same emotional reactions I had experienced. I began to feel empathy and sympathy for what they could possibly still be dealing with.

After much prayer and meditation, I felt spiritually led to spearhead our first ever family reunion, where we hopefully could come together to air some needed heartfelt emotions, and we could share and support each other through this reminiscent time. Hopefully, this would free us of those encumbrances and allow for healthy spiritual evolvement. I was ready to take the lead in making this family reunion a reality.

As I grew older, the disintegration of my family and not having the joyful pleasure of a more intimate relationship with them began to weigh more heavily on me. I began to realize the importance of *putting my house in order*—shedding and ridding myself of secrets about things that kept my family unit from being close-knit. Uncle, who shared many stories about the family prior to his passing, was delighted when he learned I was writing a book about my life, my memoir.

After I made the decision to commit to be the leader for coordinating our first ever family reunion, I began research on how to approach it. I had never planned a family reunion before, and this was my first time attempting to do anything together with my family. I believed seeing the family all together once again would be healing for me and would definitely create healing in their lives as well.

This tremendous and lofty task I knew would take much hope, faith, courage, and lots of support from my family. I thought a family reunion would help me in feeling more confident, secure, and accepted. It was now time to meet with and exchange information with family members and to rediscover the love of family.

I had to raise my confidence because *I didn't know these people*. I had been estranged from most of my family for much of my adult life. I was still angry about some things I had chosen to be rid of, but I didn't yet feel healed or free. Prior to making the commitment to lead our family reunion, I had to become clear about why I took on this project. *What was in it for me? After all, it's not like my family has been there for me,* I grappled. The chatter in my mind was loud and reminded me of how I had felt abandoned by my family for so many years.

My view of my family had been myopic. My small world consisted of my siblings and my deceased parents. Because family consists of all types of important relations, I concluded I wanted to bring together family members who had not seen one another for some period of time. I also wanted to renew and strengthen old relationships and start forming new ones as well, creating memories for the next generation.

As I dug deeper into my thoughts, I realized my main reason for spearheading the reunion was that *I* wanted to feel more stable, gain a sense of perspective, and reconnect with my intrinsic roots. I wanted to feel and prove to myself that I belonged to a family, and I wanted to experience my whole family together in one place. I wanted to catch up, reestablish, and grow family relationships.

Prior to this time, I had gathered with certain family members periodically for Thanksgiving or Christmas holidays, but I wanted to connect with more family members. I had felt drawn for a long time to initiate a family reunion, but I had resisted. The resistance and doubt in my head gave me permission to complain: *This should be handled by someone else in the family, certainly not me.* I was obviously still not quite ready to let go of the negative emotions, but this endeavor was what I needed for my transformation.

Through social media, I reached out to certain family members and called a group of like-minded folks to check their interest and get their feedback on being a part of a planning committee. I was pleasantly surprised that most of them were receptive to the idea of a family reunion. I was especially pleased that six family members agreed to be a part of the reunion planning committee. We agreed on a date to meet, and our first committee meeting was scheduled for the third Sunday in January 2015.

Though I was excited to spearhead our family reunion, I was also very nervous. I had only been on a group call once with some of my siblings regarding a family matter but had not moderated a call with other family members.

During the days leading up to the call, I worried that I was not prepared. The unwanted chatter in my mind told me I might not do a good job. I was afraid they would criticize and judge me. I badly wanted to please my family by doing a good job and to convince myself they saw me as worthy and valuable.

Six excited and motivated family members attended our first group call. It was an energetic and productive meeting. We established that the group would be responsible for planning, organizing, and creating a structure for our family reunion. In addition, we were open to receiving any information or ideas that anyone in the family wanted to share and contribute to this event. The year, date, building a mailing list, the venue, accommodations, and finances were among the things we discussed. We settled on the third weekend in July 2016, as the official date for our first ever family reunion.

We agreed to meet on a bi-monthly basis on Sunday evenings for our ongoing committee group call. Once it started, the process demanded I promise to be in it for the long haul. I vowed to see it to completion. I also decided to document the wide variety of things I would have to cover to make this dream of our family reunion a reality.

It is a collective family dream for all of us to have a bonding connection to the energy of who we are and where we came from. Having come from a family of dreamers, it was our parents' dream for us to be together as a loving, healthy family. *Isn't this what all parents want for their children and what families want for each other?* I pondered in my mind.

It took us a while for our committee to come up with a name and theme. One family member suggested we think of something we were told by our mother. Immediately, insecurity raised its ugly head. I could not think of anything my mother had told me. It made me upset because I could not recall a phrase or a lesson Mom had taught me. I felt ashamed. Most of what I knew and remembered, I learned from my sisters or had learned on my own. Eventually, we settled on "Together We Stand" and opened a private Facebook group.

I suggested "Coming Home" as a reunion theme. However, a member felt it was not a good theme because the younger generation couldn't identify with that theme—they didn't know anything about *home*. They were just beginning to establish a connection to the broader memory of home regarding family lineage. I tried hard not to take it personally and to understand that each member would have their own opinions, as well as me.

During our first call, we agreed to utilize social media to reach and tag family. I was surprised to see how many family members we had and how they were scattered over much of the world. I believed my task was to connect with each of them. Each group member would begin to compile a list with names and emails of their immediate family and anyone they knew. This would begin our master contact list.

During our second call, I became very nervous. It was now ten minutes after our call time, and I was the only one on the call. I thought that no one would show up.

The nervousness was not new. I had hoped to persevere regardless of my present fear. As Marianne Williamson said: *Feel the fear and do it anyway*. I breathed deeply and waited. Shortly after, four members joined the call, and I felt relieved. By the time we had our third family call, I was feeling calmer.

However, I worried again that no one would show up for the call, especially since each member was asked to pay dues. The purpose of the dues was to help us get started as well as to create an account for miscellaneous expenses. Thus, began the endeavor of planning our family reunion.

As I continued with my daily practice of speaking this technique, Ho'oponopono, my heart was expanding, and I was becoming more thankful for how my life was manifesting. I began to realize the gift of having life and the blessing of having the chance to heal myself and live my life in peace.

My back surgery took place in 2016, and I was afraid I would not be able to continue leading the planning committee. But, as the Universe would have it, it was time to ask for help and delegate to members of the committee. To my surprise, my family was delighted and quite able to support me in my delegation of duties in order to bring the reunion to fruition without my being so physically involved in the process. The delegation of duties really aided in uniting the group to work together and bond more quickly.

During my recovery from major back surgery, I continued with daily affirmations and guided meditations. One of the ways I took care of myself during recovery was by administering Reiki and QT healing energy to myself.

I was pleased with the love and support I received from the members of the planning committee during my recovery.

While in recovery, I decided to document my experience of having a laminectomy. I was able to write on my computer while lying on my back. I wanted to share some of my reasons for choosing to have back surgery from among other options by contributing a chapter with other global contributors in the book, *Life SPARKS: Life Stories to Illuminate, Inspire and Ignite, Volume I,* in the summer of 2016.

In addition to my exuberance about being a contributing author, I received a phone call from my favorite cousin Lenore with whom I hadn't spoken since childhood. She was living in England with her husband and children. She expressed regrets for not being able to attend our upcoming family reunion but said she would make every effort to attend the next one.

Our family reunion was held for five days from June 29–July 4, 2016. It was a big success for the Lynch, Charles, and Beazer families who came from many places: London, St. Thomas, Antigua, and the States. On the first day, we held a meet and greet at my sister's house as people came in from near and far. We enjoyed a delicious West Indian meal, which was reminiscent of home. It was quite a joyous occasion. The rest of the itinerary included a picnic in the park, a banquet, a visit to Coney Island, family members attending church service, and a brunch together.

During the banquet, I acknowledged and expressed thanks to family members who worked on our planning committee to bring the reunion to fruition. I thanked them for stepping up during my illness and keeping things moving. They showed me support, care, and love in action. My heart was full as I realized how much my family did indeed love me.

After the reunion ended, one of my brothers, who said he enjoyed all of the festivities, suggested the next reunion should be just for the immediate Lynch family so that we could hash out the things that badly needed resolving within our family to bring about more healing. I felt that it was a great idea since there had been some discussion among the committee members that we plan our next reunion for 2020 in Antigua.

Subsequently, a conference call was held with my siblings and me, and these are some of the details we discussed:

We each had the chance to talk about how life had been and the ways we'd coped with loss and grief on our individual journeys.

I shared with my siblings my fear that I would die by my 58th birthday, which was the age that Mom died. One of my brothers also admitted he, too, had that fear.

One of my sisters revealed that she felt angry for years at our family for not sticking together. She had made peace with Mom's death after her last daughter was born. She shared that she had seen Mom's face in her baby's face and at that moment, she knew Mom was protecting them in spirit.

Another brother shared that he felt abandoned not only by the death of our parents, but because he was the last sibling to leave our island country.

One sister revealed how sad and broken she felt that she was not able to make it to Mom's funeral because she was undocumented and could not leave the States for fear she would not be able to return. She was eventually able to go home and visit Mom's grave.

After each one had their chance to voice their feelings and share their thoughts about their journey, I realized how devastating the disconnection with my family had been, even though they had gone on to live their lives and build their own families. I also realized how strong my siblings were and how much they had been through.

The same sister shared that she honors our parents daily by acknowledging them. She has placed their photos, sacred objects, and frequently places fresh carnation flowers on her altar in honor of their memory. I realized then I had never had photos of my parents or anyone in my family in my home. I thanked my sister for this wonderful idea and determined I would adopt that practice in honor of our parents as well.

Each family member embraced and developed their own individual journey in coping with the trauma of our losses. It was then I realized the amount of love, care, and intimacy there was among my siblings. At that moment, I felt for the first time I did still have a family. I also had a completely different perspective of my earlier years growing up on the island. For example, as a child, I saw our family as very poor, but my older siblings felt that our family was considered rich in our neighborhood.

I began to see my family differently. I realized how beautiful we were as a family. The foundation our parents set was still in place.

The Moonlit Path
In January 2017, along my journey of seeking ways to become my best self, I enrolled in an online master class offered by spirit guide messenger Michelle Currie, who focused on "being who you are here to be." The Moonlit Path was a ten-week program that afforded me the opportunity to participate in a support group with like-minded individuals in a sacred space.

I wanted this class to provide tools I could implement to help free myself of my self-inflicted denigration. I discovered I had experienced a lot of shame in my life and needed to be rid of this albatross that was preventing me from succeeding and moving on with my endeavors in life.

During the program, I focused on understanding and connecting with my intuitive voice, visioning, manifesting, and creating ways to expand my holistic wellness business. My business is based on inspirational supportive consulting, introduction to nutrition, energy healing, and special events, which include: silent and interactive retreats, rhythm circles, spoken word, and creative writing coaching with the sole objective of supporting and benefiting myself and others who are aspiring to be confident in our own skin.

After completing The Moonlit Path program in the spring of 2017 with Michelle, I enrolled in her five-day offshoot masterclass, which included "Developing Your Clairs" and intuitive coaching sessions.

I learned that developing my *clairs* through focused exercises and practices allowed me to receive messages directly from God Source. These messages can come through sight (clairvoyance), audio (clairaudience), feeling (clairsentience), and knowing (claircognizance). Prior to this class, I had little knowledge of clairs and their functions, and I was skeptical about the accuracy and value of messages I had received.

With Michelle's gentle encouraging guidance and the group process, I was inspired to trust and open my heart even wider to see, accept, and embrace the valuable messages I received.

Not only do I now have a better understanding of the clairs and their functions, but my ability to listen has deepened and I am more grounded and motivated to tune into my clairs.

During one of my intuitive coaching sessions, I shared my feelings of anxiety and frustration with Michelle. I revealed my habit of procrastination and how vulnerable I felt because I was not further along in my business. She helped me dig deeper to see the messages I'd been saying to myself and how to differentiate between my voice and that of intuition.

She helped me be aware that I needed to identify the things I said to myself. Until I changed what I was telling myself, I wouldn't move forward because I was held hostage by shame. That was when I decided to explore and read more about shame.

Brené Brown, PhD, LMSW, describes shame as "the intense painful feeling or experience of believing we are flawed and therefore unworthy of love and belonging."[1]

Ridding Shame

Seeking to know, understand, believe, embrace, and love myself started my letting go of shame. I had convinced myself that I wasn't good enough. I told myself that something was wrong with me, and that is why I could not feel happy. Because I was so afraid of rejection, humiliation, and embarrassment, I concluded others wouldn't like me if I were truly honest about how I felt about things. These shameful thoughts occupied my mind and tormented me like a hungry ghost for more years than I care to count. In *Psychology Today*, Mary C. Lamia, PhD, Clinical

---
1. Brown, Brené. "shame v. guilt." *Brené Brown*. 14 January 2013. brenebrown.com/blog/2013/01/14/shame-v-guilt/

Psychologist, in Marin County, California, referred to shame as a self-conscious, contagious, and dangerous emotion.[2] Shame informs us of an internal state of inadequacy, unworthiness, dishonor, regret, and disconnection.

Research shows that shame leads us to hide and conceal. In the *Jung Page*, James M. Shultz, MD, a Jungian analyst, points out that the word shame comes from a word that means "to cover," that is to hide.[3]

Dr. Lamia further pointed out that "Shame can lead us to feel our whole self is bad, flawed and subject to exclusion and can motivate us to hide or do something to save face." Some feelings that can accompany shame include: envy, anger, rage, anxiety, sadness, depression, depletion, loneliness, isolation, and emptiness.

In order to get rid of shame, we first have to be aware of it. According to Dr. Lamia, our response to shame is shaped by all of our emotional memories of when it was previously experienced. Dr. Lamia postulated, "The accumulation of emotional experiences that reside in our memory, script our responses when a particular emotion is activated in the present."[4]

In her book, *Daring Greatly: How the Courage to Be Vulnerable Transforms the Way We Live, Love, Parent, and Lead*, Brené Brown, PhD, LMSW, says that we must "bring shame into light."[5] She

---

2. Lamia, Mary C. "Shame: A Concealed, Contagious, and Dangerous Emotion." *Psychology Today*. 4 April 2017. www.psychologytoday.com/us/blog/intense-emotions-and-strong-feelings/201104/shame-concealed-contagious-and-dangerous-emotion
3. Shultz, James M. "Shame." *The Jung Page*. 27 October 2013. www.cgjungpage.org/learn/articles/analytical-psychology/776-shame
4. Lamia, "Shame."
5. Brown, Brené. *Daring Greatly: How the Courage to Be Vulnerable Transforms the Way We Live, Love, Parent, and Lead*. Penguin Random House, NY. 2012.

points out that if we cultivate enough awareness about shame to name it and speak it, we've basically cut it off at its knees.

Dr. Shultz, who explores shame from a Jungian perspective, argues that by recognizing and acknowledging shame, we can stop defending ourselves against it and open a window on the shadow.

Shame goes deeper than guilt and deeper than any one instance or action. We must be persistent, consistent, and mindful of our thoughts and emotions. It is, therefore, important to learn ways to deal with shame and to build healthy barriers against it.

Michelle challenged me to get in touch with what I was telling myself about myself. She challenged me to take a hard look inside myself for answers. This made me dig deeper inside to really understand the deep shame I'd felt for most, if not all, of my life.

As I continued to deepen my intuition and develop my clairs, I began to recall feelings of shame as they came up to the surface. There were deep-rooted experiences from my childhood that traumatized me, and I was still holding on to those experiences of guilt and shame.

As I examined my life, I began to identify the outdated beliefs and negative messages I was feeding myself. I recognized that the feeling of shame was not in my heart, but in my mind. I needed to change my mindset. Michelle challenged me with exercises to look within for the answers and to let intuition guide me. I started paying more attention to what I was thinking, looking at my behavior and how I related to others. I had to practice mindfulness in order to stay present and aware of my thoughts and actions and not be in denial.

What I was telling myself was shocking! I found out I was telling myself lies! By examining the negative messages of *not being good enough* and *stupid* combined with all the events that shamed me, I suddenly became clear about what I was doing to myself. I entertained the two biggest lies of all: 1) no one loved me, and 2) I was not enough.

I was determined to reclaim the parts of me that had been lost and swept under the rug. I was on a mission to continue reinventing myself. As I chipped away at the core of my shame thoughts, I began to see how these thoughts and memories began in my childhood.

I felt shame when I learned my father could not read. I felt shame when I thought I had given incorrect change to a customer while helping Dad sell his fish when I was only eight years old. This, to me, meant that I could not count or was not good in arithmetic. I found out later in life that I had given the correct change to the customer.

I recalled my childhood educational experiences in the British school system. I felt shame for having difficulty in comprehension. I felt anger and shame about the corporal punishment I received in school—the frequent physical confinement of standing on the bench or kneeling on the stage to be punished, the beatings with the thick leather belt by the head mistress, being whacked across my knuckles with a ruler, and not being allowed to express myself to teachers—all made me feel powerless, which resulted in the lack of self-love.

When I understood that shame is a form of fear, and not loving or liking myself is a form of emotional abuse, the chain of self-abuse began to unravel. I agreed that I was worth more than that. Eventually, I adopted the mindset that: *I'm valuable, lovable, good enough, and I am always connected to God.* I know the sinking emotion of not feeling good enough, but because I'm here to embrace the divine spark within me, I am able to choose which feeling or emotion I listen to.

When I learned that shame is a fear of disconnection, I realized the guilt and shame I felt were created in part by a sense of separation from family. Consequently, I began to reach out more to my family and friends. Making connections allowed me to accept myself and others. Being connected meant we could be there for each other when the need arose.

Repeating affirmations and mantras helped me to be more introspective and honest in getting rid of shame. The more I believed, embraced, and loved myself, the more liberated I felt. I also noticed I was able to love and accept others more readily.

The practices of self-compassion and forgiveness were tools I used to help me handle shame so as not to give in to its messages of *I am not good enough*. I forgave myself for taking so long to embrace my beauty, to embrace my whole truth, and to accept that I am a Soul child of God.

I came to like myself. I realized that I had to like all of myself with all my flaws and weaknesses. To like me more is to acknowledge the beauty in my human imperfections and to love me anyway as I keep moving forward. By liking myself more, I have stopped defining myself by what I do or what others may say about me.

I came to accept that I am a human being and not perfect. I came to know that I am good enough and will continue to heal as I move forward. I chose to release the power that fear, guilt, and shame had over me and to embrace the powerful gift of my faith.

Steps to Get Rid of Shame

1. Acknowledge and talk about your feelings of shame
2. Be mindful of your thoughts and emotions to avoid shame triggers
3. Stop thinking negative thoughts and don't put yourself down
4. Practice self-compassion and forgiveness
5. Accept love and kindness from others
6. Consider going to individual or group therapy
7. See your beauty and fall in love with life

My business was growing at a comfortable rate as I continued to harness my energy to help enrich my work.

I was facilitating cooking classes and laughter yoga classes, as well as practicing Reiki healing and distant Quantum Touch energy work. In the spring of 2017, CreateWhole Wellness Services, LLC, offered a one-day wellness retreat on self-love and self-care in South Carolina. Everyone left expressing the desire to love and care for themselves unconditionally.

Later, in the fall of 2017, I contributed another chapter in the #1 International best-seller, *My Big Idea Book*, which was inspired by global bestselling authors and compiled by Viki Winterton.

Thinking you're not good enough is a disempowering, outdated belief.

Over time, the support and encouragement from my mentors, coaches, teachers, tutors, books, workshops, seminars, and retreats helped me to arrive at the place where I could say enough is enough. My teachers of both parochial and religious institutions were also instrumental in helping me to see myself more clearly, follow my inner guidance, and to realize that I mattered and was more than enough.

They all encouraged a sense of mastery in me and helped open my mind and heart to many ideas, knowledge, and spiritual practices. I was learning to embrace my god-ness.

My Beliefs About Love

Belief is acceptance that a statement is true or that something exists. Beliefs come from our environment and how we are reared. I held some core beliefs that guided my life that needed to be transformed.

I believed I had to be a people pleaser to find love. Being a people pleaser, I was programmed to behave a certain way. I was definitely preoccupied and spent too much time worrying and thinking about what others may have thought of me. I got caught up in believing I was responsible for people's opinions of me. I thought, like me, they believed I was not enough.

My Belief About My Birth

I believed that because I was born breach, there was something wrong with me—so I believed I was not lovable. Somehow, I told myself that when I was born, there was no singing, dancing, or partying, though it was customary in our family to celebrate the birth of a child with a party.

When I shared this belief with my sister, she corrected me and said that my birth was especially celebrated because Mom hadn't had a daughter in four years. There was a big party following my baptism where all our friends and my godmother came to celebrate my birth.

"Mom was ecstatic about your birth," my sister said proudly. "She was very attentive to her little baby girl."

Then I recalled Miss Ella saying with a smile, "You mother loved God first, then her children. She called you her little one, her little rose." I was slow to recognize that "little rose" referred to me. It is a part of my middle name. Recalling this made me feel loved and happy. After this recollection, my mind began to shift, and I began to consider how to communicate with Mom.

I don't know when I created those beliefs, but it certainly was relieving to know they were not true. I needed the connection with family to discover some truths and unfounded beliefs, which helped me begin ridding myself of the shame of not being loved and celebrated as a child.

My Beliefs About Death

At an early age, I had set core beliefs about death. I believed death was terrifying and terrible. I did not pray for Mom after she died because I saw death as final, and in my mind, praying seemed useless.

Before I stopped going to church, I hardly ever entered Green Bay Church from the south side because I couldn't stand to see Mom's grave site. It made me too sad. Hearing of anyone dying seemed to have compounded my fears and debilitating sadness about death. What an emotional, heavy-weighted existence I lived.

Death brought change into my life at that early age, and I was not ready for it. I tried to block it out and deny it, yet I could not deny the vacant space Mom's death left in my heart and in the family. I did not understand death and was too young and afraid at that time to explore further. I had old, outdated beliefs about dying and the dead. There was always the fear of knowing that I, too, will die.

The Power of Change

> *If you choose to see things differently, it will be different.*
> – Gabrielle Bernstein

I was still tired of feeling unhappy, and I wanted to change. I knew that I couldn't continue feeling as badly as I did, so I had to make a choice to feel better. I knew I had to return to my roots of faith that my mother had laid and prepared for me. I began to pay more attention to my thoughts and to see how they kept me from focusing on feeling better.

It became clear to me that I was practicing the vibrational frequency of negative beliefs and creating what I did not want. My charge, therefore, again, was to rid myself of fear-based beliefs and focus on love-based beliefs so I could change my vibration of fear into the vibration of love.

First and foremost, to change my thought patterns, I had to undo the old beliefs I held before coming to America, as well as the ones I developed here. Recognizing my negative thought patterns, I vowed to move out of my comfort zone and be more patient in facing my fears. I decided to focus on how I wanted to feel and to do better for myself. I wanted to change the way I thought.

I wanted to better manage negative behavioral patterns like resistance, self-sabotage, poor judgment, and self-loathing that often stymied my movements. I understood that my core story is the way I show up in the world, and the core story I was showing and telling myself and others was not my most powerful, credible self.

In order to get rid of old and outdated beliefs, I first had to look at my core beliefs in all areas of my life. I had to know how I was functioning in the areas of family, social and interpersonal relationships, career, creativity, community involvement, and so forth. I began to explore the underlying themes that defined who I was. Among these themes was a deep sense of craving to know myself, to find truth and justice, and to be honest with myself.

Secondly, I had to rid myself of beliefs based in fear. My challenge was to understand my core beliefs and the associated behavioral patterns that were difficult to change.

Thirdly, I had to open my heart and mind and become more willing to allow bigger changes in my life. I had to experience a breakdown of the old self in order to let the new ideas and ways of being come in. With faith, I allowed myself to believe again, and I set out to consciously change my fear-based beliefs.

Change Thoughts

To get rid of mind chatter, I had to allow myself to be present. We become present by training our mind to seek out and dissolve any thoughts that take us against the direction in which we want to go. I began to see that I could use mind chitter-chatter as a tool to reinforce a desire or want. By making an adjustment in my mindset, I released mindless chatter and turned my mind chatter into positive affirmations.

I let go of limiting beliefs and installed new, empowering, and abundant beliefs. I stopped focusing on the non-truth that I had no confidence, and I began to focus on what I had accomplished in my life thus far.

I gave up striving for perfection. This unrealistic expectation is an illusion, for it does not really exist. Most of all, it results in worry and anxiety. This kind of energy must be released.

I no longer see my conditions and issues as complaints. These life challenges are my stepping-stones and not my stumbling blocks.

I noticed a change in my thought patterns, and I now think and see things differently.

Coming Out of Hiding: Willing to Change

After I released fear and learned how to trust God and others, I came out of hiding. I learned that trust is important to restoring safety. This was not a one-time event because trust, like faith, is ongoing. Coming out of hiding meant I had to allow myself to be transparent and willing to change.

During my quest to know myself, I discovered the "5 WILLINGS" (5-Ws). The 5-Ws are my own life-changing steps I embraced in order to make profound changes in my life.

My Five WILLINGS

1. I am willing to forgive myself and others.
2. I am willing to give voice to my thoughts and words.
3. I am willing to be open to giving and receiving love.
4. I am willing to let go of shame.
5. I am willing to change and move from excuses to opportunities.

In order to change, I had to allow myself to be vulnerable. Being vulnerable meant giving up resistance and being willing to let someone in to support me.

Ask for Help

It takes great strength and courage to ask for what we want and allow others to support us.

I did not ask for help nor allow anyone to help me because I did not want to be responsible or accountable to them. Allowing people to help me made me feel obligated to them. I had to have faith, and I had to believe that allowing people to support me would enhance my growth and trust in others.

The Power of Faith
There are many definitions of faith. My definition of faith is to take a chance and watch it work for my greater good.

Faith is stepping out on nothing, believing something is there.

Faith empowers you to hold onto knowing the manifestations of your heart will be met if you believe.

Faith gives you the fortitude to be persistent and consistent with an attitude of expectancy. Expectancy is the act of looking for something and believing you are going to receive it. Expectancy yields results.

Faith is like a muscle that can be strengthened and developed through exercise, routine practice, and trusting.

Faith creates a sense of hope and results in mini and maxi miracles daily.
Faith is an action word. Faith without action is a form of resistance.

Exercising faith is a process. The following steps can help you in developing and strengthening your faith muscle.

Six Steps to Cultivating Faith

Step 1. *Conceive* – Get a clear picture in your mind of what you want or need, then thank the Universe or God for it. Believe you deserve to have it. Visualize yourself with it. Take the necessary actions to do your part in bringing this request to fruition. The action may just be thanking God for the blessing as if it is already manifested. Be patient and trust the process.

Step 2. *Daily Occurrences* – Look for daily occurrences that make you say, *Huh! What a coincidence,* though we know there are no coincidences. These are blessings or miracles from the Universe because you've taken the time to pay attention, observe, and acknowledge these miracles. They can be as simple as receiving an unexpected check just when you needed it most. Be grateful, thank the Universe or God and watch the blessings, miracles, and occurrences increase.

Step 3. *Acceptance* – Accept that faith is a powerful tool that brings about daily miracles, so expect them to occur. What you think about, you bring about. Practice making little requests of or expressing gratitude to the Universe. A stronger level of faith can bring about miracles faster. You may wonder, *how can my life be filled with daily miracles when I have days that are not so pleasant?* Every day and every experience are opportunities for growth and spiritual evolvement.

Step 4. *Mindset Shift* – Affirm that you need and deserve miracles in your life. A miracle is a shift in perception from fear to love. Experiencing the occurrences of miracles will increase and strengthen your faith. This will afford you the luxury of living in a state of expectancy of daily miracles.

Step 5. *Take Action* – Do something every day that will get you closer to what you desire and expect. Practice and have fun with testing the practices of the faith process.

Step 6. *Faith Journal* – Create a faith journal to keep a record of the daily miraculous blessings that will occur in your life. Being thankful for your miracles will bring about more blessings and miracles.

A formula for cultivating faith is: (C+B+E) x A = M
(Conceive + Believe + Expect) x Action = Miracles

Seeing

After reading the book, *Zero Limits* by Joe Vitale and Dr. Hew Len, I began to understand that not everything we see with the natural eye is what it appears to be. Then I realized I was experiencing my memories and the world differently than my family. I was experiencing my thoughts through the filter of my subconscious mind. I had a different memory of my childhood than most of my family!

After all the time I thought that my family did not care about me, I later learned that my family loved me. I also learned that the elders in my family were so devastated after Mom's death, they communicated their concerns for the well-being of my younger brother and me.

Practicing H'ooponopono helped me see I was so preoccupied with myself and the thoughts in my head, that I was not able to communicate my feelings with myself or with others. I came to understand that I was responsible for everything in my mind.

As I continued to actively practice my new prayer techniques, the light of awareness began to shine brighter into my being. Meanwhile the power of being present was increasing. I recalled reading, *The Power of Now* by Eckhart Tolle and his work on the power of presence. I also remembered some of the mindfulness breathing meditation exercises by Deepak Chopra I had learned.

Meditation brought me to a state of mindfulness and presence where I was a little more open and able to connect with my heart essence. All of the negative rules and beliefs I held were dissolving. Gradually, all of my doubts were replaced with new and more positive beliefs.

The grace of the Universe transformed my wrong belief systems, thoughts, thinking patterns, and cultural norms that kept me from growing my wings and flying. Finally, I was ready to take the leap and fly off the ledge into the fullness of my life.

Some of the actions I took for survival skills included:
- Getting an education
- Loving myself unconditionally
- Listening to intuitive guidance
- Developing my faith muscle
- Embracing the energy of my loved ones
- Transforming my life
- Seeking energy from support groups

As an alumnus of IIN, I agreed to join a weekly support group along with four other health coaches who were alumni of IIN. We started our group to provide emotional support, share recipes and tips, and to allow us the opportunity to alternate group leading.

Later, I understood that I magnetized myself to attract what I wanted when I took action. From then on, whenever I got an idea or nudge in my awareness to do something, I recognized it as a gift and a blessing and tried my best to do it then.

Honesty

It wasn't until I became honest with me that I took action. To be honest with myself, I had to dig deep and decide what I wanted. I could not worry any longer about what others thought, but I had to decide what was important to me. It was important to be honest with myself and others. I allowed myself to be honest by checking in with what I was feeling at any given time.

I had not been squeaky clean. Being honest with myself was hard. At first, I was not honest because I was not ready to look at myself. I did not want to take responsibility for my experiences and was not willing to hold myself accountable.

Being honest with yourself is not easy. When you're honest with yourself, you may experience a feeling that may not be pleasant. Being honest is a process.

Having the experience of spearheading and moderating our family reunion, I learned how to be vulnerable, honest, and open to giving and receiving love. The experience allowed me to move inward. Yet, in a way it felt like I was coming out. I realized I was tentative with my family in the past. I did not get too close to anyone because I did not want to get involved in their dramas. I wanted to be connected to family, but I did not want to feel intruded upon. I realized this behavior was a large part of my resistance and feeling estranged from my family.

I recognized that I had to come clean and be truthful about how I felt about my family. I admitted I was angry because I felt ignored and abandoned by them. I had to allow myself to feel my pain. It was now time for me to be open and honest with my family about how I felt.

CHAPTER 10

Soul Stuff — A Recounting of What I've Learned

Family Relationships

There were times when I isolated myself and stayed disconnected from my own family. Immediately, fear stopped by and consumed me, and I wore a mask of secure self-sufficiency. I told myself they did not care about me and I did not matter. I continued to believe the fear-based idea that I had to go it alone.

I said I didn't like people because I didn't like me. I did not trust people because I did not trust me. I said people were mean because I saw myself as mean. I now understand that I am a mirror image of what I see in others. I bring about what I see. I came to understand that, because I felt Mom abandoned me, I abandoned myself and all my memories of any positive thoughts.

As I continued my spiritual practice, over time the restorative and corrective power of Ho'oponopono was becoming more visible in my relationship with my family.

Like the book, *The Secret*, this technique operates on the premise that we are wholly responsible for our memories, and we need to make things right with ourselves and others. I wanted to develop a better relationship with my family. It helped me to be completely honest with what I deeply felt and desired. I knew then I had to communicate my feelings wholeheartedly, not only with myself, but with others to allow my truth to flow through me into the world.

There were times when my pride became more important than my relationship with my family. Refusing support at times, I allowed my pride to get in the way.

Solitude and No Isolation

I came to understand I needed people and people needed me. I needed my family because no one can survive alone. People are social beings.

I have learned we can't do for others what we haven't done for ourselves. It is a lesson of the heart that we must first love and accept ourselves before we can love others. Don't isolate yourself. You learn through exposure and dealing with others. That is a way to receive your blessings. Come out of isolation. When you isolate yourself, you shut yourself off from the best gift you can receive, which is love from others.

Isolation is more than just being alone. If prolonged, it puts you at risk for loneliness, and it can erode your well-being. Social connections can help to end loneliness and isolation because when people connect, they affect each other.

Solitude is different from isolation. Solitude is bliss. Solitude is a great way to soothe yourself when you need the space to become centered and in alignment.

> **What social connections can you build to help to end loneliness and isolation?**

Along with love, I wanted to have compassion for myself. Compassion for myself and others gave me the ability to look at my stuff with acceptance and kindness.

Armed with compassion, I vowed to be kinder to myself. I am now able to choose more clearly and creatively how to handle whatever issues arise in my life. I believe I was teaching myself self-love, acceptance, and compassion.

Responsibility and Blame

As I continued my journey and incorporated the ancient healing problem solving tool, Ho'oponopono, I became more and more convinced that I was responsible for the world I saw and the emotions I was experiencing.

My frequent chanting of *I'm sorry* seemed weird at first because I was apologizing to me. It made me acknowledge my state and not deny what had to be done. In order to move on, I knew I had to forgive. Being steadfast in my daily practices opened my heart even more, and I became more willing to receive.

Responsibility and accountability came with knowledge. As a part of acceptance, I took responsibility for my situation.

At first it was hard to accept I had a lot to do with producing the issues and problems I experienced. It was difficult to admit something in my subconscious had caused these issues.

I continued to ask for self-forgiveness because I didn't realize and wasn't aware of the love that I *was*. It was necessary to look inward, take responsibility, and be more accountable for my emotions and experiences. By not blaming anyone, I was able to move out of the role of victim and into the role of taking responsibility for my actions.

I finally accepted that as an adult, I was solely responsible for my self-worth. Becoming aware of my uniqueness gave me a sense of my own self-worth. For the first time, I felt unconditional love for me.

I had to learn to embrace and accept myself for who I was. I had to accept myself with all of my flaws. Finally, I had to accept that I was special enough for God to choose me. I began to see myself as worthy. I did not need anyone to validate me because as a child of God and the Universe, I was born worthy.

I learned that it's okay and good to be different. It's okay to be myself. That is what makes me special. That is what makes me amazing. I now accept myself as a whole person. After I accepted myself as unconditionally lovable, I set out to move out of the mindset of fear.

The Energy of Grief

If we don't grieve properly, we can become caught in a constant flux of emotional turmoil. The emotional waves of grief can be a perpetual experience. For many years, I was caught up in the ferocious energy of grief, and from that standpoint, I created much of my adult life. That experience of grief lasted what seemed like a lifetime.

Grief is a personal experience, and we all grieve differently. My grief was tied up with my many losses. My ego played into my fear of the unknown and what was going to happen to me.

Impermanence of Death

There was one last fear I had, and it was fear of my own death. I had to release my fear of dying and come to grips with my impermanence. I had to accept the fact that death is inevitable, and I had to live with the knowledge that one day I would not be in my current form.

Talking about death was morbid, and I felt that if I talked about death, I was wishing it upon myself, yet I thought a lot about it. I saw death as a kind of punishment and not a reward. Some people look at death like it's nothing to worry about, and it'll be all right. I saw death as a finite event and never considered death as a celebration of one's life.

My resistance to accepting death began early in my life. Prior to my mother's dying, I was afraid of death because it represented an unwelcomed change. Because I accepted the many superstitious beliefs of my native island, I was caught up in the quagmire of the fear of death. I viewed death as an ending instead of a new start. Even though I knew about God, Christ, and the resurrection, I still viewed death as the end. I didn't seriously ponder the birth, life, and death cycle. I had only focused on what I thought I had lost: parents, home, family, and country.

At the Masterheart Writer's Retreat, I was told about the *Tibetan Book of Living and Dying,* by Soyal Rinpoche, and I ordered it. After reading it, I became more open to thinking about and facing death.

I know it is important to think about my own death and have mature dialogues around this subject. I now know death does not have to be seen as morbid or frightening. I now believe comfort can be found in the unknown.

Planes of Consciousness
When I met my spiritual teacher, Katye Anna, I became inspired and motivated to continue to do my Soul work. Taking her classes helped me see the importance of seriously caring for my Soul.

In class, I also learned and understood about the existence and names of different bands of angels, druids, spirit guides, ascended masters, and other metaphysical beings and objects like the Akashic records and their roles, meaning, significance, and purpose.

I recalled the time in the 80s when I received a single angel earring from a complete stranger who was exiting as I was entering a metaphysical bookstore in Brooklyn. I took the angel earring as a sign to mean that angels were with me, and I carried it in my purse for years as a reminder.

Katye Anna taught that there are many planes of consciousness within God and physical death does not end the journey of the Soul. Dying a physical death is part of the journey of the Soul. For many years, I was so angry that I did not allow myself to hold Mom's transition as comforting. I did not see it from a deeper believing that she went ahead of me and I would eventually see her again.

I did not understand that after my mother's death she was experiencing consciousness on another plane. I did not perceive death as a transition and continuation of life; I saw death as final and complete.

A few months after Mom died, she appeared in my dream for the first time. I was startled and ran away. I was afraid she would take me back with her, and I was not ready to go. She looked the same but in a glow of halo. I should have known she represented light. I was afraid to see light. I was afraid of the unknown, and the old superstitions raised their ugly heads and created a fear of seeing and communicating with someone from the spirit world.

Eventually I came to understand that even though her life on the physical plane of consciousness was gone, spiritually she was always still around.

Facing Loss and Grief

Death, dying, loss, grief, and transitions are all common and inevitable. Death is a fact of life.

When I learned that death is only the end of life as we know it in the physical form and there can be continuing communication, I began to be open to the possibility of Mom visiting me again in my dreams.

After reading *The Grief Recovery Handbook,* by John W. James and Russell Friedman, I completed a graph of my loss history and recounted the many losses that had occurred in my life. Other resources that were helpful to me in coping with grief were: *You Forever,* by T. Lobsang Rampa; *Emerging Heart: Global Spirituality and the Sacred,* by Beverly Lanzetta; *The Denial of Death,* by Ernest Becker; and *Birthing into Spirit,* by Katye Anna.

I feel proud that, as a family, we organized and implemented our first family reunion. We are currently working on our next family reunion, which will be held in Antigua in the year 2020.

Being a part of our family reunion helped me gain clarity and focus. I saw I had moved forward in communication with my family. Having come in contact with many of my nuclear, extended, and blended family members—mostly the young generation—I realized they are educated, smart, spiritual, and loving, and they, too, believe in family. I had to play full-out, expose my mistakes and weaknesses, and be vulnerable and secure. *After all, this is my family by blood. We are one,* I said in my mind.

I came to believe that love is God and family.

Forgiveness and Grace
Since childhood, I have been plagued by the fear mindset and the need for grace and forgiveness.

In her book, *The Unmistakable Touch of Grace,* Cheryl Richardson talks about the role grace plays in life. I am reminded that it was Divine grace that has brought me to this juncture in my life. I believe we are all covered by Divine grace and for nothing that we have done. We are blessed with Divine love.

I learned that forgiveness is freedom. I had to free myself from the past by forgiving myself. I forgave myself for allowing fear to keep me in hiding and for not embracing my uniqueness and speaking my own voice.

I forgave my parents. I forgave my mother. Mom brought me here, and I am grateful for the time I had with her. Today, I hold her memory in grace with love.

I have learned to draw strength from my pain through forgiveness.

When I first began repeating my prayer, *Please Forgive Me*, I believed I was asking the Divine Source for forgiveness, but I soon understood I was asking myself for forgiveness as well. Asking me to forgive myself was a new and awkward concept to embrace at first. However, I soon understood clearly that asking for forgiveness was for me as well as for others to find peace. Though I was learning to forgive myself, I still had a tinge of anger toward a family member.

In order to dispel this tinge of anger, I allowed myself to experience the angry feelings instead of denying them. I started by recalling a family member who once threatened to call immigration on me; it required multiple efforts on my part of praying at home, kneeling at the altar, crying, and asking for forgiveness to loosen the anger.

I was then willing to let go of the anger against my family member and let God handle it, for real.

I had to let go of limiting beliefs and install new empowering abundant beliefs. I gave up anger at my childhood self. I let go of blaming myself for not having a voice or being able to speak my truth.

I let go of my feelings of abandonment by my parents and family.

I let go of Mom's death. I knew Mom left because she had done her work here. It was her time to move on to another state of consciousness. Her mission continues even today in all her offspring. Her dreams are still being realized.

I let go of old languages and ways of behaving because today I am a different person. I am not who I used to be, even a year ago. Reinforcing limited beliefs undermines the person I am now.

Awakening

Letting go was also my path to awakening. Deep inside my heart, I believed I was being called by unseen forces, a greater power, to transform my life. It was an awakening within my heart that was teaching and guiding me. Such guidance was there to help me overcome the challenges I was facing in my life, so I could live without fear, stress, and worry.

By allowing my greater power to guide me, I was able to transform my obstacles into opportunities using the power of my intuition.

Surrender to Divine Will

I had been carrying a heavy load around for a long time, waiting for something to happen. I eventually had to give up and let love in. By accepting my own humanity, I opened myself to a power beyond myself because it was time to surrender to the Divine.

Surrender is an act of freedom and liberation—without need to control or take over any situation. The act of surrender recognizes the wishes of my Soul. I understand that when I let go, I allow Soul to lead. When I surrender, I put my Soul Self in charge. The moment I surrendered I was liberated. When I surrendered, I freed up space within me for Divine love to come in.

I began to integrate all the lessons and wisdom I understood from my upbringing as a youngster in the church. After I let go of control, I opened myself to a new relationship and communed with the Divine Source. As I continued to integrate my new experiences in my relationship with the Divine, I came to know Divine love as the same as the conscious awareness of the love of Christ—the same consciousness I had at Bright Light Church. Divine love was always there and accessible to me.

When I surrendered my will to God, things began to change. I asked God to lead me and let the Divine Will be my will. "Dear God, Source of all that there is," I prayed. "I'm willing to see this differently."

By surrendering control, I acknowledged I could not control my perception or experience of others nor was it my responsibility to do so. Realizing I could not control anything, I had to let go and let God handle everything.

Surrender is not weakness, nor is it giving up, but it is allowing the Universal energy to flow through you. When you are in complete surrender, you're in harmony with Source, and you feel a Oneness.

When we surrender, we accept everything exactly as it is without resistance.

Resistance

At any given time, we're either in resistance or acceptance. Acceptance is a big part of surrendering. Resistance is refusal to comply with something. Acceptance is the act of believing something, like a thought or an idea.

Resistance prevents us from taking action and usually comes from fear of the unknown, of what might happen.

Give up resistance. Simply observe your thoughts and emotions without worry.

Things I Let Go

Some of the fears and emotions I had to release included:

> *Anger*, which was underlying fear and became poisonous. If you have anger, don't try to deny it. Face your anger and let it go.

> *Self-doubt*. At times, this was incessant and held me hostage. It was easy to be held hostage because I was under the illusion that I was alone.

Defensiveness made it difficult for me to let go of the need to be right or to win because I expected everyone would then accept my point of view.

Worry is a form of resistance. By staying in the moment, I allowed what is to be and replaced my resistance with acceptance.

I gave up resistance by becoming aware of and noticing what I was afraid of. When I witnessed the feeling and accepted it without expectations, I was able to give up resistance.

To break through resistance, I had to be open and willing to change. When I became willing to change, I was open to love. By giving up resistance, love began to bubble up in my heart. That is when I decided that no longer would I allow outdated beliefs and expectations to define who I was or would be. Finally, I created positive affirmations that programmed my new beliefs.

> **What might you choose to let go of in your life?**

Wake Up

Fell asleep,
Had to wake up
A spiritual crisis,
For a while
Quite rough.

Cracked, yet not broken
Had lost my way,
A false sense of safety
Yet I constantly prayed.
Wandered quite far
Outside of the fold,
Lost my false self, but
I didn't lose my Soul.

Awake On My Spiritual Journey

While studying with my Soul work teacher, Katye Anna, I began to realize my issues went way beyond my earthly woes and had their origins somewhere in a past life. I also realized my Soul is only continuing its journey on this plane. What I have come to understand is that I have lived many lifetimes. I understand I am incarnated into a physical body, and I have a calling on my life.

My Soul had chosen these experiences for me to grow in this lifetime. Before I came here, I made agreements with others that must come to pass. Breaking these Soul contracts is not easy. I understand I'm here because my Soul requires me to be here. I am here because I am a bearer of the sacred.

I Am Soul

My Soul is a spark of Divine Source, which I call God, the creator. My Soul is the individual essence of who I am. My Soul is alive and guiding my life. My Soul is working with me in amazing and profound ways to empower me while I experience being in my own authenticity.

I have had to remember that I am a spiritual being having a human experience. As such, I am an incarnated Soul. My body is the vehicle for my Soul.

I understand that there are two points in the language of the Soul—the human emotions of love and fear. I had to decide if I were going to continue to live unconsciously in fear or consciously in love. I chose love. When I am in fear, I am not in alignment with love. When I am in fear, I am putting my trust in human power rather than in the higher power, which is God.

When I am in fear, my mind is in control, and I'm not allowing my heart to lead. My mind then has freedom to think about whatever strikes its fancy, sometimes making up stories that are not true. When fear is gone, light and love appear.

What Is Love?

Love is a deep, pleasurable feeling inside your heart. Love is expressed through the heart. It is a noun and an action word.

It is not a preposition or adjective. Love is something you do and experience, not just what you say.

Love is the most profound energy in the Universe. Love can make a Soul feel whole and complete. The highest frequency you can emit and hold is love. It is the spiritual energy that can create and shape our experiences.

Unconditional Divine Love
We all want love without conditions. I desired to love myself unconditionally. I used to put conditions on my love for myself and on others as well. *You have to be and do such and such for me to love you*, I said in my mind.

However, when I understood what love was, I was ready to open to love. I learned that love was not as complicated as I had made it out to be. I found out that love can be simple, self-explanatory, and has redemptive power. Love has no conditions, expectations, or requirements. I came to understand if I didn't learn to love myself unconditionally, I wouldn't learn to love others unconditionally either.

Unconditional love, which comes directly from God Source, opens your heart and removes judgment.

> **How can you love yourself unconditionally?**

Soul Growth
I have to be diligent and consistent because sometimes I forget that my Soul chose my life experiences for its own growth and expansion. I endeavor to remember and pray constantly for clear

sight and vision. By clarifying and aligning my message, truth, security, and connection with my Soul, fear continues to lessen.

At this stage in my life, I have chosen to stand up, rise up, and embrace all of who I am. Grace gave me exactly what I needed, when I needed it. I am allowing ease, flexibility, and grace to flow through me.

Being consistent with my spiritual practices, I have noticed an expansion in my overall awareness. Spiritual practices are about discovering, probing, and looking inside to reveal and embrace the real person.

At this time, my spiritual practice consists of:
- Mindfulness to help keep me aware of my thoughts
- Daily, guided meditations
- Reciting affirmations, which help calm my mind
- Ho'oponopono to help with forgiveness
- Fasting and abstaining from solid food once a month to help detox and cleanse my body
- Prayers, which have shifted from asking to gratitude and praise

As a child, I had a religious foundation that taught me God would give me miracles along the way. These miracles were provided for me to fully embrace faith. The Divine Spirit of God kept me going. People and my angels guided me along the way until I was able to stand on my own.

All the time I was complaining about how things were not perfect in my life, I was being groomed by God. I now know that every experience I've had in this lifetime here on earth was designed by the Creator, for me to learn. These experiences didn't happen *to* me, but *for* me. They were not stumbling blocks, but stepping-stones. These experiences happened for my greater good.

I began thanking God for being my partner in creating my life. The more things I was grateful for, the more present I became. I am grateful because I get to practice being and living from my heart. I am grateful because instead of living in fear, I have learned how to act out of faith, hope, and love.

Steps to Move From Fear to Faith and Love
1. Release anger and doubt
2. Forgive yourself and others
3. Dispel judgments and criticisms
4. Let go of guilt, shame, and control
5. Learn compassion for self and others

It was not until I found love for myself that I began to release fear. When I opened my heart, I began to release the fears and doubts that held me back. I had to release that which was not in alignment with love. I released any fear that kept me from being in my power. After releasing fear, I allowed myself to love and trust others.

Today, I allow love, joy, and happiness to flow from my heart because all the answers I seek are already there. I have learned love has no bounds. Before, my heart was filled with sorrow, sadness, anger, and shame; now, I am open to giving and receiving love.

Opening My Heart

It is important to open our heart because the Soul speaks to us through the heart. The heart is a portal or pathway for the Soul to shine through. Opening my heart meant I had to be in a state of love. When I embraced love for myself, my heart opened.

When I opened the door to my heart, love became accessible to me.

When I opened my heart, I allowed myself to feel.

When I entered the depths of my heart, I found my love inside. This love was *me*.

When I opened my heart, I chose love.

When I opened my heart, I allowed myself to refocus on my conscious awareness.

When I opened my heart, I allowed my mind to quiet and let go of the pressure and pain.

When I allowed my heart to open, I allowed Divine light to enter in, and it opened the channels of connection to my Soul. Then I was able to use my inner knowing to guide my life.

When I opened my heart, I connected with my Soul to clearly know my direction. With clarity, I could discern which way to go.

For too long, I hid my light under a bushel. I was afraid to shine my light because I believed people might not be pleased. Yet, I believed this light within me was Divine. I believe the light within *you* is Divine.

When I opened my heart, I connected with and allowed myself to merge with the full light within. The light in my heart is like a lantern, guiding me in the right direction.

Discovery Process
Opening my heart was a process of self-discovery. Through this discovery process I learned to come into awareness of the real purpose of my Soul and to become a conscious thinker. I found the tools to live a purpose driven life.

By opening my heart, I helped others and emanated my light with whomever I encountered as well as people whom I had not yet met through a ripple effect.

By consistently working on myself, I changed the negative vibration to love vibration. Over time, in my mind, I shifted from anger, comparison, competition, jealousy, and judgment into connection, support, and trust through personal accountability and self-love. Love for myself brings about alignment with my Soul, which brings about healing.

When your heart is open, you can raise your vibration to feel self-love too. Self-love leads to alignment. To align means to bring that which is scattered into order. When you align with your inner power, you will feel whole and fulfilled. To move into alignment, you must turn your desires into beliefs, making sure your actions are in alignment with your heart.

While working with Katye Anna, I discovered I needed a Soul alignment. I accepted it was safe to align my will with Divine Will. My misalignment had to do with my thinking

SOUL STUFF—A RECOUNTING OF WHAT I'VE LEARNED

everyone else was more important than me and being ashamed to use my voice, though I was bursting inside to speak.

I realized I needed to stop modeling others and discover what was right for me. I had to rid myself of the heavy energy of depression. When I stopped criticizing and judging myself, I was able to change my vibration and have better control over the circumstances in my life. When I focused on feeling good enough, I enjoyed vibrating on a higher level.

We all are energy. Everything is energy. Everything is vibration and frequency. If our energy is split or unfocused, we are out of alignment and we lose power. I am familiar with feeling scattered, unfocused, tossed about, and out of balance. If we are out of balance, we are not in harmony with oneness.

Alignment is a state of expansion, an emotional state that feels good. If you raise your vibration, you will feel good.

We all want to feel and experience the vibration of love. Love comes from Divine energy. When we vibrate at a high level, we can express Divine Love for ourselves. Self-love is to know our purpose and have the confidence to be our authentic selves. When we love ourselves, we are in alignment with our Soul's purpose.

We are here to share and experience love for ourselves as well as others. Love can be expressed in many different ways. I believe we're all seeking the feeling of love in our hearts. Divine self-love is about being in alignment. When we're in alignment, we experience the energy of love.

Getting what you want is about alignment because when you're aligned, you become an energetic match to what you want. Being in alignment is law of attraction in action. When you're in alignment, you're less afraid to change, and you see every opportunity as a chance for growth.

Breakthrough Message of Love

Even though I received the message at Breakthrough, I didn't know how to open my heart. At that time, I was still having trust issues and not totally believing in myself. Somehow, I confused the message with the messenger. Messages get lost. The Breakthrough message to open my heart came directly from love itself. I came to understand that the deeper message was to embrace the quest of my unfolding into who I am meant to be.

It was not until I allowed love back into my heart that I began to feel better and trust again. Things began to shift. I embraced love for myself and vowed to treat myself better. I committed to send messages about love to myself. *I love you*, I whispered to me.

Human Condition and Empathy

Because I believed that empathy and compassion were keys to transforming my life, I wanted to show empathy for the human condition. As humans, we can be hard on ourselves. We must remember that we all make mistakes. I have always been very hard on myself and often blamed myself for mistakes or failures. As I was told at Breakthrough in 2014, I came to see my experiences were not failures or mistakes, but lessons to help me become who I am supposed to be.

Loving Me

Because I was looking at myself through human eyes, I could not see the whole of who I was. It was not until I began to see myself through the eyes of my Soul that I was able to love myself unconditionally. Unconditional love is Divine.

Seeking to know, understand, believe, embrace, and love me started my letting go of shame. By letting go of the negative, sad story I was telling myself, I began to realize that I was more than I could imagine, and with that awareness, I moved more into alignment.

By letting go of the things that no longer served me, I discovered who I was. When I understood who I was, I fell in love with me. That was when I became free from the illusion of fear and separation. When I allowed myself to be me, and moved out of my own way, I began to trust and not just survive, but thrive.

All the answers I was looking for were always, and still are, in my heart. It's about finding love for me. To me, love means living each moment from a consciousness of oneness. I believe that Soul creates only love.

Why I Am Here

I am love and have always been loved. I cannot avoid being infinitely loveable because God is love. I am made of Love. I am here to share my love. This is why I'm here. I am here to love. I am here to love first myself then extend my love to others through the overflow of the love within me.

Love is expressed through the heart. When my heart opened, I allowed myself to give and receive love. I now show and share my love, not only in my smile, but in my hugs, gestures, and by saying, "I love you."

Love is sharing Divine energy. Love has no end. Love has no bounds. Once I understood what love was, I fell in love with me.

I believe it's in loving ourselves we can have peace and joy. Love for ourselves is the power that heals us. Self-love nourishes our bodies, minds, and souls. Self-love is aligning our actions with the urging of our souls.

Your Soul wants to empower you to love yourself and give you the life of joy, peace, and happiness you want. Your Soul wants only good for you. Your Soul is waiting to heal all the stress and trauma in your body on a cellular level if you will empower and trust Soul to lead and direct your path.

Human Condition

The human condition has been at the forefront of my mind these days. As humans, we are all afflicted with human frailty, and to make a shift in consciousness is to remember that we are Spirit.

We humans all have the Divine spark of love within us. All of humanity is an expression of Divine God. You can see God in everything—in people, in service, in negative behavior, and even haters.

Until recently, I could not imagine making such a shift in my consciousness. Instead of berating, judging, and criticizing, I now accept and meet myself and others with patience, kindness, and compassion.

Clear Vision

Eventually, I realized that my gift of the transparent heart pendant served as a symbol to remind me my heart was filled with love and I was to seek this clear heart. Clear vision would allow me to open my mind, heart, and eyes.

Having searched for a long time, I came to realize I was looking for something that was there all the time. I was seeking the essence of *me* because I was not in alignment.

Now in harmony, I choose to seek clarity. This clarity comes from alignment. When I'm in alignment, the emotions I feel are love, joy, and fun. When I'm out of alignment, I feel dislike for others, sadness, and boredom. When I align my head with my heart, I experience the resonance of all that I am. When I am in harmony with oneness, I experience my Divinity.

When you're aligned, you will have clarity. Clarity is freedom. Feel the sensation of being in alignment. When in alignment, you will feel your oneness with the Creator of all things and the frequency of love and light that abounds within you.

Gratitude Awakening

My gratitude has been awakened. I am grateful for all the blessings in my life. I am grateful for every bit of experience that I've had. There are so many things I am grateful for: my life, health, strength, and the activities of my limbs.

I've also chosen to be grateful and thankful for the possibilities and choices and for the abundance that allows me to choose what foods I like.

I'm also grateful for all the experiences that flow into my life and for the people who enrich my experiences.

I am grateful I had aspirations of achieving my dreams and goals. I am grateful I was able to maintain hope in the midst of despair to achieve my dreams.

I appreciate all my successes. I saw clearly that success meant achieving my dreams and goals. By appreciating what I already have, I send a message to the Universe that I want more of this blessing. Feeling grateful changed my vibration. The more gratitude I expressed and offered, the more present I became.

It is important that you sincerely appreciate what you already have. The spiritual practice of gratitude is one of the single best ways to instantly change your vibration. Feeling good is a vibration, and when I feel good, I endeavor to sustain the good feelings as long as I can. You, too, can revel in your good feelings.

Give thanks. Living in a state of gratitude, I am able to constantly raise my vibration. I usually begin with saying the word, *Thanks*. Consistently repeating *Thank you* made me more grateful for my existence as I know it.

Instead of complaining, criticizing, or judging myself, I began to feel grateful for the opportunity to share any wisdom that came through me. Today, I thank God for being my partner in creating my life.

A benefit of being grateful is that our brains can be trained to look for what is going right instead of problems to solve. There are many people today who are bitter and constantly complaining about what is not going well in their lives. They don't yet understand when they focus on the negative, nothing positive can result from it.

The key is to focus on what you already have and be grateful for it. This is a better strategy to help you cultivate and live in a state of gratitude.

Everyone, including you, can find something to be grateful for. For one thing, you are breathing the breath of life. You are alive. Yes, there might be some challenges that your Soul chose for you to experience, so that Soul can experience manifestation on the earth plane. Soul wants you, as a human person, to learn something about grace and gratitude. It is Soul that gifted you the amazing grace to breathe every single second of the day.

You, too, have a lot to be grateful for. Starting a gratitude journal is a great way of cultivating gratitude.

Seven Gratitude Tips

1. When you get up in the morning, give thanks.
2. Write in your gratitude journal.
3. Share your gifts with others–i.e., smile, kindness.
4. Eat well and give thanks for the meal.
5. Laugh out loud at least three times a day.
6. Give thanks for the end of the day.
7. Carry a gratitude rock to remind you to be grateful.

What are you grateful for today?

The Power of Thoughts

Think of good things. When I'm centered and thinking of what is good, loving, and pure, I'm without fear and can't be influenced by my negative thoughts nor the negative thoughts of others. When I think good thoughts, I love myself.

It felt as though my perception was changing because I believed love and light were being activated within me. I noticed a change in my thought patterns. I was now seeing things differently than I once did. Over time, I came to understand most of the feelings of neglect and abandonment, sadness, and grief I entertained were the fear-based beliefs I harbored in my head.

The belief that I had no support and was without love was not the truth. This way of thinking only augmented the fear-based thoughts of abandonment in my head. I came to realize most of the emotions I entertained were also an illusion. There were people who always loved and supported me. I had support that I was not taking advantage of.

Over the years my attitude changed. I now have a new attitude. My beliefs are now based on love and not fear. I came to know that my sex, age, or income did not define me. I came to know that I am as worthy of receiving love as I am of giving love. I also noted that despair, confusion, lack of confidence, and self-worth were some of the old methods that didn't work anymore.

After finding love for myself and others, my heart opened to a deeper relationship with myself and the Divine. It happened when I began to believe in myself again. I began looking at all I had accomplished. I suddenly saw myself as more valuable.

Love-Based Thoughts
My life is proof that thoughts can become real. I've come to realize I am the creative force in my life, and my thoughts create my reality. I accepted I can only control my own thoughts, feelings, and perceptions. Therefore, I chose to ditch negative thinking, turn negative thoughts around, and replace them with gratitude. I am grateful because I get to practice being and living from my heart.

When your mind and heart are fully open, you begin to feel joy, wonder, recognized, and grateful. Negative thoughts reside in your subconscious, and your Soul knows what they are. The instant you recognize the negative thoughts, the Divine stands ready to replace them with positive thoughts.

For example, I thought I was not proficient in mathematics. I knew basically how to count, but underneath I didn't think I was smart, worthy, or good enough to learn it. This negative and limited way of thinking hampered my desire to be more proficient in this subject.

Ridding Negative Thought Patterns
Here are some techniques that helped me to recognize and breakthrough those blocks to catch, flip, and let go of non-productive thoughts that arose. Some of the things I had to let go of included my negative thoughts and patterns.

I began to transpose negative thoughts to more positive statements. For example, see the negative statements below and note the transposed positive thoughts in the second column.

Negative Thoughts and Patterns to Let Go	Positive Thoughts and Patterns
• I don't speak well enough.	• I am clear and express myself well.
• I am not good enough.	• I am more than good enough.
• I am not smart enough.	• I am intelligent and full of divine wisdom.
• People will think I don't know what I'm talking about.	• People express how knowledgeable and powerful I am.
• No one wants to hear what I have to say.	• Everyone loves listening to me.
• I am doubtful and afraid.	• I am brave and courageous.

Before I could change my negative thoughts, I had to acknowledge, based on my psychosocial and core story, that these negative patterns and negative elements colored my self-image. These habits were not easy to give up because they constituted the known and familiar. For me, they were security.

Some of the forces that blocked my growth included stagnation, excuses, blaming others, procrastination, and resistance. I always sabotaged myself and did not allow myself to be me, but when I allowed myself to be me and moved out of my way, I felt more in the flow of my life.

Don't give credence to negative thoughts. Instead, be willing to explore why you are having those negative and fearful thoughts. Thoughts like resenting, judging, criticizing, blaming others, and not loving yourself are self-limiting beliefs. These thoughts can be changed.

Reading the book, *Zero Limits: The Secret Hawaiian System for Health, Wealth, Peace, and More* by Joe Vitale and Ihaleakala Hew Len, deepened my understanding of the Ho'oponopono healing system and how it relates to limiting oneself. The technique helped rid my mind of the past, outdated beliefs and memories that held me back.

I had to let go of limiting beliefs and install new empowering beliefs to be used as a clearing tool. Ho'oponopono helped me to consider the possibility that in the past I may have absorbed the negative programming of others. Practicing this clearing technique helped me find clarity to forgive myself and others and move on.

Clearing and freeing my mind is a continuous process. Adding the forgiveness exercise to my daily spiritual practices had a profound impact and helped me to open myself to love.

We all know that thoughts are things. They originate from our emotions, which are built from life experiences. Our thoughts are our memory. Thoughts and emotions can affect us on many levels. If you look at the core of a thought, you may find it does not have power over you and may not apply to you anymore.

Create Your Life

I have come to know that my choices can dictate the outcome of the circumstances in my life. I now see how I created my own resistance and upset.

I learned that with hope, faith, and hard work you can be empowered to create the life you want. It is your choice to be the creative force in your life. Ridding yourself of the inhibiting, internal blocks that stop you is also a matter of choice. Blocks are made up of outdated beliefs that impede your movements or evolvement. Though it may seem like the world is not in your corner, don't marginalize yourself and aid in retarding your growth. You too, can take charge and turn your challenges and struggles into triumphs. You can transform your life.

You must be open and willing to change. Willingness means to take a chance on yourself and to allow for ideas or thoughts that might be helpful to you. It means opening up and creating the space inside you to grow.

Often, the old, outdated beliefs will revisit the new changes taking place, which could create emotional upheaval that will need to be managed. This will be a valuable time to explore what you're feeling.

Change is a matter of choice. You have within you the power to change. *You have it all.*

Ego and I

Ego, how quickly you entrapped me
You had me under your control,
Leaving me little room to escape
I've become a bumbling fool.

Ego, so easily you tricked me
Robbed me of good fortune and luck

SOUL STUFF—A RECOUNTING OF WHAT I'VE LEARNED

I didn't know the power of my mind
And you kept me small and stuck.

Ego, you took my negative emotions
My doubts, sadness, and my pain
Caused a tug of war between us
I was caught in a cycle of blame.

Ego, in my mind I've felt confused
Misused, refused, and rejected,
Criticized, objected, disconnected,
And, of course, disrespected.

Ego, you had me believing in a
False sense of self deep like a well,
Addicted to compulsive thinking
Rooted deeply under your spell.

Ego, you are not the whole of me
You're a smaller version of me
I am more than my mind,
Emotions, and physical body.

Ego, you took all of me for granted
You refused to let me live free, but
You're not my equal nor on my terms
I am stronger than you could ever be

UNDOCUMENTED

Ego, a lot of stuff was in my head
Where you and fear reside
In a space not made for battle
Where you and my spirit collide.

Ego, you are the culprit of my worries
The catalyst of insecurity and shame
You are the root of my sufferings
My true self you tried to replace.

Ego, I choose to take back my life,
You no longer rent space in my head
Not even a solitary moment of dread
I choose love for my life instead.

Ego, just as I created you
I can easily rid and let you go
I will only now deny you
You no longer run my show.

Ego, I aspire to a calling
Of the highest version of me
I no longer need a blanket or
A sense of fake security.

Ego, you've served me well
From a time not so long ago
I've taken back my power
To let divine inspiration flow.

Ego, I'm integrated and calibrated,
reinforced with forgiveness and grace,
I am finally happy and free
and you have been replaced.

My only sin was forgetting
To remember who I use to be
Without fury, fuss or having a row;
Armed with grace and mercy
Ego and I are best friends now.

Using the creative power of my mind
I allow my highest self to shine,
The self I choose to run my show
Is both human and divine.

Attuned with love, truth, and faith
I'm free of your control,
In every moment of unfolding
I speak the language of my Soul.

Illusion and Fear

Fear, a condition of the mind, is a choice. The *Cambridge English Dictionary* defines fear as "a strong emotion caused by great worry about something dangerous, painful, or unknown that is happening or might happen."

For many years, I swam in the emotion of the illusion of fear. Drowning in pools of emotions, fear was in control, and I was under its spell. I came to see clearly that fearing anything gives it energy and keeps it present in your life.

Recalling the teachings of Dr. Linda James Meyers and being inspired by her work and perspective of the world, her book, *Understanding an Afrocentric World View: Introduction to an Optimal Psychology,* shaped my world view and helped transform my thinking. This book helped me share my perspective and gave me a different base for increasing my self-knowledge. I came to understand that my fear, guilt, anger, anxiety, resistance, ignorance, and frustration were due to my lack of self-knowledge.

According to Dr. Meyers, negativity and fear are temporary illusions that can be dispelled with greater knowledge of self. I saw how many of my choices came from fear, and sometimes it was from unconscious fear. When I understood that fear was also a choice, I made a conscious decision to release fear and focus on love, acceptance, faith, and hope. I acted out of hope instead of living in fear.

I chose to no longer focus on the illusions that created my fear. I know now that it was my ego, not the real me, who was unvoiced. I have come to know the difference between my ego and Divine inspiration. By my faith in God, the Divine Source and His grace, my Soul tells me all I need to know.

As I learned more about myself, I began to feel more confident. Confidence comes from knowledge. Knowledge comes from the presence of God.

I have learned that confidence is empowered by taking action, and unless I act, there will be no satisfaction. I believed it was my confidence that kept me holding onto my faith.

The journey is all about discovering, uncovering, and embracing your divinity, which leads to peace. In the midst of despair, I kept hope alive. I held onto hope that I would achieve my dreams and goals, and for the most part, I have.

I dared to visualize and dream of having a comfortable, joyful life and to live that life with determination and strength.

Let Go and Conquer Fear
It is only when we conquer our fears that we can begin to live and practice the power of letting go. I had to let go on route to my freedom. Letting go of grief and fears was a choice I made so I could embrace my freedom. I saw how these fear-based beliefs and illusions kept me enslaved in my mind. I eventually understood that to let go meant letting go of who I used to be and embracing who I was becoming.

Letting go is the opposite of trying to make something happen. So, when feelings of fear come up now, I stand up and face the fears by acknowledging them, then I let them go. Every time I let go, I open my heart to receive the blessings that were blocked when I could not see. Now, I clearly see it was God's favor and mercy that brought me to this point in my life. God's Grace led me to where I needed to be at the right time. I now understand that all those sad, traumatic events that happened to me were evidence of God's grace coming into my life.

Letting go allows grace to come into consciousness. Once you let go, it's like you're lying back and resting in the process, knowing that a higher power has your back. Letting go allowed me to heal myself.

As an undocumented black immigrant, there were times I felt powerless, as if I had no human rights. I felt I didn't belong in America, and in every which way, unspoken and otherwise, I felt invisible and unvoiced. Every day, I heard and felt the unspoken invisibility words, like *alien* and *garrot*, pop their heads up everywhere.

I gave away my power by marginalizing myself. I marginalized myself by hiding and living in fear, anger, and frustration, as well as avoiding connections with my family. By marginalizing myself, I created paranoia, anxiety, mistrust, resentfulness, and self-loathing. The many years of fear and worry, compounded with PTSD syndrome, kept me sad and unhappy.

I gave my negative thoughts, emotions, and energy too much power. I felt powerless. I became my own victim in spirit. I created it all. It was my own creation. I allowed it to happen. Though I was cracked, I was not broken, and I still wanted to feel free and be at peace.

Gradually, I became more aware of how I had given my power away. I spent so many years focusing on getting rid of the fear, and the only thing that showed up was more fear because I concentrated on what I did not want, to not be afraid.

Having watched *The Secret* (Prime Time Productions, 2006), I learned we bring about what we think about. I became more aware of how my thoughts were making me feel. I did not feel good.

Since my entrance to America, I've had to hold onto my belief systems. Though I had strong faith and believed that everything would always work out for my greater good, there were many times when things got really hard and my faith waned, but I learned those were the times when I should hold onto my faith strongly.

I found power in rediscovering my own voice and that no one had the power to shatter my dreams. I had to embrace my uniqueness and the ways I was different from others. Then I came to know that to be different is golden.

Creating Reality

Knowing we can use the power of our mind to visualize and create what we want, we're free to make our own choices to create our own fate. It took a long time for me to realize that in order for me to have a peaceful life in America, I needed to change my perspective about the acculturation process.

Success

Ultimately, I came to understand that success is living life to its fullest and embracing my joy and happiness. Happiness, I concluded, is a state of mind.

The secret to happiness is to know that no matter what the condition is, there's always a solution. I've lived long enough now to know that happiness is a continuum. Happiness is to know who I am on a deeper level. Happiness is a choice.

Finding happiness also took courage. I learned that courage is a sort of endurance of the Soul. I developed courage, which comes from the core of my heart, to stand in my authority. I found courage and trusted God to help me through the pain of events in my life.

Family and Communication

The most important, intimate, and loving relationship begins with me. Before I could love anyone, including my family, I had to first find love for myself.

I love you; I love you, I whispered under my breath as often as I thought about these words.

Reflecting on the phrase, *I love you,* transformed my awareness and expanded my understanding of love for me and the Divine Source within me. When I think this phrase, I feel more aware of my inner emotions and know that I am loved.

I have come to know the importance of family support. For many years, I did not talk to my sister because she said she would put immigration on me. So much time was lost. Eventually we made up, and we've been like two peas in a pod ever since.

Over the years, Third Sister and I have become closer. More than anything, we have developed a loving friendship that we could not have imagined. The level of respect we both wanted is very present in our communication.

I learned that communication is simply talking back and forth. The key is listening. I am learning to talk less and listen more. Though I prided myself as a good listener in the work environment, I had to admit I needed to improve my psychosocial skills on a personal level. In the past, I was so busy thinking about what my response would be that I did not hear what another person was saying. My ego fooled me into believing I was listening. I began to hear better when I was being quiet and still enough to listen to what was being said. Listening, I came to understand, is a virtue.

Recently, my oldest sister and I were talking about our mother's dream.

"She had the insight and forethought to get us all out of the neighborhood, out of there early," my sister reminisced.

"She was a wise woman, way ahead of her time," I agreed.

"It was her dream that we would all have better opportunities than she had," she continued. "What Mom did was a success because we all got out of the neighborhood."

"Yeah, we made it out," I smiled.

"Our mother was a phenomenal black woman. She was an artist in her own right, and baking was her art," she said proudly.

"Dad, too, was an artist," I agreed.

"We came from creative parents," she continued.

For a moment, my mind wandered to the thought that we all have personal power to create and be our own artist. We all have the creative source within. "Indeed," I said.

"We are a creative people," we said in unison. We hugged.

The thought of Mom no longer makes me feel sad. Thinking of Mom brings a smile to my face. I believe I have reached another milestone in my life because I have embraced Mom.

I have come to believe love is God and family, whether extended or biological. I now see the importance of opening myself to the love of my family. I feel loved by everyone, and I feel their concern for my well-being. My family showed up in my world because I allowed them in. It felt as though I had found my home. I now know that my family is my family for the remainder of my life and theirs. The lines of communication are more open among my siblings since our family reunion in 2016. It feels good to care about others, and it's rewarding to share and show family love.

Intuition

Over time, I found out that trust requires me to follow my heart and let the Universe take care of the rest. I had to let go of self-limiting beliefs. I had to be willing to let someone in. Therefore, I began to trust what I felt and act on it.

My intuition comes from inside my heart. My Soul speaks to me through my feelings. The download I received at IIN in 2006 from God was to *create whole,* and I kept it in my heart. My intuition was increasing as God was speaking knowledge and wisdom into my consciousness.

My intuition was providing me inspiration to move forward toward my own creative gifts. I am more in tune with my intuitive feelings and know I am going to be okay if I just follow my heart and let the Universe take care of the rest. I understand my intuition is the voice of my Soul. Intuition is direct guidance from my Soul. Intuition is my deep inner knowing, my inner compass. We all have this intuitive spark inside us.

Trust what you feel and act on it without doubt. You must remember you are Spirit, and you must be open to listening to and trusting your intuition.

Patience

Patience is usually followed by trust. I had to trust God; I had to trust the Divine Source and not allow myself to be pulled into victim energy and impatience.

You need patience to exercise faith because things manifest in their own Divine timing and not always in our timing. You must believe in the bigger picture and trust the outcome.

I spent many years being impatient, wanting to know everything at once and to be there *now*. It took almost my lifetime to realize there is no *there* to get to, and I need to be in the here and now.

Life is a process of creation. My job is to create, unfold forward, and have a joyful time being with people I love. Growing older has taught me not knowing all the answers was actually a good thing that allowed faith to hold space for me, while being patient and following the intuition from my heart and Soul.

Intuition is not a thinking energy. It is a feeling, sensing, hearing, and knowing energy.

Be open to your intuition. Trust what you feel. We often get the information from within but don't trust what we hear. Trust, act on it, and don't doubt.

> **In what areas of your life can you exercise more patience?**

Power of Words

Gradually, I came to accept and embrace the power of my words as expressed in my poetry and journaling. Over time, I decided to use the power of words to better communicate with others. I was not able to express my thoughts and feelings easily. As a youngster, I didn't have the confidence to speak freely for fear I'd be rejected or diminished. Fear kept me silent.

Being silent no more is about courage to be my authentic self.

I had to come to the understanding that words have power and using my authentic voice would enable me to create the life of my desires. I began to use my words more openly without fear of being judged, criticized or reprimanded by others. The more I spoke with my true authentic voice, the more confident I became and less apprehensive about taking up space. In learning to use my authentic voice, I had to implement using diplomacy because I wanted my words to be non-threatening, comforting and healing to others.

Your words have power. You can believe in the power of your words. With the power of faith, you can speak and visualize into existence what your heart desires.

Spoken Word

We've all heard the old saying, *Sticks and stones may break my bones, but words will never hurt me,* but words are powerful and they can hurt.

Spoken words have the power to bless, harm, and uplift. The words you speak are energetic.

In his book, *The Four Agreements: A Practical Guide to Personal Freedom (A Toltec Wisdom Book),* Don Miguel Ruiz points out we must be impeccable with our words. With our words we can love, hate, create, and communicate with each other and to the masses. When words are spoken, they can show love, kindness, or displeasure.

My Spoken Words
In addition to meditation, I began listening to affirmations written by others and decided to write my own spoken word affirmations and poetry.

Being mindful of the words I used to describe myself helped me personalize my affirmations. I did not want to use words like: *Things are hard, Life is a struggle,* or *You can't make it,* which were past habitual ways I sabotaged myself.

I began to write, create, and memorize positive affirmations that became my mantras. I spoke and sang them daily to reprogram my mind and create a new way of being.

When I share my story with people, they want to know how I made it in America. People want to know how to do it.

"You bring so much light and energy," they comment. "How do we bottle your essence?" "Give me some of that," they joke.

Here are the action steps I took to find my way:
1. I had hope.
2. I had faith in God.
3. I joined a church.
4. I went to school.
5. I became a civil servant as a social worker.
6. I wrote in my journal.
7. I went to therapy.
8. I began a spiritual practice.
9. I became an entrepreneur.
10. I continued to serve others.

Affirmation Exercises

Today I use affirmations for releasing and healing any self-limiting thoughts and beliefs that I have. Speaking affirmations helps me to stay clear about my intentions, which are to have a sense of fearless courage, inner strength, and the power to conquer any challenges I am facing.

I know my Soul wants me to succeed in whatever I do for the greater good.

The practice of affirmations helps me to be doubtless, to believe more, to be clear, to have clean thoughts, and to connect with my heart and Soul, which allows me to let go, release fear, and awaken to the power of the amazing God Source inside me. I have accomplished a state that has brought me the benefit of clarity and well-being.

Here are some of my personal spoken words and affirmations.

Spoken Words for Self-Love/Acceptance

I love myself.
I trust myself.
I forgive myself.
I believe in myself.
I accept myself.
I appreciate myself.
I empower myself.
I deserve happiness.
I think good thoughts.

Spoken Words for Courage/Confidence

I believe and trust myself.
I open myself to others.
I speak in my authentic voice.
I create my experiences.
I allow myself to be seen.
I am a spiritual warrior.
I am confident in every area of my life.
I am courageous.
I rock.

Fearless Affirmations

I am courageous and stand up for myself.
I am a spark of the Source of all abundance.
I am powerful and unstoppable.
I am a fear conqueror.
I am valuable and worthy.
I speak my truth.
I am proud to be uniquely me.
I motivate myself.
I inspire myself and others.

Spoken Words for Self-Praise

I am smart.
I am bold.
I am successful.

I am whole.
I am clear.
I am being myself.
I am authentic.
I am able.
I am love.
I am conscious.
I am forgiving.
I am present.
I am secure.
I am mindful.
I am self-assured.
I am accomplished.
I am great.
I am focused.

Affirmations for Self-Love/Respect
I am proud of being uniquely me.
I have positive regard and respect for myself.
I am ethical and honest.
I am worthy and valuable.
I am strong and powerful.
I matter.
I am more than good enough.
I love myself, bunches.

Affirmations for Abundance

I am healthy, wealthy, and wise.
I am limitless.
I am successful.
I am making all the right decisions.
All that I need is inside me.
I have everything in abundance.
I am accomplished.
I am prosperous.

Spoken Words for Health/Wellness

My body is healthy.
I prioritize my wellness.
I am strong.
I am aware.
I release all my fears.
I accept the things I cannot change.
I feel supported.
I think good thoughts.
I am more than my thoughts and emotions.
I move with grace, confidence, and ease.

Spoken Words for Well-Being

I am blissfully blessed.
I am pure consciousness.
I am love and light.

I am holy and eternal.
I am Soul, incarnate.
I am guided by my Soul.
I am one with the divine.
I am an awakening spirit.
I am witnessing presence.

Spoken Words for Gratitude
I am grateful for my family and friends.
I am grateful I have a caring heart.
I am grateful I am guided by my Soul.
I am grateful I am clear and intuitive.
I am grateful I have all that I need inside me.
I am grateful for my life's lessons.
I am grateful I have peace of mind.
I am grateful I am in harmony and complete.
Thank you, thank you, and thank you.

> **What positive affirmation can you write to recite daily?**

Beauty and Goodness in America
It is sometimes good to take time to reflect on your life. Reflecting over the years since my hopeful entrance into the States, I have seen how the Universe is always on my side.

The opportunity of coming to America gave me the chance to get an education, which I appreciate and value highly because there are parts of the world where women and girls don't have rights to an education. My education has given me the ability to grow as an individual and a professional.

Cultural Pride

As a Caribbean woman, I knew how to survive, and I came to America in pursuit of my goals. There's a certain pride the Caribbean woman exudes that I wanted to maintain. It was not grandstanding nor boasting but basking in my right to exist.

I learned my pride from my parents. We were taught as a family to be proud. My mother's influence propelled me to set high standards for myself.

When I look at what I have accomplished in America, I am proud and grateful for the blessings.

African Queen

In 2017, I completed my heritage DNA test, and learned I am over 90 percent African from the Bantu tribe. I am a queen, born into freedom. My ancestors were taken from our homeland in Africa, brought oversees, and landed on the island of Antigua. Becoming aware of my uniqueness gave me a sense of my own self-worth.

As an African, Caribbean, American woman, I have freedom to pursue my dreams. Now, you can see the pride in my eyes and the happiness and joy on my face. I now see it when I look in the mirror.

America is unique in the history of humankind. There is no place like America. The American dream is still alive, and the sky is still the limit to dream.

Stillness

Be still and know that I am God.
—Psalm 46:10, KJV

During times of stillness, I stop to reflect on how I came to love and accept myself. I came to love myself when I learned I was responsible for my own well-being, the importance of taking care of and putting myself as a priority, and to be more selfish in a healthy wholesome way so as not to be selfless. When I began reciting positive affirmations, it resulted in my seeing more of my own worth, beauty, and in my liking *me*. I realized it was my responsibility to love myself.

The road to loving me was hard. First, I began by releasing what I thought I knew about love. I needed to come into the understanding of what love was and was not for me. Somehow, I convinced myself that love was conditional. I had to be willing to change my way of seeing things, know my value, and embrace my divinity. I had to be willing to allow my life to be transformed.

I believe that in order to hear you must be still, because it is in the stillness we hear the message. God speaks through stillness. Stillness is being silent. It is being alert and aware of each present moment.

I carved out quiet time to hear the inner voice for guidance. That inner voice, I call the Divine God Source. Silence is the language through which God Source speaks. When I take the time to be still, I realize how blessed I am to be here in this moment.

You hear better when you are still. When you allow quietness

SOUL STUFF—A RECOUNTING OF WHAT I'VE LEARNED

in your spirit, you can hear the calm voice within. In the quiet stillness, your energy can meet with the energy of the Divine.

The spiritual practice of meditation allows God to speak to me in silence. God's response manifests in my intuition, which guides me when I trust what I hear. In meditation, I spend time with myself to know my needs, strengths, and weaknesses so I can keep myself in harmony with my Soul's calling. After meditation, I experience an alert and spacious calmness. It is my way to tap into my divinity.

The valuable practice of mindfulness enhanced my awareness of the present moment. Mindfulness heightened my awareness and helped me tune into my feelings. Mindfulness also helped calm my mind, refocused my thinking, and replaced those bad habits of negative thoughts with positive uplifting thoughts about myself and others.

The spiritual practice of mindfulness helped me cultivate awareness of my breath, thoughts, feelings, and other aspects of my life experiences. Mindfulness reduced my symptoms of anxiety, sadness, pain, and feeling detached from everyone. Mindfulness helped me create a state of non-judgmental awareness of myself.

Everything I was seeking: love, joy, peace, harmony, and truth required the capacity of being in the present moment.

My practice of poetry writing allowed me to practice trusting God with my thoughts and to listen for the Divine guidance that always came.

> **How can you become more mindful?**

Counseling

Going to therapy was my saving grace. I sought counseling when I needed clarity in my endeavors.

As I went about my journey and found weaknesses or lack of confidence, I sought remedies, such as going to counseling, reading self-help materials, eating well, and associating with people who were aspiring for joy and happiness in their life.

Spiritual practice is about discovering, probing, and looking inside to reveal and embrace the real you. I found God the Divine Source within me, and I held on for dear life.

Utilizing spiritual practices such as mindfulness, prayer, meditation, being compassionate, and listening, I learned how to stay centered in my authentic self and discovered it was possible to transform my fears into awareness and love.

Laughter Yoga

I love to laugh. It has been said, *laughter is the best medicine*. Because laughter brings joy and happiness, I became a Laughter Yoga leader. Using laughter yoga as a spiritual practice provided an outlet to deal with my sadness and pain. Somewhere along my journey to freedom, I heard: *The best person to laugh at is you*. I believed laughing at myself would be liberating and could free me up inside. I am now able to see my own drama and laugh at my own mind patterns.

Laughter is the sound of the human Spirit. Laughter is the music of the Soul. I also love to dance.

Dancing

When I am dancing, I'm not silent for there is a message in my movements.

When I am dancing, I'm not quiet, but voiced, speaking my body's language of ritualistic bliss and moving to experiences.

When I am dancing, I feel liberated, bringing out my true spirit, capturing words with my rhythmic dance moves, creating new messages.

When I am dancing in the physical plane, I allow my spirit to shine.

When I am dancing, I'm feeling free, allowing others to see my authenticity.

When I am dancing, I give gifts to the world, bringing in Spirit, embodying my Soul.

Connect to Source

Nothing can ever separate us from God's love.
– Romans 8:38, NLT

We all want to connect and carry the vibration of what we connect to. The Universe is the Source of all things. There were times when I secretly thought I was not connected to the Divine Source. This was only a sense of fear and separation because I am never disconnected from Divine Source energy. We cannot be separated or disconnected from Source, though sometimes we disconnect our awareness of it. It is our own perception of separation that makes us feel disconnected from Divine Source.

Taking the time to commune with your Spirit on a regular basis will keep you feeling connected to Divine Source. Spiritual practices, such as praying and being present, ensure you stay connected to Spirit moment by moment. Reaching out and asking for help and support from family and friends can help you feel connected to Divine Source as well.

Connecting to Source also requires practicing the right attitude. When connecting, do so from your heart and not your mind. Whenever you feel disconnected from God, it's because you're out of alignment with the Divine Source.

Someone to Rescue Me
I was waiting for someone to rescue me. I was looking for someone to set me free, but I realized I am my own rescuer. I had the power to set myself free. As a result of practicing Ho'oponopono, the ancient Hawaiian practice of forgiveness, I felt more reconnected to Divine Source and gained profound benefits in my personal life.

My Gift
Despite going to school and receiving an education and credentials from the best institutions, I could not figure out what I had that was special and unique. I often wondered what my gifts were, what filled my Soul and made me thrive.

My education did not liberate me, my credentials did not liberate me, and naturalization did not liberate me. I wanted liberation for my Soul. I became liberated when I finally accepted that I am *the light*. Not only do I have a light, but I *am* the light.

I became liberated when I realized I am the expression of the One Divine Consciousness, which I call God.

Every time you smile at someone, it is an act of love, a gift to that person, a beautiful thing.
– Mother Teresa

Sharing My Gift

I never considered that when I smiled at someone, I was showing love to that person. It was not until I began to appreciate my worth and value that I recognized my beautiful smile was a gift to the world.

Now I understand that my whole life is a gift. My gift is my light. Showing and sharing my love is also a gift.

Today, I want to share my story and message through teaching. My life is in progress, and I want to share with my readers my experiences and to impart wisdom and knowledge that can be excavated from my spiritual journey.

"What am I here to do?" I consistently asked myself.

"To live a more joyful life," I whispered to myself.

It was then I understood the difference between a pleaser of people and a server of people. I am a server of people, but I now know I must serve myself first.

Being willing to open and share myself freely is a gift and an honor. Whenever I take time to help anyone, we are both blessed. It is also my gift to research and share information that helps people bring comfort and peace into their lives so they may live in a blissful way. If I share from my heart to help someone along the way, then my living shall not have been in vain.

I'm here to tell you: *you are enough*. No matter what you may think, what you may feel, I'm here to say, you are enough. No matter where you're from, your dreams are valid and valuable.

You are already what you're looking for. You must see that truth about yourself. Stop looking at where you came from and look at where you are now and where you want to be.

Share Your Gift
Your life is a gift. Your free will is a gift. You, too, can do something. You can show your love. You can share your gift. You may think you have nothing to contribute just like I did, but you have special gifts. Your gift is your light.

You don't have to be working behind a desk or in a social worker's office; you're still giving back in a profound capacity, whether it is a smile, laughter, a kind word, or a gentle touch.

> **What are your gifts? Identify them.**

My life has been an emotional journey that's personal, individual, and unique to me. I have shifted my mindset from the need to compare myself with others to accepting that I am enough.

While we may attempt to identify with each other's experiences, the truth is there is no duplication to our life's situations, and that's the beauty of it all. However, we can all benefit from hearing someone else's situation. *We are all on the same journey to find out who we are.*

Life is a journey and everything happens for a reason. We are all becoming what we're supposed to be. We are here to experience the expansion of our Soul as we continue to discover and reinvent ourselves.

Through traumas, I've found an inner strength that I know came as a result of my desire to succeed. I am strong, but not because of my ego or false sense of self, but because I have courage and fortitude.

My Transformation

There has been a clear transformation in me. Not only am I thinking differently, but now I care enough to do and give to others through sharing. I have opened my heart and am not so guarded and restrictive, though I must employ my spirit of discernment for spiritual protection. My heart is open, but I'm still observant of ways to help ward off unpleasant emotions like fear and anger.

The fact that I endured all I did along my journey showed my strength. I learned that strength comes from knowing who I am. This experience showed me that I am resilient and courageous. I have changed from worrier to warrior. I am a strong, brave woman who has lived a life of triumph.

Being Me

Through my life experiences, I learned who and what I am and how to be me, which is my purpose. My spiritual journey has been one of continuous learning and purification. My life has been a journey toward self-acceptance on all levels.

Today, I accept everything as it occurs because the Universe has it exactly the way it should be.

I learned that all I can ever be is me. Self-love is about being my authentic self. After I reached a deeper level of understanding of myself, I realized that acceptance of love was always a choice.

I chose to accept myself as I am and to continue to improve myself. All I know is that nothing is ever finished.

Feeling Free

When we're sometimes not confident, it's probably because we are not comfortable in our own skin. Being comfortable in your skin means not being attached to any outcomes and feeling okay about what others may say, do, or feel about who and how you are being. To be comfortable in your own skin means liking yourself, caring enough to praise yourself, and feeling free to be you.

I have come to know that I'm self-assured, resilient, and comfortable in my own skin. Being comfortable in my own skin means I am absolutely sure I am a child of God, and in that, I can take comfort. I know I am never alone because God is always with me.

You too, can be assured of this.

Creating change in my life and business requires courage, faith, a sense of humor, and consistent action. I acknowledge and celebrate myself, and I am grateful for those who have supported me and held me accountable.

Now I live with the knowledge and understanding of how the Universe works. I believe I am intuitively guided by the Universe. Through daily meditations, visualizations, repetitive mantras, spoken words, and affirmations, I raise my vibration and experience feelings of peace, ease, and grounding.

The constant repetition of the spoken words shifted my attention from my head and focused it within, to the physical center of my heart. I came to know my heart was the doorway to connect with my higher power, and I believed that by opening and dropping into the portal of my heart, I would find clarity, stillness, and answers.

In my heart, I could let go of judgments and fears. I trusted and believed God would take care of me and that all would be well within. When I dropped into my heart, I let go of control and surrendered to the power of God within me. In my heart, there is only love. There is no fear or judgment.

The quest to find my freedom turned out to be the journey of my life. This quest for freedom was mystical in nature for it became clear I was seeking freedom from the illusions of fear and grief. The real freedom quest was to learn to love and be loved. I then understood I had been on a freedom quest to embrace my love.

Letting go of all encumbrances was my path to spiritual freedom. We all have our own path. My path is mine and your path is yours. None can walk my path but me. And none can walk yours but you.

I desire to manifest fearlessness. I believe that because I kept going toward situations and things that rejected me I showed bravery. Now I am ready to jump into my authentic nature and prepare myself for my holistic transformation.

I realized I had not been totally silent but dared not speak my truth because I needed clarity about who I was born to be. Where there is clarity, there is no confusion. I now embrace freedom to be who I'm born to be and that's me.

No matter what, I knew I had something to say. *Silent no more* was my path to authenticity.

I am free to be authentically me, and true peace comes from freedom. Freedom is a state of mind. My process of transformation had many layers, like an onion. Transformation took place when I no longer felt the same emptiness I experienced after Mom's, Dad's and Uncle's deaths. Transformation occurred when I moved from individual, solitary grief to collective family grief.

Coming from a place of severe emotional trauma, including abandonment, loss, and grief, I want to convey the kind of transformation that has occurred in my life, bringing me to where I am today—a confident, secure woman, who had the courage to open her heart.

My transformation is that I now stand and speak in my own voice and am no longer guided by the shadows of old ways of being but creating my own new way of living and being. My life has been transformed. I have moved from unvoiced to voiced.

I am silent no more. I have accepted I am a Soul having a physical experience with the ultimate aim to align my body, mind, heart, and spirit.

I know my Soul has many beautiful qualities, including wisdom, peace, love, and creativity, and I want to be in constant alignment with my Soul.

Soulful Messenger

I am a soulful messenger
The path marked out for me
My goal is to align with Spirit
So can my wholeness be.

I am a soulful messenger
Source planned it all that way
To allow my light to shine
Bright and brilliant each day.

I am a soulful messenger
'Tis a yearning in my heart
Despite my ups and downs
It's been there from the start.

I'm here to share a message
Of love Divine and true
Of amazing grace and mercies
And good intentions too.

To become a soulful messenger
listen to the whispers you behold
Trust the deep call inside your heart
You too are a messenger of Soul.

ACKNOWLEDGMENTS

I wish to honor my deceased parents, all my siblings, and extended and spiritual families for their love and support throughout my life.

I would like to express my sincere thanks and gratitude to all of those who took this book along the road to publication: Christine Kloser, my mentor and coach has been relentless in giving love and support. Carrie Jareed, Julie Clayton, Karen Burton, and the editorial staff for their patience, humor, tact, skill, and support in bringing this publication to life so effortlessly.

A special thank you to Dorothy Randall Gray, my mentor and friend, who told me, *"The world is waiting for the star of your soul to shine brighter than the sun."*

I am grateful for my teacher, Katye Anna Clark, for her wisdom, inspiration, and encouragement.

Very special thanks to my soulmate, Joyce O. Chavers, whose love and faith in me made it possible to bring this book to fruition.

I honor all documented or undocumented immigrants who feel invisible and have no voice.

Deep thanks to the Divine Creative Source whose energy has been my sustenance and silent comforter within.

BIBLIOGRAPHY

The following is a partial list of the books intended for quicker access:

Achebe, Chinua. *No Longer at Ease.* Greenwich, CT: Fawcett Publications, Inc., 1969.

Akbar, Na'im. *Chains and Images of Psychological Slavery.* Jersey City, NJ: New Mind Productions, 1984.

Aldred, Cyril. *Egypt to the end of the Old Kingdom.* New York: Thames and Hudson, Inc., 1982.

Angelou, Maya. *I Know Why the Caged Bird Sings.* New York: Random House, 1969.

Bach, Richard. *Jonathan Livingston Seagull.* New York: Harper Collins Publishers, 1973.

Bell, Derrick. *Faces at the Bottom of the Well: The Permanence of Racism.* New York: Harper Collins, Inc., 1992.

Bennett Jr., Lerone. *Before the Mayflower: A History of Black Americans*. Chicago: Johnson Publishing Co., 1982.

Cameron, Julia. *The Artist's Way: A Spiritual Path to Higher Creativity*. New York: G. P. Putnam's Sons Publishers, 1992.

Colbin, Annemarie. *Food and Healing: How What You Eat Determines Your Health, Your Well-Being, and the Quality of Your Life*. New York: New York: The Random House Ballantine Publishing Group, 1986.

David, Marc. *Nourishing Wisdom: A Mind Body Approach to Nutrition and Well-Being*. New York: Bell Tower, 1991.

Davis, Angela Y. *Women, Culture & Politics*, New York: Random House Publishers, 1984.

Diop, Cheikh Anta. *The African Origins of Civilization: Myth or Reality*. Edited and translated by Mercer Cook. Westport, CT: Lawrence Hill & Co., 1974.

Friday, Nancy. *My Mother, My Self: The Daughter's Search for Identity*. New York: Dell Publishing Co., 1978.

Gibran, Kahlil. *The Prophet: Life and the Human Condition*. USA: Alfred & Knopf Publishers, 1923.

BIBLIOGRAPHY

Gordon, Richard. *Quantum Touch: The Power to Heal.* Berkley, CA: North Atlantic Books, 2006.

Graham, Lloyd M. *Deceptions and Myths of the Bible.* New York: Carol Publishing Group, 1991.

Harris, Joseph E. *Africans and Their History.* New York: The New American Library, Inc., 1972

Hay, Louise L. *Heal Your Body: The Mental Causes for Physical Illness and the Metaphysical Way to Overcome Them.* Carson, CA: Hay House Inc., 1984.

James Myers, Linda. *Understanding an Afrocentric World View: Introduction to an Optimal Psychology.* Dubuque, IA: Kendall Hunt Publishing Co., 1988.

James, George G. M. *Stolen Legacy: Greek Philosophy is Stolen Egyptian Philosophy.* Newport News, VA: The African Publication Society, 1980.

James, John W. and Russel Friedman. *The Grief Recovery Handbook: The Action Program for Moving Beyond Death, Divorce, and Other Losses.* New York: Harper Collins, 1986.

Jenkins, Albert H. *The Psychology of the Afro-American: A Humanistic Approach.* New York: Pergamon Press, Inc., 1983.

Karenga, Maulana. *Introduction to Black Studies*. Los Angeles: University of Sankore Press, 1982.

Lanzetta, Beverly. *Emerging Heart: Global Spirituality and the Sacred*. Minneapolis, MN: Fortress Press, 2007.

Mandino, Og. *The Greatest Salesman in the World*. New York: Bantam Books, 1974.

Mbiti, John S. *African Religions and Philosophy*. Portsmouth, NH: Heinemann Educational Books Inc., Portsmouth, 1989.

Moore, Thomas. *Care of the Soul: A Guide for Cultivating Depth and Sacredness in Everyday Life*. New York: Harper Collins Publishers, 1992.

Morrison, Toni. *Songs of Solomon*. New York: Alfred A. Knopf, a division of Random House, 1977.

Morrison, Toni. *The Bluest Eye*. New York: Holt Rinehart and Winston, 1970.

Pagels, Elaine. *The Gnostic Gospels*. New York: Random House, Inc., 1979.

Peck, M. Scott. *The Road Less Travelled: A New Psychology of Love, Traditional Values, and Spiritual Growth*. New York: Simon & Schuster, 1978.

Pinderhughes, Elaine. *Understanding Race, Ethnicity & Power: The Key to Efficacy in Clinical Practice.* New York: The Free Press, 1989.

Richardson, Cheryl. *The Unmistakable Touch of Grace.* New York: The Free Press, 2005.

Rinpoche, Sogyal. *The Tibetan Book of Living and Dying.* New York: Harper Collins, 1994.

Ruiz, Don Miguel. *The Four Agreements: A Practical Guide to Personal Freedom.* San Rafael, CA: Amber-Allen Publishing, Inc., 1997.

Sadleir, Steven S. *The Spiritual Seeker's Guide: The Complete Source for Religions and Spiritual Groups of the World.* Costa Mesa, CA: Allwon Publishing Co., 1992.

Shinnie, Margaret. *Ancient African Kingdoms.* New York: St. Martin's Press, Inc., 1970.

Stone, Merlin. *When God was a Woman.* New York: Barnes & Noble Publishers, 1976.

Sutphen, Dick. *Radical Spirituality: Metaphysical Awareness for a New Century.* Malibu, CA: Valley of the Sun Publishing, 1995.

Thurston, Mark. *Discovering Your Soul's Purpose: Finding Your

Path in Life, Work, and Personal Mission the Edgar Cayce Way. Virginia Beach, VA: A.R.E. Press, 1984.

Tolle, Eckhart. *The Power of Now: A Guide to Spiritual Enlightenment.* Vancouver, BC: Namaste Publishing, 2004.

Van Sertima, Ivan. *Black Women in Antiquity.* New Brunswick, NJ: Transaction Books, 1984.

Van Sertima, Ivan. *They Came Before Columbus: The African Presence in Ancient America.* New York: Random House, 1976.

Viorst, Judith. *Necessary Losses: The Loves, Illusions, Dependencies, and Impossible Expectations that All of Us Have to Give Up in Order to Grow.* New York: Simon & Schuster Inc., 1986.

Whelan, Richard, ed. *Self-Reliance: The Wisdom of Ralph Waldo Emerson as Inspiration for Daily Living.* New York: Crown Publishers, Inc., 1991.

Wigmore, Ann. *The Healing Power Within: How to Tap the Infinite Potential Within Yourself.* Wayne, NJ: Avery Publishing Group Inc., 1983.

Williams, Chancellor. *The Destruction of Black Civilization: Great Issues of a Race from 4500 B.C. to 2000 A.D.* Chicago, IL: Third World Press, 1987.

Williams, Eric. *From Columbus to Castro: The History of the Caribbean.* New York: Random House, 1970.

Williams, John A. and Charles F. Harris. *Amistad I: Writings on Black History and Culture.* New York: Random House, Inc., 1970.

Woodson, Carter G. *The Mis-Education of the Negro.* Trenton, NJ: African Press, 1990.

Zukav, Gary. *The Seat of the Soul.* New York: Simon and Schuster, 1989.

ABOUT THE AUTHOR

Dr. Veronica R. Lynch is an award-winning author and the founder of the "7 Balancing Acts to Wholeness: A System of Personal Revitalization." She lives in and manages Blissed™, an Inward Sanctuary and Wellness Retreat Center in the Low Country of South Carolina.

You may schedule a distant energy healing session with Dr. Veronica at: vlynch@createwhole.com

For information about her retreats, special events, and other services, visit: www.blissedretreats.com

CONTACT AUTHOR

Contact Dr. Veronica R. Lynch
Address:
CreateWhole™ Wellness Services, LLC
P. O. Box 6363
Beaufort, South Carolina   29903
Phone:
(347) 526-5116

Emails:
vlynch@blissedretreats.com
vlynch@createwhole.com

Main Websites:
www.blissedretreats.com
www.createwhole.com
www.veronicarlynch.com

FREE RESOURCES

Guided Blissful Meditation

If you're feeling stressed or overwhelmed and want to experience a mini retreat, get your FREE guided audio meditation to help you relax, be calm, and feel peace and bliss.

Visit www.blissedretreats.com and enter your name and email on the right side of the homepage.

10 Steps to More Bliss Guide

If you want to learn how to bring more balance, harmony, and bliss into your life, you'll want to download this FREE special resource: "10 Steps to More Bliss Guide." Visit www.blissedretreats.com and enter your name and email on the right side of the homepage.

www.ingramcontent.com/pod-product-compliance
Lightning Source LLC
Chambersburg PA
CBHW071954110526
44592CB00012B/1087